Translation in Lar
An Argument for

Published in this series

Translation in Language Teaching

An Argument for Reassessment

GUY COOK

OXFORD
UNIVERSITY PRESS

OXFORD
UNIVERSITY PRESS

Great Clarendon Street, Oxford OX2 6DP

Oxford University Press is a department of the University of Oxford.
It furthers the University's objective of excellence in research, scholarship,
and education by publishing worldwide in

Oxford New York

Auckland Cape Town Dar es Salaam Hong Kong Karachi
Kuala Lumpur Madrid Melbourne Mexico City Nairobi
New Delhi Shanghai Taipei Toronto

With offices in

Argentina Austria Brazil Chile Czech Republic France Greece
Guatemala Hungary Italy Japan Poland Portugal Singapore
South Korea Switzerland Thailand Turkey Ukraine Vietnam

OXFORD and OXFORD ENGLISH are registered trade marks of
Oxford University Press in the UK and in certain other countries

ISBN: 978 0 19 442475 2

Printed in Spain by Unigraf S.L.

To Henry Widdowson

Contents

Acknowledgements

Three people in particular—David Baker, Denise Santos, and Michael Swan—have been intimately involved in the genesis of this book and given me detailed and helpful suggestions for changes at every stage. For this help, encouragement, and constructive criticism, I am profoundly grateful. Writing a book is always a difficult and lonely labour, and their interventions made the whole process much easier and more enjoyable—and gave me the confidence to continue.

I am also grateful for (one or more of) commentary, information, discussion, encouragement, help, criticism, and correction to Khalid Al-Balushi, Mona Baker, David Block, Martin Bygate, Guozhi Cai, Ron Carter, Victoria Castillo, Elena Poptsova Cook, Regine Hampel, Nisreen Hassan Ash, Marie-Noëlle Lamy, Jieun Lee, Theresa Lillis, Andrew Littlejohn, Barbara Seidlhofer, Tony Smith, and Joan Swann. My thanks go also to Ann Hunter for her skilled and insightful copy-editing.

This is the first book I have ever written which has not benefited from detailed critical commentary by Henry Widdowson. But I have been aware at every stage of the influence of his ideas on mine. For this reason, and with great affection, this book is dedicated to him.

The authors and publisher are grateful to those who have given permission to reproduce the following extracts and adaptations of copyright material:

pp. 12–13 From *The Penguin Russian Course: A Complete Course for Beginners* by J. L. I. Fennell (Penguin Books Ltd, 1961) Copyright © J. L. I. Fennell, 1961. Reproduced by permission.

p. 14 From *Teach Yourself Italian* by Kathleen Speight (English Universities Press, 1963) Copyright © 1963. Reprinted by permission of Hodder & Stoughton Ltd.

p. 60 Adapted from *A Linguistic Theory of Translation* by J. C. Catford © Oxford University Press, 1965. Reproduced by permission.

p. 62 From *Communicate 1 Students'* by Johnson and Morrow, Cambridge University Press, 1979. Reproduced by permission.

p. 68 From pp. vii–x of *Pushkin: Eugene Onegin* by Vladimir Nabokov, 1964.

p. 127 Article first published in *El Gazette*, March 2000. Reproduced by permission of *El Gazette*, editorial@elgazette.com.

p. 141 Extract from www.able2know.org. Reproduced by permission.

p. 141 Extract from http://slowtalk.com. Reproduced by kind permission of www.SlowTrav.com.

p. 146 From p.178 of *Multiple Voices in the Translation Classroom* by Maria Gonzalez Davies, 2004. Reproduced by kind permission of John Benjamins Publishing. Company, Amsterdam/Philadelphia, www.bejamins.com.

p. 147 From *Using the Mother Tongue* by Sheelagh Deller and Mario Rinvolucri, 2002. Reproduced by kind permission of Delta Publishing.

Although every effort has been made to trace and contact copyright holders before publication, this has not been possible in some cases. We apologize for any apparent infringement of copyright and if notified, the publisher will be pleased to rectify any errors or omissions at the earliest opportunity.

Prelude

I begin this book anecdotally by recounting a communicative disaster which befell me many years ago. It is a story which sheds light on the subject matter of this book: the role of translation in language teaching and learning, and the pitfalls of communication across languages and cultures. It is intended to show that where there is potential for misunderstanding in such communication, awareness of the problems and nuances of translation has a key role to play in avoiding conflict and promoting understanding—and that where it is absent, it can have the opposite effect.

I was a young volunteer with VSO (Voluntary Service Overseas), a British international development charity recruiting idealistic and enthusiastic young people to 'help' in poorer countries. I asked to go to Jamaica, but was sent to teach English language in a secondary school in Upper Egypt. It was 1974. I had just graduated. It was my first job.

Before leaving for Egypt, I was sent on a one-week crash course in spoken colloquial Egyptian Arabic. The course was up-do-date and state-of-the-art for the time. It was taught by native Arabic speakers. It focused on speech not writing. There was a great deal of repetition, role play, and visual aids. There was no use of translation or English language explanation. We learnt some rudimentary Arabic—how to introduce ourselves, say where we came from, ask the way to the station, and so forth. And we acted out 'authentic' situations, role-playing waiters and diners, bus-conductors and passengers. In the course of this enjoyable week, we several times encountered a phrase that sounded like *in-shâ'-llâh*. We gathered, from our teacher's hand gestures and facial expressions (of the sort teachers have to use if they do not translate) that this phrase denoted some kind of uncertainty. There was no way of telling, in a course like this, how many words were involved. This *in-shâ'-llâh* seemed to have three or four syllables—so presumably it could be any number of words up to four.

I surmised that it meant something like 'perhaps', but I wanted to know the meaning more precisely—I had a problem with the vagueness and imprecision of the 'knowledge' we were acquiring, and I was yearning for some explanation and translation. But because there was strictly no English allowed and we were banned from asking such questions, I had to wait. Then in conversation with our teacher outside the classroom, I asked in English what this sequence of sounds meant. The teacher answered that yes, *in-shâ'-llâh* means in effect 'perhaps'. Then he added that literally it means 'by the will of God'. More specifically, word for word: *in* = if; *shâ'* = *wish*; *llâh* = God—'If wishes God'.

Nevertheless, he hastened to add, when Arabic speakers say *in-shâ'-llâh*, they basically mean 'perhaps'. Conversely if I wanted to say 'perhaps', I should say *in-shâ'-llâh*.

Pupils trust their teachers—and I trusted mine. When I was living in Egypt a few months later, however, I had a difficult encounter involving this phrase. In the block of flats where I lived together with another British volunteer and two *coopérants* (the French equivalent of VSOs), there was a janitor called Mahmoud, a friendly old man whose job was to do various things around the flats, such as clean the stairs, collect bottles, and chase away dogs and small boys. So when one of the water pipes in our flat developed a leak, we asked Mahmoud to fix it—but nothing happened. Every day we asked him when it would be fixed, and every day he answered that it would be soon, *in-shâ'-llâh*. Eventually I became frustrated and said in my pidgin Arabic that we needed a definite answer, not *in-shâ'-llâh*. To my shock, the apparently easy-going Mahmoud was suddenly very upset, so much so that my previously good relations with him never recovered. Even with my limited linguistic resources I understood the reason—too late. For him, *in-shâ'-llâh* did not just mean 'perhaps', but was part of a deeply felt religious view of the world and everything that happens in it.

This anecdote illustrates a number of truisms, and raises a number of questions about the strange state of language teaching at that time, which for many pupils and teachers still persists. The first point concerns excluding the student's first language from the classroom. Would it not have been easier and more instructive to have told us what *in-shâ'-llâh* means, both literally ('God willing') and pragmatically ('perhaps'), at the time it was introduced, with some caution as to the balance between the two? And why should students be refused a translation in class if they feel it might be helpful? A second point concerns the inadequacy of a purely transactional approach to translation which does not take linguistic and cultural differences into account. By ignoring both the literal word-for-word meaning of the original and the identities and belief systems of the individuals involved in the communication (an arrogant young Englishman and an elderly, religious Egyptian), a rough, pragmatic translation (like 'perhaps') can cause rather than resolve conflict.

Interlingual and intercultural contact and communication is a very delicate matter, especially in relations between Arabic and English speakers. (Sadly, this is no less true as I write now in 2009 than it was in 1974.) To avoid conflict and misunderstanding, we need a knowledge of the two languages involved to be as accurate and explicit as possible. It is not always enough to have a vague, rough idea what a word or phrase means 'communicatively' or 'pragmatically'.

Encounters between individuals at the micro-level reflect and feed into those of nations and cultures at the meso- and macro-levels. This vignette was part of larger communicative failures all around me at the time: between Islam and the West, between British and Egyptian governments, between VSO and the Egyptian Ministry of Education. Late in the first year of my teaching post at the Luxor boys' secondary school, I discovered that we were not really wanted. The school had never asked to have two untrained monolingual 'volunteer' teachers from England. To make room for us, two incumbent trained teachers had been moved out—a cause of anguish to them and their families, as city posts were much sought after and the schools they had been moved to were out in the surrounding villages. But I was not too shaken by this—partly through the confidence of youth, and partly through a firm belief that, as a native speaker, my English and therefore my English teaching, must be better than that of any local teacher. My pupils probably thought otherwise. They did not do well in their exams.

INTRODUCTION

Introduction

Why learn another language? What is the best way to do it? What counts as success?

These are big questions which a book assessing the role of any activity in language teaching and learning needs to address—and this book, in the course of its argument, will attempt to do so. But the answers given here are rather different from those to be found in the greater part of the current language-teaching literature. I shall argue that for most contemporary language learners, translating should be a major aim and means of language learning, and a major measure of success.

This argument is a radical break with tradition. Translation in language teaching has been treated as a pariah in almost all the fashionable high-profile language teaching theories of the 20th century—so much so that towards the end of that century, other than at university level, it was no longer discussed in the academic literature as a serious candidate for aiding the learning of a new language. The reasons for this ostracism need some interpretation, for they are seldom made explicit. Translation was often simply assumed to be bad, and if mentioned at all, was held up to ridicule. Some of the reasons for this seem to have been pedagogic—a belief that translation was dull and demotivating; others seem to have been cognitive—an idea that it hindered successful language acquisition and processing; others still were practical—that it was not an activity which students might need in the real world. Strangely, however, there was very little research or serious argument to back up these beliefs.

Nevertheless, despite this ostracism by the most prestigious and trend-setting theorists, especially those concerned with the teaching of English, translation has continued to be used in many contexts around the world (Benson 2000), especially in classes—still the majority around the world—in which students share one language, and the teacher knows both this language and the one being taught. The use of translation remains the norm at university-level language teaching (Malmkjær 2004) and in the teaching of many languages other than English, and even in the teaching of English and other widely taught languages it is still common. In other contexts, however, it has almost completely disappeared. This has created something of a division in language teaching, with those on one side treating the superiority of monolingual teaching as a given, and those on the other—either in ignorance or defiance of this development—continuing to teach bilingually, using translation.

My arguments for reassessing the role of translation are various, and are broader in range, I hope, than those advanced against its use in the past. I shall certainly counter each of the unsubstantiated charges against translation. Thus I shall try to show that translation has pedagogic advantages both for teachers and learners, that it is both a stimulus and aid in the cognitively demanding task of acquiring a new language, and that for many language users it is a very practical and much-needed skill. But I also hope to show that the reasons behind the rejection of translation in the 20th century were more political and commercial than pedagogic or linguistic, and that now, at the beginning of the 21st century, there are powerful political reasons to reinstate it. If we want a more tolerant and peaceful world, translation has an important educational role to play.

There are two apparently contradictory perspectives behind these claims: The first perspective relates translation in language teaching to the specific circumstances of our time. Answers to my opening 'big questions' about motives, means, and measures cannot be absolute, but vary between individuals, places, and historical periods. Language learning is not the same now as it was when the currently dominant ideas about it were formulated. A student's reasons for learning a language in 2009 (the year in which I am writing this book) are likely to be different from those that were common fifty or a hundred years ago; and the same is therefore true of measures of success. This is the era of electronic communication, mass migrations, an exponential growth in the use of English, and a consequent complexification of identity for many individuals. This book therefore sets out to answer the 'big questions' for the opening decades of the 21st century, when many aspects of the linguistic landscape are dramatically new. As time goes on, things will change again, so the arguments in this book are not necessarily true for all time.

The second perspective relates translation to factors in language learning which have remained constant throughout history. Although this seems at odds with the first perspective, it need not be so, for the simple reason that although some things have changed, others have not. Despite all that is so strikingly new about our times, many of the common reasons for language learning remain—and consequently so may some of the best ways of facilitating learning or of measuring success. Throughout history, as today, people have learned languages for a variety of reasons, some born of necessity, others of choice: as the subjects of conquest and colonization; as economic migrants; as slaves and captives; for trade and profit; for prayer and worship; to keep watch on actual or potential enemies; to learn from others' achievements; for marriage outside their own community; for travel; for pleasure; for social advancement; for mental exercise; and to understand how languages work. The persistence of these ancient motives for language learning means that we would be well advised, when answering the 'big questions' above, to look back beyond recent language teaching theory, which has in general tended to reject and ridicule the motives and methods of the past. It is worth bearing in mind that whereas academic understanding of language learning may be cumulative, in each individual learner the task begins anew, and there is no evidence that any one generation has been better or worse at it than any other.

Translation in language teaching raises complex issues, and as with any such topic, lines of argument inevitably intertwine. The many strands which compose our understanding need to be unpicked and rewoven many times, and in a variety of ways. Though for reasons of clarity and organization, I shall endeavour to group various themes in particular chapters, each will appear and reappear under different headings, viewed from different angles and through different lenses. There will thus be frequent—though I hope not irritating—use of formulations like 'as we shall see in more detail later'. But if the reader will reserve judgment, I hope by the end of the book to have done some justice to each of these many strands.

How the book is organized

Part One: 'History' explores both current attitudes to translation and their historical origins. In language teaching, the 'latest', 'cutting-edge' ideas often have their roots in much earlier times, reflecting ideologies which their adherents may neither be aware of nor sympathize with (Kelly 1969). It is my belief that to understand what is currently happening in language teaching, we need to understand its origins. Therefore, this first part is historical, dividing the course of the recent history of translation in language teaching into three periods (though the boundary between each period cannot be precise, as there are always those who are behind or in front of their time, as well as considerable variation between different places and sectors).

Chapter 1 describes the rejection of translation by theorists and practitioners at the end of the 19th and turn of the 20th centuries.

Chapter 2 investigates the long silence on the topic of translation in language teaching theory in the 20th century, asking why, in what was otherwise an era of intense activity and open-mindedness, translation was largely ignored by ascendant movements such as second language acquisition theory (SLA) and communicative language teaching (CLT).

Chapter 3 examines the possibility of a climate for revival of translation in language teaching offered by the new 'social turn' in applied linguistics (Block 2003a: 1–3), which has been gaining strength from the 1990s and into the 2000s, and which is more concerned than the applied linguistics of the past with the politics of language use and learning, and with the complex identities of language learners in late modernity.

Translation is not easily defined, and certainly not easily understood—but an argument for its use in language teaching needs to engage with the linguistic and social processes involved, so that we can be clear about what is being advocated.

For this reason, Chapter 4 to some extent steps away from the main theme of the book—the use of translation in language teaching—to examine the difficult question *What is translation?*, drawing upon insights from both translation theory and translation studies.

Part Two of the book returns to language teaching more directly, examining arguments for and against translation. This is done under three headings: evidence, education, and pedagogy.

Chapter 5 investigates evidence-based arguments, considering in particular the available evidence on whether it aids or hinders the acquisition of a new language, and whether it is liked or disliked by teachers and students.

Chapter 6 assesses educational arguments, considering the degree to which translation can answer both societal and individual needs, further personal fulfilment and development, promote positive values such as cross-cultural understanding, and extend linguistic knowledge and awareness.

Chapter 7 examines pedagogical arguments, assessing how translation can help and motivate students in a variety of pedagogical contexts. Although it is not the purpose of this book to provide a practical instruction manual on how to use translation in language teaching—for that the reader should look elsewhere—this last chapter is an attempt to grapple with some of the practical issues that arise. First, it considers ways in which translation is suited to different types of teachers, and different ages and stages of students. Second, it discusses a range of translation activities which can develop both linguistic knowledge and communication skills in student-friendly ways.

Lastly, a brief conclusion draws together the implications of what has been said in Parts One and Two, summarizing some of the many questions about language learning which the ostracism of translation for the last hundred years has left unanswered.

Matters arising

There are a number of questions about the argument in this book which will inevitably occur to the informed reader. I have certainly encountered them frequently while giving lectures on this topic. So I will tackle the most fundamental ones at the outset, as the answers are relevant throughout. They concern: the relation of translation to other uses of the first language; whether translation is a means or an end of language learning; and whether my arguments apply to the teaching of all languages, some languages only, or just English.

Is this book just about translation and/or using the first language in the classroom?

While many of the most influential 20th century theories of language teaching strongly advocated exclusively monolingual teaching, at the beginning of the 21st century there has been a resurgence of support for bilingual teaching. A question thus arises as to how an advocacy of translation relates to these more general arguments for 'using the first language in the classroom'—to borrow the title of an influential article on the topic by Vivian Cook (V. Cook 2001a).

Though clearly related, they are not exactly the same. Translation entails use of the student's language, so it is *a kind of* own-language use, but it is by no means the only one. Teachers may use the student's language in a variety of other ways too—for explanation, for classroom management, to establish personal relationships—none of which necessarily entail translation. Thus translation *can* be seen as separable from other ways of using the students' own language, and those advocating bilingual teaching are not therefore necessarily advocates of translation. There are some making a case for own-language use who are sceptical about translation, or have little or nothing to say about it.

A further question then arises as to whether this book accepts this distinction—especially as many of its arguments relate to bilingual teaching in general, rather than translation in particular. My view will be that the two cannot and should not be treated separately. Translation cannot in practice be kept neatly compartmentalized as the 'translation versus other uses of the own language' dichotomy seems to suggest. It is one of many strategies for negotiating and mediating between languages which, while they may be distinguished in theory, go naturally together and blend into one another in practice.

Translation cannot, in any case, be precisely defined or confined, and attempts to do so have run into all sorts of problems. There is a well known and long-established continuum with the tightest word-for-word translation at one end and the loosest paraphrases and interpretations at the other. At this loose end of the spectrum, translation merges into types of communication which are not usually included under its heading. Mindful of the theoretical impossibilities of precise definition, some translation theorists (Jakobson 1959; Steiner 1998) have argued for even broader definitions by which translation *between* languages merges metaphorically into translation *within* languages, encompassing any reformulation of one piece of language as another, embracing intralingual reformulations such as paraphrases, summaries, simplification, and updating (for example rendering Shakespearean English into contemporary English). The concept of translation is, in short, difficult to keep within boxes, but of its nature spills over into a host of neighbouring activities and uses of language. This is not surprising. Translation a living, moving activity, not a dead one to be pinned down in a museum. It is this dynamism which can make it so interesting and so stimulating, not only to linguists and translators, but to teachers and students too.

This book takes a similarly broad approach to translation in language teaching, and does not treat it as a neat and separate sub-area of first language use. The two necessarily go together. Once the students' own language is allowed and encouraged, it is unrealistic to suppose that it can be confined to some uses of the mother tongue and not allowed in others. Explanation, commentary, and management will inevitably make use of translation (in the tighter senses) and translation is by definition one of the main ways to bring back students' own language into the classroom. Translation is not envisaged here as a compartmentalized and enclosed area of activity, but one which is an integral part of the language teaching and learning process as a whole.

So this book will attempt to have it both ways. It is in part about translation defined in a reasonably tight way and as a distinct activity. But it is also about translation as a part of a general revival of bilingual teaching.

Is this book about translation as a means or an end?

Traditionally, a distinction has been made between the teaching of a language for translating on the one hand, and for general purposes on the other. In the former case—so the argument goes—it makes sense for students to use translation as part of their studies, in the latter case this is not necessarily so. But this is a very unconvincing distinction. An ability to translate is part of everyday bilingual language use—in personal, professional, and public life— and is needed by all learners, not just translation specialists. For someone to claim that they have learned a language successfully but cannot translate it would be bizarre, akin to the situation of those learners who can speak a language but not read it, or read it but not speak it. Such people exist, but they can hardly be said to have a rounded ability. Being able to translate is a major component of bilingual communicative competence. So one argument here is that translation should be a part of language teaching because all students will need to translate. Another, complementary argument, however, is that translation in language teaching not only develops translation skills *per se* but also deepens general knowledge of the new language and improves monolingual communication too. For the successful language learner, bilingual knowledge is always implicated in monolingual use, and it makes little sense to think that one can exist without the other. For these reasons I do not accept a neat division between translation as a means and an end. The discussion throughout this book assumes that a use of translation always has the potential to improve the ability to use the new language both monolingually and bilingually.

Is this book about teaching English or teaching any new language?

Much of the book is about translation in language teaching in general, and the arguments are relevant to the teaching and learning of any new language through translation. However, a good deal of it relates specifically to the teaching of English. This is for two reasons. First, English is now so widely known, used, and needed, that setting out to learn it increasingly raises different issues from those involved in learning other languages. In addition, and related to this, is the fact that for more than a hundred years the most innovative ideas about language teaching have been developed in relation to the teaching of English, and have then spread to a greater or lesser extent into the teaching of other languages. In particular, the rejection of translation has been strongest in the teaching of English, and perhaps its reintroduction will be in that area too, and it will then be accepted elsewhere. There have been similarities between the teaching of English and that of other big international languages such as French, especially in the use of native-speaker teachers who do not know the language of their students, and/or teaching to mixed-language classes. So, many of the arguments relating to these phenomena could apply there too. Smaller and geographically confined languages tend to be taught to single-language classes by bilingual teachers who make use of translation anyway.

Controversial terms

The terms involved in a discussion of translation in language teaching are like traps for a writer on the topic to fall into. The established terms encode the established view, reflecting the close historical links between language-teaching research, direct-method teaching, and SLA. A writer who seeks to question the *status quo* is therefore faced with a dilemma: either question existing terms and propose alternatives, or use them for brevity and accept with them the world view they entail. Despite its dangers, I shall follow the former path, in the belief that defining the terms of a discussion is part of the discussion itself. To conclude this introduction then, I briefly introduce some of the key terms and the reasons for them—though more will be said about some of them in the course of the argument.

TILT (translation in language teaching)

As a general rule I do not favour acronyms, but the phrase 'translation in language teaching' occurs so often in this book, and its initial letters so neatly form a real word that I shall refer to it from now on as 'TILT'. I could as easily have called this book 'Translation in Language Learning' and used the acronym 'TILL'. 'Teaching' and 'learning' may not be reciprocal verbs, like 'give' and 'take'—it is possible to teach someone who learns nothing from being taught—but the two do generally go together. There is no significance in my choice of TILT rather than TILL. The book is about both.

'Own language'

All language learners, other than children acquiring their first language(s), are by definition speakers of at least one language and aspire to know at least one new one. In talking about TILT we are inevitably therefore talking about the relationship between two languages. But how best should we refer to them?

For the known language, the most widespread terms in the language-teaching and SLA literature are 'first language' (abbreviated to 'L1'), 'native language', and 'mother tongue'. All these terms are unsatisfactory however. The medium of the classroom may not be the 'first' language of all its students, in the sense of being the language they encountered first in life. German, for example, is the main language of German secondary schools, but not necessarily the 'first' language of Turkish students in those schools. The term 'native' language is notoriously muddled and imprecise, as it unites three criteria—language of infancy, expertise, and identity—which do not necessarily go together (Rampton 1990). 'Mother tongue' is not only an emotive term but is also inaccurate—for the obvious reason that many people's 'mother tongue' is not their mother's 'mother tongue'! For these reasons I shall use the term 'own language' to refer to the language which the students already know, and through which (if allowed) they will approach the new language. I use this term even though, as in the example of Turkish students in Germany above, many students may also know and identify with another language as well.

'New language'

What about the language being learned? The commonest terms are 'second language' (abbreviated to 'L2'), 'foreign language', or 'target language'. These too are unsatisfactory. 'Second' wrongly implies that all learners know only one other language, when many are already bi- or multi-lingual. When applied to recent immigrants, the phrase 'second-language learners' may have unfortunate connotations of 'second class', even though the word 'second' describes the word 'language' rather than the 'learners'. In addition, the traditional distinction between English as 'second' and 'foreign' language becomes harder to draw as the use of English becomes ever more global (Crystal 2003). For these reasons, I propose the simpler term 'new language'.

Direct Method versus bilingualization

At the heart of this book is the issue of whether new languages are best learned by relating them to students' own languages, or by doing everything in the medium of the new language only. As with the two languages, we need terms to refer to these two extremes. (There is of course an infinity of intermediate positions.)

Terms in current use for the first option include 'cross-lingual' (Stern 1992), 'inter-lingual', and 'bilingual' teaching, or—as it is often a question of a process of reintroducing students' own languages—'bilingualization' (Widdowson 2003). I shall also use the term 'code-switching' to refer to movement back and forth between languages in classrooms, though there are those who would reserve this for naturalistic settings only.

For teaching without use of students' own languages, the terms 'monolingual' and 'intralingual' are used. The term 'Direct Method' was coined at some point around the turn of the 19th and 20th centuries, but is often reserved to refer only to certain specific teaching methods of that time, implying that the approaches which have followed are somehow very different. I shall use the term 'Direct Method' more generally however to refer to any approach which eschews the use of students' own languages. I do this as a deliberate way of highlighting the continuity of the belief throughout the 20th and into the 21st century, that students' own languages should be ignored. This continuity is considered in much more detail in Part One below.

PART ONE
History

I

The rejection:
'Reform' and Direct Method

The outlawing of translation

What does it mean to say that translation has been outlawed? For many teachers and learners it may seem a strange claim, because in many language teaching contexts translation has never disappeared and in some it is over-used. It is still central to many syllabuses and examinations around the world, still practised in many classrooms, often in such dry and mechanical ways that independent-minded teachers, understandably yearning to escape its grip, perceive the advent of alternative approaches as a welcome liberation. Translation is also still the staple of courses of self-study, such as (for English speakers learning other languages) bestselling series such as 'Teach Yourself', 'Made Simple', the Penguin language courses and, more recently, the phenomenally successful audio courses by Michel Thomas 'tutor to the stars', whose technique includes constant repetition, translation, and own-language explanation (see Thomas 2006; Block 2003b). And translation is still the means as well as the end of courses training translators and interpreters—a fact worth pointing out despite its self-evident nature! In all these instances, translation in language teaching (TILT) lives on as a legitimate activity, with institutional blessing.

Translation also continues to be used unofficially in many language classes which claim to do without it going as it were, underground. Thus even in the most hard-line monolingual classrooms, teachers who have been trained and contracted to teach without translation nevertheless occasionally resort to it when all else fails, which may be quite often. In addition, students are still generally allowed, and indeed assumed, to use bilingual dictionaries outside these classrooms, to 'see what a word means', i.e. its translation equivalent. In addition, they are likely to seek the reassurance of translation in whispers to classmates, to seek advice outside the classroom, or—since no one can stop a thought—to translate to themselves inside their minds (Widdowson 2003: 150).

So translation persists with various degrees of legitimacy, still sanctioned in many contexts by educational authorities in syllabuses and examinations, and by publishers in dictionaries and self-study guides. But in one important arena—one to which this book aspires to belong—it has been consistently an outlaw for around a hundred years: language teaching theory. By this phrase I mean the substantial academic and professional literature on the topic of language teaching, mostly relating to the teaching of English, but also making explicit or implicit claims of relevance to the teaching of all languages. It is informed by research and theories from linguistics, psychology, and the study of Second Language Acquisition (SLA), and is for many synonymous with the term 'applied linguistics'[1]. It is in this literature, and in the teaching practices and teaching guides which are influenced by it, that translation has until comparatively recently been either criticized or ignored, with the result that, where it has persisted, it has often done so at best a-theoretically and at worst guiltily, leading to a situation where many who believe in it are unwilling or unable to defend their views when challenged.

How did this state of affairs come about? This is hard to pin down. It may have emerged in popular practice and only later been given an academic rationale. Butzkamm and Caldwell (2009: 27) refer to the practice of speaking Latin all day long in medieval monastery schools; to punishments handed out to pupils in an English 16th-century grammar school for not speaking French at meal times; and to colonial and indigenous minority schools where everything was to be done in English, or French, or Latin. Phillipson (1992: 186–7) quotes an English country school report from 1808, stating that in compliance with the 'strict instruction' of the parents, '... not a word of [the students' first language] was allowed to be spoken in the school.' As we shall see shortly, it was in the practical programmes of language schools rather than in the theoretical writings of academics that these ideas became most firmly entrenched, raising the depressing possibility that movements in language teaching theory may be driven more by economics than by scientific findings or rational debate.

Self-proclaimed heroes: the Reform Movement

The most influential academic reasons for abandoning translation were the ideas formulated at the end of the 19th century by the self-styled 'Reform Movement', a group of phoneticians and linguists, who also had some experience of teaching. Prominent among them were Wilhelm Viëtor and Hermann Klinghardt in Germany, Otto Jespersen in Denmark, and Henry Sweet in Britain. The ideas of the Reform Movement (ably chronicled by Howatt 2004: 187–210) were based upon the latest linguistics and psychology of the time, and the reformers were in that respect applied linguists, though that term was not to become current until the 1950s and 1960s. In particular they drew upon the relatively new science of phonetics, and the idea of the 'primacy of speech'[2], to describe and emphasize the importance of the spoken language. From psychology they drew upon 'associationism', a theory of memory current at the time, which claimed that information in connected texts is more likely to be retained than that in isolated sentences, and that memorization is aided by links made between texts and events (Howatt 2004: 203–204).

In the light of these ideas the reformers advocated a radical shift in language teaching practice, away from an exclusive emphasis on written language and the deductive teaching of grammar rules artificially embodied in invented sentences, towards an emphasis on speech, on connected texts, and on learning through the medium of the language being taught, confidently claiming that such changes would be both more popular with learners, and more successful. In an early example of an 'intervention study' (though the term is an anachronism), the so-called 'Klinghardt experiment', the new ideas were put into practice with a beginners' class of fourteen-year-old boys in a *Realgymnasium* in Silesia. Though we are not told much about how the pupils reacted, there is no reason to suppose that the enterprise was not a successful one.

What is strange about the influence of these ideas is not so much that they caught on at the time, nor that these scholars sought to apply their academic insights to the real-world problem of how to teach and learn languages. What is odd, given the usual short shelf-life of ideas in language teaching, is how long they have persisted without challenge. The linguistics and psychology on which they were founded have been through numerous revolutions and counter-revolutions since. These reformers were old-style 19th century diachronic philologists whose ideas about language were yet to be overturned by the new linguistics of the next century—whether structuralist, functionalist, or generative. Much of what they had to say about language would hardly pass muster now. Sweet for example (1899/1964: 194) talks of some languages having 'defects', of some languages being less 'logical' or 'simpler' than others—ideas which the new linguistics was to reject. Yet somehow, in marked contrast to the ephemerality of most subsequent ideas in applied linguistics, the essence of the reformers' ideas about language learning has continued almost unquestioned for over a hundred years.

In its own period, however, the Reform Movement was in many ways a valid reaction against pedagogic excesses. There was unquestionably a sterile over-emphasis in secondary schools on grammatically accurate writing and a concomitant neglect of spoken language and fluency. And despite their rather heavy-handed insistence on the use of phonetic transcription with beginners, the reformers were not excessive or fanatical in their attitude to translation, acknowledging a role for it, and allowing for its judicious use. As Howatt (1984: 173) comments: 'The teacher was expected to speak the foreign language as the normal means of classroom communication, retaining the mother tongue only for the glossing of new words and explaining new grammar points'. And one of the leading publications to emerge from the movement, Henry Sweet's *The Practical Study of Languages*, first published in 1899, contains a whole chapter on translation (1964: 197–210) advocating judicious use of translation for both beginner and advanced learners, and such moderate statements as:

We translate the foreign words and phrases into our language simply because this is the most convenient and at the same time the most efficient guide to their meaning.
(Sweet 1964: 201)

Self-proclaimed heroes: the Direct Method

The excesses began, in a pattern which has since repeated many times, when the financially disinterested ideas of the academic reformers merged with developments in the commercial sector, where publishers and language schools had a vested interest in an altogether simpler and harder-line approach. It is no coincidence that this pattern of simplification and financial interest appeared as English language teaching embarked on an unprecedented expansion and rapidly became a major commercial activity. Over one hundred years after the Reform Movement, a British Council report estimates the number of people learning English worldwide to be heading for two billion (Graddol 2007: 14) and in 2008 the total annual revenue generated in the English-speaking countries by private language schools alone was estimated to be US$10 billion (Baker 2008).

The Reform Movement had developed its ideas with reference to secondary school teaching. The impetus for the new developments, however, was a new market of adult language learners outside the regular education system: immigrants to the USA, traders, and tourists in Europe. Both groups needed to learn a language fast and for very functional reasons: to survive and prosper in their new homeland, or to do business and cope with the communicative demands of travel. It was to cater for this market that a new type of language learning establishment appeared: private language schools. Most notable among them were the Berlitz Schools, named after their founder Maximilian Berlitz. Established in the USA in 1882, the schools rapidly expanded both there and in Europe. By the end of the century there were 16 in the USA and 30 in Europe, teaching at first a variety of European languages, but increasingly concentrating on English. It is in the ideas put into practice in these schools, the so-called 'Berlitz Method', that we find the first true hard-line rejection of translation. There was quite simply to be no use of translation at all, a focus on speaking rather than writing, and, significantly, all teachers, without exception, were to be native speakers of the languages they were teaching. In addition, these teachers were to follow rigidly the guidelines in the teachers' books, with the result that across this Berlitz empire, courses were regulated and co-ordinated to such an extent, that (ran the Berlitz boast) a student leaving one Berlitz School and entering another, however far away, could be guaranteed to pick up the course exactly where they had left it. In this way, the Berlitz method curiously foreshadowed the Fordist principles of assembly-line factory production, which were developed from 1908 onwards (Watts 2005). So strict was the supervision of teachers that at later times in the development of Berlitz schools, microphones were used in classrooms to monitor what teachers were doing and to stamp out any use of translation by making it a dismissible offence.

The relation between the Reform Movement and the Berlitz methods is not a straightforward one of cause and effect, and indeed cannot have been such, as the two appeared simultaneously: Viëtor's 1882 pamphlet *Der Sprachunterricht Muss Umkehren (Language Teaching must Start Afresh)*, which launched the Reform Movement, was published in the same year as the foundation of the first Berlitz School. So we must assume that they developed separately and for different reasons: the one out of academic and pedagogic concerns, the other out of commercial imperatives. And their focus of attention was different too: the Reform Movement was concerned with language teaching in secondary schools, where there was less need or pressure for fast results or student satisfaction, whereas the Berlitz schools catered for paying clients. Yet the ideas and practices of these two streams, one academic and one commercial, merged to yield a strong and coherent new programme for language teaching which became known as the Direct Method.

The Berlitz Schools did not use the term 'Direct Method', nor is it clear who first coined the term (Howatt 2004: 210); it somehow emerged as the description of these practices, initiated by Berlitz and rapidly taken up elsewhere. 'Direct Method' will be an important term in this book, but it is also one which—like most important terms—is used in different and even contradictory ways by different writers. So it is important to clarify here exactly how I intend to use it. By 'Direct Method' I shall mean any and all teaching which excludes use of the students' own language from the classroom, whether for translation or for explanation and commentary. And I shall regard 'Direct Method' as synonymous with terms such as 'intralingual teaching' (Stern 1992: 279) and 'monolingual teaching' (Widdowson 2003: 149) which are contrasted with 'crosslingual' and 'bilingual' teaching respectively. As such, my use of the term 'Direct Method' embraces much more than these early methods developed just before and just after the turn of the 19th and 20th centuries, but extends to include almost all major methods and approaches initiated since, including major approaches such as graded structures, situational teaching, audiolingualism, communicative language teaching, task-based instruction, lexical syllabuses, and so forth, as well as some—though not all—alternative 'ways' of the 1970s (Stevick 1981) such as the Silent Way and Total Physical Response. All of these apparently disparate approaches and methods are, in my terms, Direct Method in the sense that they use neither translation nor first-language explanation. (For surveys and commentaries on the history of 20th century methods and approaches see Richards and Rodgers 2001; Johnson 2001: 188–190.)

Four pillars of the Direct Method

The Direct Method was founded on a number of strong, confidently held assumptions—about language use, language learning, and effective language pedagogy—that have held sway in various degrees of strength ever since. As these assumptions are so crucial to all the arguments that follow in this book, it is worth spelling them out in detail, and giving each one a name: monolingualism, naturalism, native-speakerism, absolutism. We shall encounter and analyse these assumptions in more detail many times during the course of the book, so for the moment it is sufficient to give a brief outline of each in turn.

Pillar one: monolingualism

The first assumption is an implicit one about language use itself: that it is predominately monolingual, and that movement backwards and forwards between languages, including translation, is peripheral. It follows from this assumption that the teacher's main task is to prepare students mainly for situations in which the language under instruction is being used on its own, rather than for situations in which there is use of more than one language.

Pillar two: naturalism

The second assumption, which is sometimes made explicitly, is one about language learning, that it is best if it proceeds 'naturally'. By this is meant a variety of things, to which we shall return in more detail in Chapter 6, but for the moment let us note two. First is the notion that the classroom can in some way reproduce what happens to someone who 'picks up' a language through immersion in a context where it is used; second is the notion that the classroom can in some way reproduce what happens to the infant during their acquisition of a first language. Within this assumption is nested another implicit one—that the typical course of first language acquisition is monolingual. Direct Method discounts, in other words, the language acquisition of infants who grow up exposed to more than one language, and whose mastery of their communicative environment includes knowledge of when and how to switch between languages.

Pillar three: native-speakerism

This idea of the child being a good model relates to the third assumption which we shall call native-speakerism. This is the notion that the aim of language learning is to approximate as closely as possible to the language use and abilities of a native speaker of the language in question. It is a notion to which we shall return, but for the moment we need to note three consequences of it in Direct Method: that the native speaker is the best model for the learner; that emulating native-speaker acquisition is the best route for the learner; and that native speakers make the best teachers. These beliefs raise an enormous number of issues, not least how the native speaker is to be defined, and have been roundly challenged by many in recent years (Coulmas 1981; Rampton 1990; Davies 1995, 2003; Seidlhofer 1999; Braine 1999; Medgyes 1994).

Pillar four: absolutism

The fourth assumption, held with absolute confidence but no substantial evidence, is that Direct Method is the one true path to success, and that students will prefer it to bilingual approaches. The untested—and arguably untestable—nature of this assumption seems doubly strange when one considers that Direct Method (in the general sense defined above) has thrived alongside an apparently new scientific approach to the study of language teaching and learning, in which rigorous (even experimental) testing has been applied to all hypotheses, especially to those concerning SLA, and evidence has been required for all claims, however self-evident they may seem. Yet for some reason, despite this climate, the superiority and popularity of Direct Method has remained largely immune from investigation until recently. However, as we shall see later, some recent studies suggest that, at least in some circumstances, it may be less effective, or no more effective, than translation (Rolin-Iantizi and Brownlie 2002; Kaneko 1992; Källkvist 2008; Laufer and Girsai 2008), and that at least some student populations deeply resent it (Brooks-Lewis 2007, 2009). This absolute certainty may be further evidence of a commercial rather than academic origin for Direct Method. For this extreme self-confidence seems to have more in common with the discourse of advertising and public relations which never expresses doubt about its own claims (G. Cook 2007a, 2008a), than with the self-questioning and provisional nature of academic argument. Though claims of the unpopularity of translation are occasionally supported with anecdotal evidence (often based on the advocate's own memories of school), these tend to leave important factors out of account. These include teenager propensity to criticize the teaching they receive, whatever the method, and of each generation to reject the ideas of its predecessor. These factors are likely in time to work against any new method and to render any popularity it may have enjoyed on its introduction short-lived. There is in Direct Method a delusion that it can remain forever young.

The villain: Grammar Translation

All new movements need an old regime to replace—one they can caricature and ridicule, whose weaknesses will nicely show off their own virtues in contrast. In Grammar Translation, the orthodoxy of their time, both the Reform Movement and the new Direct Method language schools found an easy target.

Grammar Translation was the dominant way of teaching modern languages in European secondary schools at the end of the 19th century—and continued to be so, despite the attacks, long into the 20th century. It had inherited from the teaching of Latin and Ancient Greek, with which the modern languages vied for respectability, an emphasis on writing, on grammar, on accuracy, and on the ultimate aim of enabling its students to read the literary classics of the language they were learning. Grammar Translation is what people often seem to be referring to when they use the vague term 'traditional language teaching' or talk in general about TILT, though it had some rather more specific features than that imprecise designation suggests. This is despite the fact that we are now so far removed from the heyday of Grammar Translation, and have lived so long with Direct Method, that it is now surely time to call the latter 'traditional'.

Devised at the end of the 18th century for use in Prussian secondary schools (Howatt 2004: 151), Grammar Translation is essentially teaching a language through a combination of explaining and learning grammar rules and translating both into and out of the target language. It is a prime example of what later came to be called a 'synthetic syllabus' (Wilkins 1972) in which items to be learnt are formulated, graded, and presented to students in an ordered and cumulative manner.

> Different parts of a language are taught separately and step by step so that acquisition is a process of gradual accumulation of parts until the whole structure of language has been built up...At any one time the learner is being exposed to a deliberately limited sample of language...The learner's task is to re-synthesize the language that has been broken down into a large number of small pieces with the aim of making his learning task easier.
> (Wilkins 1976: 2)

The items which structure a Grammar Translation course are discrete grammar rules, graded for difficulty and presented a few at a time, starting with the 'easiest' and 'most important' first (though these are not necessarily the same thing). Each lesson or unit of the course thus revolves around a few new rules, which are first explained to the student in their own language, learnt and committed to memory, and then practised and tested through exercises involving the translation of single invented sentences exemplifying the rules currently in focus. Grammar cannot be practised without vocabulary, but as Grammar Translation revolves around grammar, its presentation of vocabulary is rather more haphazard. A few words, chosen by the course writer for a variety of reasons, are presented in each lesson or unit, together with their translation equivalents for students to learn by heart. Knowing the meaning of a word is thus conceived of as knowing its translation equivalent. The key principle of this approach is that the translation exercises should contain only words and constructions which have already been encountered. There are in other words no surprises, either for students or for teachers. Knowledge is cumulative and staged, so that by the end of the course (it seems to be implied) the language—by which is meant the grammar and how to use it for translation—has been learnt. Vocabulary can, of course, be added on independently and indefinitely, and is not generally seen as something which needs teaching. A further obvious but important point is that a Grammar Translation course is always for speakers of a particular language. So it is 'German for French speakers', 'Japanese for English speakers', and so on, rather than, as Direct Method courses are, for learners from any language background.

Though sometimes described as a 'method', it is worth noting that while the typical Grammar Translation coursebook says a great deal about *what* is to be taught, it has little or nothing to say about *how*. Much, however, is implicit, and textbook and lesson structures often mirror each other, with the units in many Grammar Translation books being called 'lessons' rather than 'chapters'. For the autodidact using a self-study guide, the procedure is to begin at the beginning and work through to the end, understanding and memorizing each rule and vocabulary list as it appears, practising and self-testing through the translation exercises (checking against the answers given at the back of the book), and taking time out periodically to revise and review. In the classroom the procedure is similar, although it is the teachers who will ensure the comprehension of new rules and who will correct answers to exercises, undertaking remedial work and further explanation where necessary, and adding further commentary and explanation of their own. All this entails a mode of learning which is highly dependent upon the authority of the textbook (Gray 2002; Santos 2004). It entails teacher-centred and teacher-led learning, with whole class procedure, lock-step progress, and norm-referenced testing (Clark 1987: 8–9). And this, in turn, implies streaming for ability within a classical-humanist educational curriculum whose overriding rationale is to pass on knowledge from one generation to the other, rather than to seek social change, adapt to new economic needs, or develop variable fulfilment for individual students (ibid: 1–100).

To make these general principles more concrete, it is worth looking at an example in more detail. As already mentioned, Grammar Translation remained the staple of self-study guides until quite recently, and the example in Figure 1 on pp. 12–13 is not from the late 19th century, but from the 1961 edition of *The Penguin Russian Course* (Fennell 1961), which remained in print until 1996, when it was replaced by *The New Penguin Russian Course*.

It is called *Lesson 1*, but assumes that students have already mastered the Cyrillic alphabet and Russian pronunciation, both of which, though they are ongoing problems for any English speaker beginning Russian, have in this book been relegated to prefatory matter and dealt with in a rather cursory manner. It begins with a list of vocabulary items assembled partly on the principle that many of the words are similar to their English equivalents. Russian класс (*klass*) for example is English 'class'; Russian лампа (*lampa*) is English 'lamp'; Russian стул (*stul*) is English 'chair' (and like English 'stool'). There follows an explanation in English of two grammar rules, expressed rather anglocentrically as 'Absence of article in Russian' and 'Omission of verb corresponding to English 'is', 'are' in the Present Tense', as though English grammar were the norm, and Russian somehow a deviation from it. (There is also a rather curious and ironic omission of the article in the heading 'Absence of article in Russian'!) These two rules have presumably been chosen as openers on the basis of contrastive analysis between the two languages, in that they are frequently encountered points of grammar in which Russian differs markedly from English. The absence of the article would not need pointing out to speakers of Chinese, whose language also has no articles, nor the absence of the present copula to Arabic speakers, whose language has this same feature. In practical terms, this early explanation of these rules is intended to spare the learner from constantly asking futile questions like 'What's the Russian for "the"?' or 'What's the Russian for "is"?' Having studied both these rules and the vocabulary, the learner is then to try out their understanding of them by translating sentences which make use of both: 'The house is here', 'The bridge is there', 'Here is the Volga', and so forth. That done, they are ready to move on to Lesson 2 where they will encounter new rules and new vocabulary which, together with those from Lesson 1, will be practised through new sentences for translation.

УРО́К 1   LESSON 1

СЛОВА́РЬ   VOCABULARY

вода́ water	Ленингра́д Leningrad
Во́лга Volga	Москва́ Moscow
вот here is	мост bridge
да yes	па́рта school-desk
дом house	план plan
доска́ board, blackboard	река́ river
и and	сло́во word
кана́л canal	стол table
ка́рта map	стул chair
класс class(room)	там there
ла́мпа lamp	тут here
	э́то this

ГРАММА́ТИКА   GRAMMAR

1. Absence of article in Russian

The Russian language has no article. The noun **дом** may mean 'the house', 'a house', or 'house' depending on the sense.

2. Omission of Verb corresponding to the English 'is', 'are' in the Present Tense

In Russian, the verb equivalent to the English 'is', 'are', etc., is not generally used in the present tense. The sentence **дом там** corresponds to 'the house is there'.

After **вот**, a demonstrative particle meaning 'here is' 'here are' and used to indicate one or more objects or persons (like the French 'voici' and 'voilà'), no verb is used. Thus

Вот дом.	**Here is** the house.
Вот дом и мост.	**Here are** the house and bridge.

The same applies to the neuter form of the demonstrative pronoun **это** which may be used to translate 'it is', 'this is'.

Это дом.	This is a house.

3. Interrogative Sentences

Questions in Russian may be denoted by intonation, the word order of the sentence remaining the same as in the affirmative statement:

Дом там.	The house is there. (Affirmative)
Дом там?	Is the house there? (Interrogative)

ТЕКСТ   TEXT

Вот дом. Вот мост. Дом там. Мост тут. Дом там? Да, дом там. Мост тут? Да, мост тут. Вот стол, стул, лампа. Там ка́рта и доска́. Это ка́рта. Тут Москва́. Там Во́лга. Тут сло́во «ла́мпа». Это вода́. Это мост и дом. Там стул, стол и па́рта. Стол тут, стул там.

УПРАЖНЕ́НИЯ   EXERCISES

Translate into Russian:

(1) The house is here.   (2) The bridge is there.
(3) Here is a house.   (4) Here is a bridge.
(5) Here is a lamp, a chair, a table.
(6) The school-desk is there.   (7) The plan is here.
(8) This is a map.   (9) Here is the Volga.
(19) The canal is here.   (11) A bridge is there.
(12) Is this Moscow?   (13) Here is Leningrad.
(14) This is a classroom.   (15) Is this a map?
(16) Are the house and the river there?
(17) Here is the word 'bridge'.

Figure 1 Fennell 1961: The Penguin Russian Course, pp. 3–4

While these explanations of grammatical rules are reasonably straightforward, it is worth pointing out that they do assume in students a pre-existent knowledge of grammatical terminology—'article', 'present tense', and so on. It is worth noting too that study along these lines is a way of teaching students a general grammatical metalanguage. While self-study books take knowledge of such terminology for granted, one can imagine a teacher using a course such as this one to teach simultaneously both Russian and grammatical terminology.

As courses progress however, the nature of these grammatical explanations inevitably becomes ever more complicated and impenetrable. Take for example this explanation of the use of the Italian subjunctive[3] from another self-study guide, the 1962 edition of *Teach Yourself Italian* (Speight 1962: 141). It is worth quoting at some length—given that prolixity is one of the features of this kind of explanation.

> The tense of the subjunctive in the subordinate clause is determined by what tense of the indicative is to be found in the main clause... We may formulate the rules as follows:
> 1 When the verb in the main clause is in the present indicative or the future or the imperative, the verb in the subordinate clause is in the present subjunctive or in the present perfect subjunctive...
> 2 When the verb in the main clause is in any other tense of the indicative (except the present perfect), the verb in the dependent clause is in the imperfect subjunctive, or in the past perfect subjunctive...
> 3 When the verb in the main clause is in the present perfect the verb in the subordinate cause may be either present or imperfect subjunctive, according as to whether it expresses a present or past action.

What the critics of Grammar Translation have pointed to is not difficult to guess. In their view, it is exclusively focused upon grammatical accuracy with no attention to fluency, and exclusively on writing with no practice of speech. It uses isolated invented sentences rather than authentic connected texts. It teaches knowledge about a language rather than an ability to use it, and is in general—it has been claimed—unnatural, authoritarian, and dull.

All of these criticisms have force, and it is easy to imagine the frustration of students faced with an explanation such as the one of Italian grammar above, particularly if they are eager to use the language in 'real' spoken communication, perhaps on a visit to a country where the language is spoken. Yet the validity of these criticisms does not mean that Grammar Translation has no merits at all, as some commentators concede (Larsen-Freeman 2000: 11–23). It is not a case of all or nothing. Grammar Translation can be adapted and supplemented by activities focusing on the aspects of language use which it ignores: connected texts, authentic examples of use, spoken discourse, fluency, student-centred activity, and so on. In its favour, it can be said that Grammar Translation does develop grammatical accuracy, grammatical metalanguage, and written translation skills, and, perhaps most importantly, that it provides a safe, structured route for both students and teachers. In this, it may be particularly well suited to those teachers who are themselves not wholly proficient in the language they are teaching and/or too overworked to undertake extensive preparation. For them Grammar Translation may prove a safe and reliable option. Lessons can be planned by just following the book; the teacher's own knowledge of material can be checked in advance; there are no linguistic surprises (as there can be in many other less structured approaches) revealing embarrassing gaps in the teacher's knowledge to the students; or, worse still, encouraging teachers to cover up such gaps by giving wrong information and explanation.

Nevertheless, Grammar Translation undoubtedly has weaknesses, and cannot provide a holistic course of study for students who want to attain a rounded proficiency. However, to use criticism of Grammar Translation as an argument against *any and all* use of translation is a logical sleight of hand. Grammar Translation is by no means the only way to use translation— indeed the kind of translation skills it develops, and the criteria it proposes for assessing them, are idiosyncratic, taking little account of time pressures or the possibilities of free rather than literal translation. So to condemn the use of translation in general by castigating its use in Grammar Translation is as unconvincing an argument as to dismiss the teaching of writing by criticizing a course using only dictation for that purpose, or to dismiss pronunciation teaching by pointing to the shortcomings of reciting decontextualized sounds. Yet this is what happened in the dismissal of Grammar Translation. On the basis of observations about its shortcomings, all uses of translation were renounced with no further argument allowed.

Sweet words

To illustrate the quality and nature of early arguments against Grammar Translation, let us move from the general to the specific, and examine a passage from Henry Sweet's *The Practical Study of Languages*, a book whose influence has been so long-lasting that it was reissued 65 years after its first publication in 1899 and is perhaps one of the most widely distributed and influential books on language teaching of all time. Sweet was a powerful and charismatic character (he was in fact the model for Professor Higgins in Bernard Shaw's play *Pygmalion* and its later musical adaptation as *My Fair Lady*). He writes with seductive eloquence. In one passage, he mocks invented sentences, of the kind which form the staple of Grammar Translation exercises. In his view, the effect of using such sentences:

> is to exclude the really natural and idiomatic combinations...and to produce insipid, colourless combinations, which do not stamp themselves on the memory, many of which, indeed, could hardly occur in real life, such as '*The cat of my aunt is more treacherous than the dog of your uncle/We speak about your cousin, and your cousin Amelia is loved by her uncle and aunt/My sons have bought the mirrors of the duke/Horses are taller than tigers.*' At one school where I learnt—or rather made a pretence of learning—Greek on this system, the master used to reconstruct the materials of the exercises given in our book into new and strange combinations, till at last, with a faint smile on his ascetic countenance, he evolved the following sentence which I remembered long

after I had forgotten all the rest of my Greek—'*The philosopher pulled the lower jaw of the hen*'.
(Sweet [1899] 1964: 73)

This is persuasive and entertaining rhetoric, effectively pillorying the eccentricities of both an individual teacher and a whole tradition of teaching, and it is easy to be carried along by it. It conveys the flavour of the book and provides evidence of why it was so successful. On closer scrutiny however, the logic—as opposed to the flow—of the argument seems suspect, and the issues more complex than Sweet suggests.

There is, in this entertaining anecdote, a glaring contradiction. First the invented sentences of grammar translation are criticized for being 'colourless combinations, which do not stamp themselves on the memory'. Then, only a few lines later, we are given an example a 'sentence which I remembered long after I had forgotten all the rest of my Greek'. Such sentences are, it seems, at once both utterly forgettable but completely memorable.

Sweet, like contemporary advocates of 'real language', favours language which is 'really natural and idiomatic' over 'insipid, colourless combinations' but the example of the latter with which he concludes his anecdote works against his own case. Whatever other Greek he may have 'made a pretence of learning', he certainly learnt the Greek in his final outlandish sentence very well. Indeed he continues in the line immediately following this passage to quote a correct Ancient Greek translation of it. My own experience of this sentence also testifies to its memorable quality. I have no problem remembering it, and do not even need to look it up when I use it as an example.

On reflection this is hardly surprising. The instances of language use which people most readily memorize verbatim are not from the mundane discourses of everyday life, where exact wording is unimportant, but are those marked by unusual, elevated, or archaic language, those reinforced by parallel structures such as rhythm and rhyme, and those with important or emotional content (G. Cook 1994, 2000: 170). The most likely stretches of language to be recalled verbatim are from genres such as prayers, jokes, literature, songs, graffiti, tabloid headlines, and rhetorical speeches (Keenan et al. 1977; Bates et al. 1980). The more bizarre the meaning, the more likely something is to be remembered. The sentence *The philosopher pulled the lower jaw of the hen*, precisely by being so absurd, seems to have gained entry to this élite category. It is remembered exactly, and can therefore serve as a reliable model for composition for other sentences in Greek. So it may be that some startlingly bizarre sentences such as *The philosopher pulled the lower jaw of the hen* are pedagogically useful, while some 'real' instances, being bland and forgettable, are much less so (G. Cook 2001a). Sweet offers no evidence to counter this possibility. Quite the contrary.

All this raises the more general issue of the relative merits of reality and artifice in learning. Sweet's assumption is that sentences which do not occur, or are unlikely to occur, outside the classroom are necessarily bad examples inside it. But the creators of sentences such as *The cat of my aunt is more treacherous than the dog of your uncle*, and phrases such as *the dog of your uncle, the mirrors of the duke, the lower jaw of the hen, the book of your uncle's gardener* are not attempting to emulate or teach the language of colloquial spoken interaction (as are the examples in many contemporary communicative courses), but rather are using them to illustrate grammatical points for pedagogic purposes. In these circumstances, it seems wrong to criticize them for not fulfilling aims which they did not espouse. What needs to be considered is the validity of the aims themselves. If assessed as models for the actual use of English, these are undoubtedly not good examples. As both intuition and corpora will testify, a pre-modifying possessive construction in which the modifier is animate (*your uncle's dog* etc.) is more typical and more native-like in English than a post-modifying possessive construction (*the dog of your uncle*, etc.). Yet as sentences for translation into a language in which a post-modifying construction is more frequent in such circumstances, as in French, Spanish and many other languages, this distortion of usual English acts as a guide to the student to produce correct translations: *le chien de mon oncle, el perro de mi tío*, etc.

Sweet's arguments against the Grammar Translation sentences however proved both effective and enduring. Mockery of ridiculous sentences for translation is a perennial favourite and guaranteed to raise a laugh in the right contexts, though the fact that a sentence is funny does not mean it is ineffective. Quite the opposite may be true.

Eminent British linguist J. R. Firth for example made the same point and the same joke in an address to the Philological Society in 1935. His argument, like Sweet's, relies heavily upon parody.

> '*I have not seen your father's pen, but I have read the book of your uncle's gardener*', like so much in grammar books, is only at the grammatical level. From the semantic point of view it is just nonsense. The following sentence gives perfectly satisfactory contexts for phonetics, morphology, and syntax, but not for semantics: '*My doctor's great-grandfather will be singeing the cat's wings*'.
> (Firth 1957: 24)

Elsewhere he argued (Firth 1968: 175) that such sentences are meaningless because they cannot be related to any 'observable and justifiable set of events in the run of experience'. We may note that both Firth and Sweet are guilty of playing the same trick. To prove their point, they deliberately create instances of sentences in which English grammar is distorted, rather than taking them from actual textbooks. The irony of this device is easily missed. These are in fact invented examples of invented examples! In addition, such unreal phenomena as cats with wings, though they may not occur in 'the run of experience', may well do so in fiction, fantasy, and play, all of which surely have a role to play in language learning. In stories, there have been plenty of winged cats both before and after Firth—for example in Henry Thoreau's *Walden* (1854) and Ursula Le Guin's *Catwings* (Le Guin 1998)—and there is no reason within their worlds why those cats' wings could not be singed.

This tradition of opposition to invented sentences has been constantly echoed ever since. Michael Lewis seems to regard them almost as sins, describing them as 'forgivable'.

> Many sentences occurred in textbooks, and were used in grammar practices which were well-formed English sentences, but which it was difficult to imagine anybody actually using.
> … While that may be forgivable, it is less so that teachers and textbook writers use such sentences themselves.
> (Lewis 1993: 13)

Grammar Translation was by no means dealt a death blow by the criticisms however, and has survived in many contexts, sometimes in spite of the assaults upon it (Benson 2000). It can still be found in many textbooks and syllabuses around the world, although ironically, some of its last bastions are now falling to Direct Method, while own-language use and translation, albeit in a different form, are being positively reassessed around the world, as we shall see in Chapter 3.

But in the language-teaching literature and in education, the extension of the critique of Grammar Translation to cover all uses of translation became deeply entrenched. The notions that monolingual instruction is better and more natural than bilingual instruction, that inductive learning is better than deductive teaching, and that the adult learner should follow the path of the native-speaker infant, run through the communicative language teaching revolution of the 1970s, and continue in many of the supposedly cutting-edge movements of the 2000s.

An attack on Grammar Translation, however, whether successful or not, is not the same as one on the use of translation in general. Indeed the Reform Movement never made such a case. Elsewhere in *The Practical Study of Languages*, as already observed, Sweet showed himself to be in favour of both translation and of explicit grammar teaching. The rationale for the complete outlawing of translation in many teaching contexts, and its almost complete neglect in theory and research for many decades, cannot claim descent from the academic arguments of the Reform Movement. We must conclude then that it was much more a matter of practical expediency, brought about by changes in learner and teacher demography.

These practical reasons for its demise included the following: translation cannot easily be used in classes composed of students from different language backgrounds, nor by native-speaker teachers who do not speak their students' language. There was also commercial and political self-interest behind the advocacy of Direct Method. It allowed publishing houses and private language schools to produce courses which could be taught to all comers by any teacher and therefore marketed worldwide. For those nations whose languages were to be taught by Direct Method, there was both political and commercial advantage in the export of native-speakers as teachers and experts, in the trend for students to learn in the country where the language was spoken, and in the general spread of influence which the new dispensation entailed. It is perhaps no coincidence that the Direct Method originated just as the English language publishing industry entered a new period of mass production, and drew upon ideas developed in Europe's two most powerful industrial nations, Britain and Germany, in the heyday of European nationalism. Direct Method was in tune with mass production, nation building, and imperialism. The chilling slogan:

'One Nation, One People, One Language'

can easily be rewritten for English Language Teaching:

'One Class, One Learner, One Language'

Notes

1 Corder's seminal *Introducing Applied Linguistics* claims that 'Of all the areas of applied linguistics, none has shown the effects of linguistic findings, principles and techniques more than foreign-language teaching – so much so that the term 'applied linguistics' is often taken as being synonymous with that task.' (1973: cover notes)

   The 2002 edition of the *Longman Dictionary of Applied Linguistics* (Richards, Platt, and Weber) gives the primary definition of the discipline as: 'the study of second and foreign language learning and teaching'. For further discussion see G. Cook 2003, 2005.

2 Later to be proclaimed by de Saussure and Bloomfield as one of the doctrines of 20th century linguistics: 'Language and writing are two distinct systems of signs; the second exists for the sole purpose of representing the first.'
   (de Saussure 1974: 23)

   Writing is not language, but merely a way of recording language by means of visible marks.' (Bloomfield 1935: 21). The primacy of speech is also reflected in the fact that we talk of someone as learning 'to speak' rather than 'to speak and write' a language, and being an 'English speaker' rather than 'English writer'.

3 As illustrated by this quotation, with its use of terms like 'subjunctive' and 'indicative', such explanations have frequently used a grammatical terminology inherited from Latin and Ancient Greek.

2

The long silence:
From Direct Method to meaning focus

The last chapter looked at the reasons for outlawing translation at the turn of the 19th and 20th centuries. The lack of any substantial pedagogic or linguistic argument against TILT in this period, and the suspicion of other driving forces behind its rejection, throw an interesting light on what happened in the following century. It is to this period, seen in this light, that we now turn.

There are times in surveys of academic literature, when an absence is of more interest than a presence. It indicates either that something has simply been overlooked, or judged to be not worth considering, perhaps on the assumption that, if it were considered, there would be unanimous agreement on its irrelevance to the enquiry in hand. Such phenomena are what French philosopher Bourdieu (1977: 164) referred to by the Greek term *doxa*: something in 'the natural and social world [that] appears as self-evident'. These blind spots in academic thinking and the reasons for them are sometimes well worth studying, and it is (or at least it should be) the job of academic enquiry to do so.

It may be that something is not mentioned because at some level—conscious or not—it is felt to be dangerous to the reigning ideology. Some have argued that it is what is *not* talked about, the gaps within discussions, which constitute the shared ideology of the participants (Althusser 1971: 136–69; Macherey 1978: 87; Fairclough 1989: 78–90). Discussions about education, for example, might raise specific issues about whether schools should teach religion, how big the classes should be, etc., but never question the whole concept of a school—the fact that almost every day children leave their homes to assemble in purpose-built buildings under the care of adults other than their parents. Once such usually unchallenged phenomena are talked about, once these gaps are filled, then difficult but significant questions may begin to be asked. Translation may be a phenomenon of this kind—absent from discussion for the damage it might do to the reigning ideology if it were not.

So successful were the Direct Method criticisms of TILT that, although translation continued to be used in many places, from the 1900s until very recently there has been virtually no discussion of it in the mainstream language-teaching literature. It is not that it was considered, assessed, and rejected, with reasons given for that rejection, but rather that it was simply ignored. It is thus difficult to take issue with explicit 20th-century arguments against TILT, as they hardly exist. This is, to say the least, an odd situation, especially given that—as argued at the end of the last chapter—the academic case for reform was based not on the use of translation in general, but on a highly limited form of that use in Grammar Translation, and that in general the 20th century was committed to a rational enquiry into all aspects of language teaching and learning. It seems fair to say that the case for translation was summarily dismissed without ever being properly heard.

Thus if we look at the current major surveys of the field, we find little or no mention of translation. Otherwise excellent introductions to language teaching, even in their latest editions, such as Hedge (2000), Carter and Nunan (2000), Johnson (2001), Richards and Rodgers (2001), either ignore translation completely or make passing reference to it as a historical phenomenon. Some others, such as Harmer (2007: 133) have introduced more discussion of it into their latest editions, responding to widespread grass-roots support for use of the students' own languages, to which we shall turn in Chapter 3. In surveys of SLA the situation is very similar. Thus in none of Rod Ellis's authoritative and comprehensive ongoing surveys of SLA research (Ellis 1985, 1993, 2003, 2008) do we find either an index entry or a section heading relating to translation, and the same is true of other widely used surveys and introductions such as Mitchell and Myles (2004) and Lightbown and Spada (2006). To be fair, the blame for this omission is not be laid wholly at the doors of these authors, as in surveying current approaches, either to teaching or to how languages are learnt, they are accurately reporting what has been said in recent decades on the role of translation—i.e. next to nothing.

Despite this lack of evidence or reasoned argument against translation, however, this chapter does attempt to chronicle and understand its absence from analysis. As a framework, it does so by characterizing 20th century language-teaching theory as having undergone two revolutions: the first was the shift from cross-lingual teaching to intra-lingual teaching (i.e. the coming of the Direct Method at the end of the 19th century described in the last chapter) and the second (still under that heading of intra-lingual approaches) a shift away from form-focused to meaning-focused teaching from the 1970s onwards. This framework may be represented diagrammatically. (See Figure 2 on page 22.)

To many this may seem an unwarranted simplification as, in its time, each revolution seemed to be composed of many very different and even irreconcilable movements. Nevertheless, I believe it is justified from a 21st-century perspective and with the advantage of hindsight; and I hope to substantiate the validity of this schematic approach to historical change in this chapter.

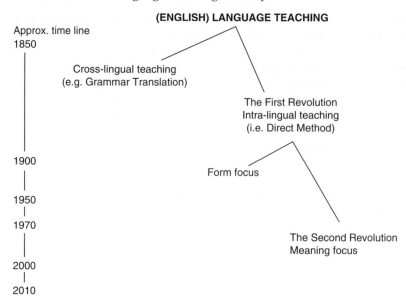

Figure 2 Major directions in English language teaching theory

It is worth noting however that while the first revolution was at its incep-
tion concerned with teaching several modern languages (both the Reform
Movement and the Berlitz Schools had applied their ideas to teaching French,
German, and other European languages as well as English), the second revolution was initially almost entirely concerned with English, though its influence
has also been felt since in the teaching of other languages (Grenfell 2002;
Pachler et al. 2008).

The first revolution: form-focused Direct Method

The first revolution, discussed in the previous chapter, was the movement
away from the use of the student's own language in favour of doing everything through the medium of the language being learnt. Yet despite its
apparent clean break with the past, ironically this shift left intact many characteristics of Grammar Translation. Though now conducted in the target
language, teaching was nevertheless still structured by an attention to form,
and a conception of the language as a set of grammar rules to be learnt. Some
say that even after the second revolution this continued to be the case (Littlejohn 1992), with successful EFL textbooks always having at their heart
a grammatical syllabus, even if it was disguised as communicative and/or
task-based. Whether or not that is true, certainly in all major approaches
flourishing prior to the meaning-focus revolution of the 1970s, the language

under instruction was still itemized and graded for presentation to students and practice by them. Examples of the language were, for the most part, still artificially constructed to exemplify a particular grammatical point, rather than because they arose 'naturally' from a communicative impetus to understand or achieve meaning. This is not to say that there were not considerable differences of teaching approaches, methods, and techniques (Anthony 1963) during this period. Thus audiolingualism saw habit formation through repetition as the best route to grammatical accuracy, while graded structure teaching favoured conscious mastery of rules, and situational teaching—as the name suggests—attempted to place structures within situations where they might occur.

Exercises might vary. They might be substitution tables, sentence transformation or completion, gap filling, or prompted responses. Yet across all these different approaches, student activity tended to be preceded by a presentation phase in which, prior to student practice, the teacher explicitly formulated what was to be learnt. This deductive process, in which rules are formulated first and put into action later, survived the outlawing of translation, but was also undermined by it. For to explain a new word or a complicated grammar rule without resort to the student's own language is notoriously and often comically difficult (as had been pointed out by Sweet 1899/1964: 201). Imagine, for example, what hope students of Italian might have of understanding the painful case of the Italian subjunctive we encountered in the last chapter if it had to be explained to them in Italian. Formulations of grammar rules are likely to incorporate instances of grammar beyond the ones they are explaining. As for new vocabulary items, they are similarly difficult to explain without translation. Classroom realia ('chair', 'desk', etc.) and other objects can be pictured or mimed ('car', 'flower'), the same is far from true of abstract terms and grammatical words. For all but the most hardened direct-method diehards, translation and first-language explanation is clearly more efficient. In cross-lingual teaching moreover, translation equivalents can be given together with commentary on ways in which they are *not* exactly equivalent, thus reducing the risk of student error when words are used in other contexts. The Russian word 'рука' (*ruka*) for example is often a valid Russian translation equivalent for 'hand' (a word likely to occur quite early in learning Russian), and this could be easily explained in a direct-method class. But unlike 'hand' it denotes the entire part of the body between shoulder and finger tips (i.e. 'arm' and 'hand' together) and is thus in some contexts best translated by 'arm'. Though this could be explained through illustration, it is much more easily done through first-language commentary.

In the many movements and methodologies which followed on from the early Direct Method, and in the many accompanying theories of how best to teach and learn a language, exceptions to the ostracism of translation were few and short lived. The highly successful American Army Method, developed for the rapid training of military personnel at the end of World War II, innovatively combined the presence of a native speaker talking to the students in the target language with that of a trained (structural) linguist who provided explanation and commentary on what was being said. While this was not exactly a use of translation in the conventional sense, and indeed in principle opposed to it, the Army Method nevertheless more generally relied on the mediation of the unknown language through the known, and in practice often made use of translation (Angiolillo 1947). In the 1970s Suggestopaedia (Lozanov 1978), a radical alternative way of teaching small groups, centred upon the notion that the reduction of student stress was the key to language-learning success. For this purpose, it used soft furnishings, comfortable chairs, background baroque music, and yogic breathing exercises. It also provided students with translations of what they heard, lest they should worry about not understanding, but did not ask students themselves to translate, lest they should worry about getting it wrong! Among other innovative techniques from this period, Total Physical Response (TPR) (Asher 1977), in which students learn by acting out instructions without speaking could, if we interpret translation very broadly, also be seen as a kind of translation—of words into gestures[1]—even though its founder, James Asher, throughout his work expressed strong opposition to TILT. Yet another alternative 'way' from this same period, Community Language Learning (Curran 1976), derived from Rogerian counselling and dedicated to the humanistic development of the 'whole' learner, argued that language learning activities, rather than being determined in advance, should arise from a process of negotiation between student and counsellor (as the teacher was called). True to this principle, it allowed translation in its inevitably eclectic repertoire, and in practice made use of translation more often than not, making one wonder in passing whether, if learners in other approaches had been more frequently consulted about their own preferences, translation might never have been sidelined to the extent that it was. All four approaches (Army Method, Suggestopaedia, TPR, and Community Language Learning) have proved comparatively minor and ephemeral in comparison with more mainstream developments.

   Within the ascendancy of the Direct Method, it is possible to talk of degrees of absolutism, and the situation was more complex than simply one of acceptance or rejection of students' own languages. In broad terms, there were two stages in the distancing of students' own languages by language teaching theory, corresponding to the two revolutions I have characterized above. In the first stage, even though students were barred from using translation as a practical way of comparing their own language with the new one, analysis of that relationship continued to inform academic research on language teaching and the design of teaching materials. In a sense, awareness of differences has always been behind the approaches to teaching one language to speakers of another, and any course produced to teach language A to speakers of language B automatically tends to base its approach on known differences. The most systematic and influential realization of this general principle, however, was the Contrastive Analysis Hypothesis which emerged out of structuralist and descriptive linguistics in the 1940s and was generally accepted until the 1970s. It is summed up succinctly by Fries (1945) as follows:

> The most efficient materials are those that are based upon a scientific description of the language to be learned carefully compared with a parallel description of the native language of the learner.

In *Linguistics Across Cultures: Applied Linguistics for Teachers*, a book widely regarded as having launched the movement in language teaching, Lado (1957) set out ways in which such systematic comparisons might be carried out and then used in syllabus design, teaching methodology, and testing. The overall assumption was—in general terms—that learner difficulties could be both predicted and remedied by an understanding of where their language differed from the one being learnt. The fact that Japanese has an /h/ phoneme but no /f/ phoneme should mean, for example, that Japanese learners of a language which has both will have difficulty with minimal word pairs distinguished by a contrast between /f/ and /h/, such as /fæt/ and /hæt/ in English. The hypothesis had a deep effect on the methods of its time. Audiolingualism for example was based on the notion that own language habits had to be replaced by new language habits through 'over-learning', and contrastive analysis determined both the content and the order of many graded structure and pronunciation courses. Work on contrastive analysis for language teaching continued actively in the 1970s and 1980s (James 1980; Fisiak 1981; Odlin 1989). Although under Chomsky's influence, there was a general shift in linguistics and first-language acquisition studies away from an interest in the differences between languages towards a quest for their similarities, even within a Chomskyan paradigm, there continued to be contrastive analysis for language learning (di Pietro 1971) and discussion of whether the learning of a new language might be influenced by similarities and differences between its parameter settings[2] and those of the student's own language (V. Cook and Newson 1996; Towell and Hawkins 1994).

While belief in the contrastive analysis hypothesis by no means entails the use of translation, and the findings of analysis were used mostly to inform language teaching rather than presented directly to students, it nevertheless maintains the presence of the students' own language, if only indirectly. A blow to even such an indirect presence was struck, and a second stage of distancing initiated, by the widespread acceptance from the 1970s onwards of new SLA theories of interlanguage (Selinker 1972) and natural acquisition (Krashen 1982), which claimed own-language interference to be only one minor source of errors, and that all learners followed similar sequences and encountered similar difficulties whatever their language. Yet although these ideas gained widespread acceptance in SLA, the contrastive analysis hypothesis has remained understandably popular outside the research world to this day, and the advent of these theories in many ways marks a point of disturbing divergence between theory and practice. Among teachers, there remains a strong interest and need for contrastive knowledge—witnessed by the success of books such as Swan and Smith's *Learner English* (2001) which sets out contrastive difficulties in English for seventeen of the world's major languages and four regional language groups as well.

The second revolution: focus on meaning

With the movement away from a structural approach to language teaching informed by contrastive analysis, the 1970s saw the advent of two related intra-lingual movements—the Natural Approach and CLT. In a kind of pincer movement between psycholinguistic and sociolinguistic approaches to language learning and use, these movements were inspired, on the one hand, by the new study of SLA, and on the other by sociolinguist Dell Hymes' theory of communicative competence (Hymes 1972). The former gave rise to a belief that language could be acquired without conscious attention to forms; the latter—at least in its most populist forms—to the advocacy of successful communication rather than formal accuracy as the language learner's ultimate goal. Despite very different theoretical pedigrees and many resulting differences, these two movements had one very significant item of belief in common: that the successful language learner should focus more upon meaning than on form. Their reasons for saying this were different. In the case of the Natural Approach, and the early SLA theory from which it derived, the idea was that a focus on meaning would activate subconscious cognitive language-acquisition processes when stimulated by 'comprehensible input' (Krashen 1985: 2). In the case of CLT, the belief was that, as the ultimate aim of language learning is to communicate, the most important activity for learners is to do things with their words, and understand what others are trying to do with theirs. Forms would be acquired in order to fulfil this need rather than for their own sake. Taken to extremes, this raises the possibility that forms with no semantic function—such as grammatical gender in French or the *s* morpheme of the English third-person present—are unimportant, or that successful formulations ('Me go sleep now') are as valid as correct ones ('I'm going to sleep now') (Taylor 1988).

Although students were not allowed to focus consciously on grammar rules themselves, the SLA research of this period was still focused almost exclusively on student acquisition of those same rules. In CLT, on the other hand, the focus was rather on the pragmatics of communication, and accurate grammar was seen as necessary only insofar as it served this 'higher' level. (Neither movement had much to say about either lexis or pronunciation.) These two influences together led to what we may validly regard as a second major revolution in language teaching theory and practice. The result was a further outlawing of form-focused teaching activities which were judged in the words of Long and Robinson (1998) to be 'associated with failure':

Grammatical syllabi, linguistically 'simplified' teaching materials, explicit grammar explanations, immediate forced student production, pattern practice, *translation*, error 'correction', and other widely used teaching devices are often asserted by their advocates to account for classroom language learning success. Attested by the ratios of beginners and false beginners to finishers, however, the same phenomena are more frequently associated with failure, suggesting that the successful students may learn through them or in spite of them, not necessarily because of them. (emphasis added)

Quite what the evidence could be for such a sweeping assertion is anything but clear. Knowing 'ratios of beginners and false beginners to finishers' not only implies access to a database of all language learners everywhere, but also a precise definition of what it means to 'finish' learning a language!

Though different in origin and in theory, however, both movements pointed towards similar activities and exposure. The language encountered by learners should be 'meaningful' and 'authentic', rather than 'artificially' focused on form. Both then presuppose an easy separation of the binary opposites:

meaning—form
real—artificial

A further common feature is the downplaying of the role of student conscious awareness and control of their own learning. Acquisition was believed to take place below the threshold of consciousness through attention to comprehensible input in the Natural Approach, and through communication in CLT. In SLA theory, acquiring a language was an automated internal biological process, rather like respiration or digestion, and this remains a widespread view today. In the words of V. Cook (2002):

Input for language acquisition mostly provides data for the mind to work on, just as the digestive system works on the vitamins in one's food. The message of the input sentences could be anything at all, provided they contain the necessary language elements on which the mind can build; it doesn't matter what your food tastes like or whether you eat liver or spinach provided you get iron in your diet...

Despite this relegation of language learning to a subconscious process beneath the threshold of consciousness, and the consequent treatment, in the worst cases, of students as language-acquiring mechanisms without will or wishes of their own, both movements presented themselves as liberating and promoting student autonomy, depicting older approaches which emphasized conscious attention to form as authoritarian and repressive.

Given the problem inherent in the first Direct-Method revolution, that it had continued to focus upon forms but deprived itself of the means to do so (i.e. first language explanation), the second revolution was, in many ways, a welcome relief from a self-inflicted wound, and clearly made sense for many people. It was also a child of the mood of the times. Occurring on the heels of the social and political revolutions and near-revolutions of the 1960s, and the ongoing Cultural Revolution in China, it presented itself, like them, as a liberation from regimentation and convention. Focus on forms was to be replaced by focus on meaning, dull and artificial exercises by 'real' and 'communicative' activities, and teacher and textbook authority by a new 'student-centred' curriculum. Yet although its proponents wholeheartedly believed in these changes, it is also possible to see this second revolution as a new form of repression posing as a liberation. Its effect was to reduce dramatically the number of 'allowed activities'. Not only was the ban on translation tightened, but a host of other well-tried language-learning activities were strongly discouraged too. Deductive teaching and manipulation of forms involved too much explicit attention to rules. Dictation, choral work, repetition, and rote learning were not how language is 'really' used. Drilling, teaching from the front, and correction were seen as authoritarian. Yet somehow this reduction of available options was hailed as an expansion of opportunities.

By confounding the many different movements of the time under one heading, I am open to the charge of overlooking significant differences between them, and no doubt veterans of that exciting era still active in language teaching theorizing today will criticize me for doing so, rather as the various factions of the 1968 revolutions do not like to be classed under one single heading as 'The Left'. Nevertheless, despite finer insider discriminations, there were sufficient characteristics in common between the different language-teaching movements, to identify this as a single and significant shift. Arguments for synthetic over analytic syllabuses (Wilkins 1972), for functional syllabuses (Wilkins 1976), natural language learning (Krashen and Terrell 1983), communicative language teaching (Brumfit and Johnson 1979; Littlewood 1981), procedural syllabuses (Prabhu 1984), process syllabuses (Breen 1984, 1987; Candlin 1984, 1987), the interaction hypothesis (Long 1983) and many others all had a great deal in common. They all preached against a graded itemized focus on forms and the use of 'artificial' examples. They all also claimed to be moving away from the demands of 'the course' or 'the language' towards those of the student. Ironically this student-centredness did not include any recognition of one of the main components of student identities—their own languages.

It is this commonality of purpose and practice, despite different theoretical rationales for them, which justifies my idealized representation of the course of 20th century language teaching as being subject to two major shifts whose influence, like those of their social and political counterparts, is still very much with us today, though waning.

Task-based language teaching

The key emphases of this era—on meaning, successful communication, student centredness, and 'real' language—can still be found in many research-driven ideas about language teaching today. Task-based language teaching (TBLT) in particular may be regarded as the successor of both early SLA-inspired approaches and CLT. Its pre-eminence among language-teaching theorists as an alternative to more 'traditional' approaches, including translation, makes it relevant to our concerns.

Standard and widely accepted definitions and exemplifications of tasks invoke one or more of these criteria, and include the notion that a task must relate to 'real-world' activities, in the sense of being something that students are likely to do when they actually use the language outside the classroom. Thus for Samuda and Bygate (2008: 69) a task is:

> a holistic activity which engages language use in order to achieve some non-linguistic outcome while meeting a linguistic challenge, with the overall aim of promoting language learning, through process or product or both.

Much TBLT theory explicitly derives from an SLA research base, and justifies its recommendations and their supposed effectiveness with reference to SLA theory (for example, Skehan 1998; Bygate, Skehan, and Swain 2001; Ellis 2003; Samuda and Bygate 2008). However, current SLA theory has made considerable advances since the early days of the 1970s and the extremism of the Natural Approach rejection of any explicit teaching of forms, and this is reflected in the more sophisticated claims of current TBLT. Following Schmidt (1990) there is now an emphasis on promoting student 'noticing' the formal features of the language they encounter and use. There is belief in the benefits of 'a focus on form', defined as drawing 'students' attention to linguistic elements as they arise incidentally in lessons, whose overriding focus is on meaning and communication' (Long 1991), although there is still rejection of a 'focus on formS' equated with the explicit teaching of discrete points of grammar. There are now also 'focused tasks' or 'structure trapping' tasks 'which *force* the use of particular structures' (Loschky and Bley-Vroman 1993), and task repetition is done in the belief that the same task 'can help different learners develop different areas of their interlanguage' (Lynch 2000) or 'lead students to integrate prior knowledge into performance' (Bygate and Samuda 2005). These advances are commendable for re-complexifying the image of the language learning process and allowing a variety of perspectives and strategies. They have certainly left behind the single monologic doctrine of all acquisition as subconscious. Nevertheless they place TBLT and SLA in the odd situation of having come full circle, paradoxically advocating that same attention to form and practice through repetition which they had originally rejected, rather than of moving on to genuinely new ground.

Given these developments, 'tasks' are in danger of losing a distinct identity from 'exercises' (of the kind often associated with 'traditional' translation or graded-structure courses), at least if the distinction between these two terms is that the former are focused upon language use to achieve a given outcome, while the latter are concerned with the practice of particular language items with no purpose as yet specified for their use. Indeed this danger is recognized by TBLT advocates themselves, who either reject such developments as apostasy:

> The use of the word task is sometimes extended to include
> 'metacommunicative tasks' or exercises with a focus on language form,
> in which learners manipulate language or formulate generalisations
> about form. But a definition of task which includes an explicit focus on
> form seems to be so all-embracing as to cover almost anything that might
> happen in a classroom. We therefore restrict our use of the term task to
> communicative tasks and exclude metacommunicative tasks from our
> definition.
> (Willis and Willis 2001)

or embrace the paradox:

> 'Tasks' are activities that call for primarily meaning-focused language use.
> In contrast, 'exercises' are activities that call for primarily form-focused
> language use. However, we need to recognize that the overall purpose of
> tasks is the same as exercises—learning a language—the differences lying
> in the means by which this purpose is achieved.
> (Ellis 2003: 3)

acknowledging that the overt purpose for the students and the covert purpose of a task for the teacher are rather different:

> In fact tasks involve a sleight of hand. They need to convince learners
> that what matters is the outcome. Otherwise, there is a danger that the
> learners will subvert the aim of the task by displaying rather than using
> language. However, the real purpose of the task is not that learners should
> arrive at a successful outcome but that they should use language in ways
> which will promote language learning. In fact, the actual outcome of
> a task may be of no real pedagogic importance. For example, whether
> learners successfully identify the difference between two pictures is not
> what is crucial to language learning...
> (Ellis 2003: 8)

Yet developments have not quite come full circle, and though there may be a partial return to ideas from before the second revolution, i.e. to the organization of teaching around language form, there is as yet no return to the days before the first revolution, i.e. to a cross-lingual syllabus which includes translation. Nowhere in the TBLT literature do we encounter an act of translation presented as a task, although this would easily fulfil all the criteria of the usual definitions[3]. Translation is a real-world activity outside the classroom. It is outcome-oriented: a successful translation is one that works. It promotes a focus on form as an offshoot of a communicative need, rather than as an end in itself. These points about the distinction between tasks and exercises, the relationship between the two, and the need felt in task-based syllabuses to re-introduce elements which will allow practice or draw attention to forms are highly relevant to an argument for TILT. Translation, as we shall see in Chapter 7, enables the apparently disparate focuses on communication and form to be reintegrated.

Another ascendant movement perpetuating confidence in the efficacy of a focus on meaning is content-based language teaching, in which curriculum subjects are taught through the medium of a new language on the assumption that this simultaneously furthers both student proficiency in that language and their knowledge of the subject in question. In many parts of the world this is specifically used for teaching English, but in Europe, where it is energetically promoted by the EU under the acronym CLIL[4] (Marsh 2002), it is also used in teaching other languages too, although English is by far the commonest choice. Drawing upon ideas dating back to the second revolution of the 1980s and early Canadian immersion schooling (Dalton-Puffer 2007: 255–261), it sees meaning as the main focus of teaching and learning. Specific attention to language form is seen as an auxiliary activity, while code-switching and translation ('trans-languaging' in the CLIL jargon) are seen as activities which will—and should—wither away (Marsh 2002: 98).

Relativity of outcomes

A considerable problem for TBLT and CLIL, and for any approach which confidently argues for the effectiveness of a focus on meaning is whether there is, or ever could be, any conclusive evidence to support such a view. Criteria for assessing language-learning success vary just as much as language-teaching strategies, and there is a real sense in which any approach can be vindicated if results are judged by its own measures. TBLT is likely to look successful if the yardstick is performing classroom tasks, and CLIL if it is discussing a particular curriculum subject, just as Grammar Translation will help if the test is the accurate translation of written sentences deploying covered vocabulary and structures. The predictions of any approach are, to an extent, self fulfilling. This charge of course cuts both ways and can be turned against any claims, including those for focus on forms, or translation. But given the strength of TBLT and CLIL claims, which are sometimes reminiscent of the absolutism of Direct Method, this weakness is particularly pertinent.

SLA has not been the only body of research drawn upon in TBLT. In corpus linguistics, automated analysis of databanks of millions of words of attested language data has effected a major revolution in language description (Sinclair 1991, 2004; Stubbs 1996, 2001) and has generated many ideas about how languages are represented in the mind (Wray 2002; Hoey 2005). Some prominent TBLT writers (Willis and Willis 2001) have also worked within this paradigm, and explicitly draw upon it in their work on language teaching, linking the corpus-linguistics concern with 'real language' to the TBLT aspiration to create 'real-world' classroom activity. Like Henry Sweet, they have an aversion to invented examples. Closely related to this brand of TBLT, there have been calls for a 'lexical syllabus' (Willis 1990) or 'lexical approach' (Lewis 1993, 1996) making use only of attested examples of the kind found in language corpora. CLIL too implies the benefits of attention to the 'real language' generated in the pursuit of a particular curriculum subject.

Yet this linking of real language and real-world activity leads to a paradox. Generally speaking, the majority of corpora, and certainly those used to inform language teaching, are a record of how people who already know the language actually use it. Learners are by definition people still in the process of acquiring a language. In addition, most corpora used for language-teaching examples also aim to be records of native-speaker use. Learners are, also by definition, non-native speakers. Despite the use of learner corpora for research (Granger 2002), those used to inform English-language teaching materials tend also to record only monolingual use of the language, rather than cases where it is mixed with other languages, although such macaronic code-switching is a common phenomenon in the multilingual societies of the real world, and will come as a natural strategy to language learners, especially if they share the language of other students. All this means that the language brought into a classroom through the mining of examples from monolingual native-speaker corpora is very different from that being used by learners struggling to carry out tasks within it. The very fact that the 'real' language use recorded in corpora comes from the world outside the classroom puts it in marked contrast with the very different 'reality' of language use inside the classroom, which may well include frequent translation. Indeed one might say there are two kinds of 'reality' in conflict with each other, rather than—as often assumed—a real monolingual world in opposition to an artificial bilingual one. A learner may well resort to unidiomatic formulations or to code-switching or translation in order to complete a task in an authentic way. Conversely, the attempt to mimic native-like constructions may have an inauthentic ring to it, and even hinder communication. What was live and vibrant when first used, becomes dead and frozen when imitated. As argued persuasively by Widdowson (1978: 80), what was 'real' and 'genuine' when it occurred outside the classroom becomes inauthentic when used inside it. Authenticity is less a quality of the language itself than of the communication which makes use of it.

Drawing upon this distinction of Widdowson's, van Lier (1996: 127–128) goes further, interestingly claiming authenticity for the most unreal language data of all—the grammatical explanations and invented sentences of Grammar Translation.

> In a curious way it seems to me that the traditional language lessons of the grammar translation type which I remember from my school days might lay greater claim to that sort of authenticity than some of the so-called communicative classrooms that I have had occasion to observe in recent years. I must emphasize that the old lessons seem to have been authentic

for me, although they may well have been unauthentic for some of my classmates.

Dissenting voices

It is not the case, however, that there were no voices raised in defence of translation during the heyday of the second revolution, from the late 1970s into the 1990s. Most were lone voices making a case for the use of translation in particular contexts such as testing (Matthews-Breský 1972), literacy (Baynham 1983), English for Specific Purposes (Tudor 1987), reading (Cohen and Hawras 1996). More general pleas for reassessment (Green 1970; Atkinson 1987; G. Cook 1991, 1997; Hummel 1995; Malmkjær 1995/1996) did not attract mainstream attention. However, there were also some striking defences of translation by major thinkers of this period.

Widdowson's distinction between the genuine and the authentic, discussed in the last section, is made in his *Teaching Language as Communication*, one of the seminal books of the communicative movement. Pursuing this distinction towards the end of the book, he makes an explicit case for translation, writing (with the generic masculine pronoun of the time):

> What is meant by the first of these [principles] is that language learners should be made aware of what they are doing when they undertake language tasks, that they should be led to recognise that these tasks relate to the way they use their own language for the achievement of genuine communicative purposes. This principle naturally leads us to associate the language to be learned with what the learner already knows and to use the language for the exploration and extension of this knowledge. To use language, in short, in the way language is normally used...The principle might also be applied to the association of the language being learned with the language the learner already knows. What we are aiming to do is to make the learner conceive of the foreign language in the same way as he conceives of his own language and to use it in the same way as a communicative activity. This being so, it would seem reasonable to draw upon the learner's knowledge of how his own language is used to communicate. That is to say, it would seem reasonable to make use of translation.
> (Widdowson 1978: 159)

This is, however, only a brief passage at the end of this influential book, appearing in the last six pages almost as an afterthought to the main argument, and neither this, nor Widdowson's further elaboration of ideas for communicative translation exercises in ESP (Widdowson 1979: 101–112), were taken up in the general practices of CLT.

Another authoritative voice for translation is that of the historian of English Language teaching Tony Howatt, on whose work I have drawn extensively in the previous chapter, whose survey leads him to the conclusion in the first edition that:

> The practice of translation has been condemned so strenuously for so long without any really convincing reasons that it is perhaps time the profession took another look at it.
> (Howatt 1984: 161)

and this is reiterated in the second edition, significantly written in collaboration with Henry Widdowson:

> There has long been a strong case for reviewing the role of translation in language teaching and particularly its educational value for advanced students in schools and universities. Properly handled, it provides a useful antidote to the modern obsession with utilitarian performance objectives, but the pitfalls that were identified by the nineteenth-century reformers have not gone away, and the activity remains a demanding one
> (Howatt 2004: 312)

Another influential commentator who touches upon the use of translation is H. H. Stern. In a survey of syllabus types and approaches, he devotes a chapter (Stern 1992: 279–300) to the relative merits of what he terms 'cross lingual' syllabuses (those which make use of the students' own language) and 'intra-lingual' syllabuses (those which do not). He sees these options however not as binary opposites, a case of either/or, but as opposite poles of a continuum, with many intermediate hybrid cases along the cline between the two. In this representation, translation is one of several possible cross-lingual activities. Others are 'comparison between L1 and L2', 'use of L1–L2 dictionary', and 'interpretative treatment of texts' in which the text is read in the L2 but commented upon in the L1. For a topic which tends to elicit extreme points of view, Stern's assessment of the competing claims of cross- and intra-lingual approaches is admirably balanced. He argues that each has merits, but which one is chosen should depend on specific purpose and situation:

> if proficiency in L2 communication skills is the principle objective the intralingual strategy will be dominant. However if the mediating skills (translation and interpreting) are the goal, a crosslingual strategy will have an important part to play.
> (op. cit. 301)

Within this framework, Stern is able to present the arguments on each side, firmly anchoring all his comments to the realistic observation that translation will take place anyway, and lamenting anti-translation dogmatism as detrimental to both approaches:

> We would like to suggest that an intralingual strategy would be more effective if its crosslingual counterpart were more clearly recognised as a strategy in its own right complementing an intralingual.

On the side of the cross-lingual option, he states the case as follows:

> Let us set out from our deeply ingrained knowledge of the L1, and
> the inevitable existence of transfer and interference, and use them as a
> psychological given. We need not deny the fact that the learner uses the
> L1 for a reference; on this basis we can help learners gradually develop a
> new L2 reference system, pointing out where the two languages are alike
> and where they are different.
> (op. cit. 284)

Most of Stern's argument relates, however, to bilingual teaching rather than
translation *per se* (about whose use he is arguably rather cool), implying the
possibility of the former existing without the other.

One final voice from the end of this period which will lead us on into the
next is that of Claire Kramsch. In her book *Context and Culture in Language
Teaching*, she unashamedly recommends the contrast of translations (1993:
163–169) arguing that:

> a way of highlighting the discourse value of the author's choices is to
> compare it with its translation into another language
> (Kramsch 1993: 148)

The remarks are made about the teaching of German rather than English, and
for advanced learners (the translations in question are of Rilke's poem *der
Panther*), but are stated in a way which implies a wider relevance.

These last two voices, those of Stern and Kramsch have another characteristic
in common other than their advocacy of translation and a bilingual approach to
language learning. Unusually among the English Language teaching theorists
of the second revolution, which was dominated by Anglo-American academic
voices, they are neither of them native speakers of English. Stern left his native
Germany in around 1933 for England (where he used his native German language in the propaganda war against the Nazis[5]), moving later to Canada in
1968, where he conducted work on French/English bilingual educational programmes. Claire Kramsch is French, but emigrated to the USA in 1963, where
she taught first at Cornell and then at MIT, and is now Professor of German and
Foreign Language Acquisition at the University of California, Berkeley.

Both have themselves been successful learners, both used to operating in
and between more than one language. Stern, who died in 1987, was in many
ways, despite his forward thinking views, of an earlier generation of thinkers
about language teaching, and his major books (1983, 1992) are grand narratives, aiming to bring order and rationality to the rather disordered history
of English language teaching in the 20th century—in ways which would find
little favour with the more deliberately local perspectives of the post-modernist approaches which have followed. The voice of Claire Kramsch however
spans the two periods and will, together with that of Henry Widdowson, be
very much in evidence in the 21st century calls for bilingualization of language teaching to which we now turn.

Notes

1 Referred to by Jakobson (1959) as 'intersemiotic translation'.
2 According to one version of Chomskyan theory, parameters are variables of an innate Universal Grammar which are given different settings within the early stages of child language acquisition. A particular setting may be shared by several languages.
3 Although some recent advocacy of TILT has discussed translation activities as tasks. See for example Howells 2009.
4 Content and Language Integrated Learning. It is also known as EMILE: *Enseignement d'une Matière par l'Intégration d'une Langue Etrangère.*
5 Juliane House, personal communication.

3

A climate for revival:
The recognition of bilingualism

In contrast to the absolutist monolingualism which dominated high-profile theories of language teaching in the 20th century, the first decade of the 21st century has seen increased interest in and support for the use of students' own languages. Yet this has not always entailed an advocacy of translation as a part of that bilingualization. Thus the long 20th century silence which followed the 19th century rejection remains only partially broken. As translation is a major and obvious way of using the two languages together in a useful and systematic manner, this failure to embrace it wholeheartedly is something of a conundrum. One possible explanation is that TILT has never really shaken off its association with Grammar Translation, whose academic formality, and almost exclusive attention to formal accuracy in writing, made it seem quite distinct from the use of language for actual communication. The early Direct Method confounding of TILT with Grammar Translation enabled it be cordoned off as a neatly separate kind of teaching and learning activity, quite different from all others, including even other uses of the students' own language. Translation came to be associated with the dry and the academic, conceived as the polar opposite of 'real-world' language and activities, rather than as something interwoven into communication in bilingual contexts.

It is not entirely surprising then, that in the recent advocacy of bilingual learning, TILT is still often kept at arm's length. Somehow the image of TILT as a discrete activity has lingered on; calls for the use of students' own languages have kept their distance from calling for the use of translation. There is no reason for this to be so, however. In addition to the insights TILT can provide into language form, as it does in Grammar Translation, it can also be a lively communicative activity, which inevitably arises from, and merges into, other kinds of cross-lingual activity. This is in line with the view, already outlined in the Introduction, that translation cannot be treated separately from other bilingual activity, and to insist that it should be is somewhat forced and unconvincing. It is hard to imagine, for example, how explanation in the students' own language can proceed without giving rise to incidental translation, nor how—conversely—when translation is the main focus of activity, it can proceed without giving rise to incidental explanation in the students' own language. In addition, many of the arguments which support bilingualization, have the same force in support of TILT, even when they do not advocate it explicitly.

This chapter examines the degree of support for bilingual and multilingual language use—in academic enquiry, in society in general, and in language teaching—and the positive environment which a change of attitude has provided for TILT. This new climate is a necessary precondition for TILT, even if it is not also a sufficient one.

The academic climate

Ten years into the 21st century there is potential for a radical change in academic approaches to language teaching and learning, and for a break with entrenched beliefs which hardened during the previous century. This new climate is influenced by directions in the study of language itself, and in a wider context by social and political changes in the world at large. In linguistics, the old preoccupation with separating language from context, as well as other rigid dichotomies in the study of language, such as those between mind and society, form and meaning, classroom and reality, native and foreign speaker, synchronic and diachronic study, are giving way to more complex and fluid analytic categories. The boundaries between languages themselves are seen as more fuzzy and less fixed (Harris 1998; Rampton 2005) as are those between language and other communicative modes such as images, music, and gesture (Kress and van Leeuwen 2001; Norris 2004). In applied linguistics, including some SLA, there is a new 'social turn' (Block 2003a) in which applied linguists increasingly draw upon other disciplines and types of enquiry such as social theory (Sealey and Carter 2004), Bakhtinian criticism (Kelly Hall et al. 2004; Ball and Warshauer Freedman 2004), sociocultural theory (Lantolf 2000), ethnography (Creese 2008), and complex systems theory (Larsen-Freeman and Cameron 2008), though without abandoning language as the main and distinguishing focus of enquiry. And from these new sources, the study of language has borrowed new concerns, perspectives, and preoccupations, taking a new ecological approach (van Lier 2000, 2004; Kramsch 2002) which sees language not as a reified object but:

> as a historically contingent phenomenon negotiated between interactants in daily conversations and daily interactions and includes consideration of language and power, language and history and the ways people position themselves *vis-à-vis* one another and *vis-à-vis* history through language.
> (Kramsch 2008)

There is a greater recognition of complexity, diversity, difference, and indeterminacy. In descriptions of international communication, this new breadth is evident in a greater propensity to talk of Englishes rather than English

(Kachru 1985), of the multiple ownership of English (Widdowson 1994), and of the validity of non-native English as a *lingua franca* (Jenkins 2000, 2007; Seidlhofer 2002, 2010).

The political climate

This change is set, as intellectual revolutions inevitably are, against the wider political and social upheavals of its time; and the revolution in language study we are witnessing now and the struggles which take place within and around it, echo and reflect these wider changes. This same period of the 1990s–2000s has been—as often remarked—one of rapid changes not only in cultural practices, the power balances between nations and economies, and the technologies of linguistic communication, but also in the very nature of cultural, national, and linguistic identity itself. Mass migration and global communication work against any simple equation of nation, culture, and language (Brumfit 2001: 55–63; Carter and Sealey 2007) of the kind which was the basis of various ideologies of nationalism in the past (Joseph 2004).

However, against a trend to acknowledge identities as more fluid and less discrete, there are powerful forces seeking to freeze, preserve, and exclude. There have been rearguard reactions by those who would prefer to halt this current of change, and whose views are still powerful and influential. Thus nationalism is ascendant in many places, manifest often in movements for monolingual purity. Around the world many of the most violent and intractable conflicts arise from an impetus to preserve older national, linguistic, cultural, and religious identities. One of the arguments of this book, already advanced in Chapter 1, is that the suppression of students' own-language use has something in common with such movements, especially in the teaching of English and other major international languages.

When one language is promoted as a means of national, regional, or international communication, there is a crucial distinction to be drawn— one which is often strategically overlooked by both sides in debates on these issues—between the promotion of that language at the expense of others, perhaps even as a means of their suppression, and the promotion of that language as a means of communication across language barriers in ways which seek not to be detrimental to other languages. It is important in the critique which follows to distinguish between those policies and practices promoting one language, which are nevertheless prepared to tolerate or even promote the use of other languages alongside it, and those policies and practices whose aim is to replace a multilingual environment with a monolingual one, by actively suppressing or discouraging the use of all languages other than the one they favour. This possible dichotomy can be seen at every level. At a societal level, for example, official status may be granted only to one language and withdrawn from others or, conversely, active measures may be taken to protect and ensure minority language rights alongside an official language[1]. In educational policy, resources might be directed only to the teaching of a national language, and not at all to the teaching of other community languages. In classroom practice, bilingualism may be discouraged or even actively banned, or it may be looked upon positively and encouraged. Within a family or a community a heritage language may be abandoned, or actively maintained. (In practice and at all levels there are, of course, many intermediate positions between these extremes.)

In the heated academic debates around these issues, there are those who argue, particularly with regard to English, that there is no such dichotomy, and the ascendancy of one language inevitably entails and indeed is instrumental in the decline of others, making the promotion of one language 'linguistic imperialism' (Phillipson 1992). On the other side are those who argue that the growth of a global language—specifically English—need not entail harm to other languages (Crystal 2003). These two opposed views have given rise to bitter exchanges (Phillipson 1999; Crystal 2000a). In this debate, while neither side overtly supports suppression, Phillipson believes that the latter view falls into the trap of inadvertently providing succour to suppression through misguided liberalism, while Crystal refutes this charge, pointing to the well established view in linguistics that, contrary to some ill-informed popular and political claims, bilingualism is in no way detrimental to either language involved, and there is therefore no contradiction in simultaneously promoting both one global or national language for general communication while simultaneously protecting and promoting others.

With this in mind, it is informative to view international English language teaching in the context of more general developments in language policy and education in the English-speaking countries. In the United States, the English-Only campaign seeks to make English the nation's only official language, rather than—as it is at present—the sole official language of 48[2] of the Union's 50 states. Though particularly active during the George W. Bush administrations, with sympathetic Senate votes in 2006 and 2007[3], the movement has a long history. One of the most extreme formulations of it can be found in a speech by President Theodore Roosevelt in 1914, significantly, we may note, during the heyday of the rapid expansion of Direct Method in English language teaching:

> We have room for but one language in this country, and that is the English language, for we intend to see that the crucible turns our people out as Americans, of American nationality, and not as dwellers in a polyglot boarding house.
> (Roosevelt 1926: 554)

The debate has inevitably also involved education policy. One resolution, known as Title III of the House of Representatives debate on the 'No Child Left Behind Act' found that:

> English is the common language of the United States and every citizen and other person residing in the United States should have a command of the

English language in order to develop their full potential (H.R.1., Title III, Sec. 3102).
(quoted in Johnson 2009)

This statement, though ostensibly moderate and reasonable, taken in the context of the English Only debate, raised concern about Federal policy towards the maintenance and encouragement of bilingualism. In the words of Johnson (2009):

> With its vigorous attention to English language acquisition for English language learners... Title III has fomented concern that developmental bilingual education will be phased out and transitional or English-only pedagogical approaches phased in.

In short, while there is undoubtedly a case for one general language known to all citizens for communication throughout the USA and good grounds to pursue this goal, there is also good reason to suppose that the English Only movement, and legislation and policy inspired by it, is aimed at replacing other languages rather than supplementing them. There is an echo in it perhaps, not unconnected to the religious fundamentalism of many of its supporters, of the attitude to multilingualism in *Genesis* 11: 1–9, the story of the Tower of Babel in which God punishes humanity for trying to build a tower to heaven. In this story, a desirable state of affairs in which:

> the whole earth was of one language, and of one speech.

is replaced by an undesirable state of affairs, in which God did:

> confound their language, that they may not understand one another's speech

Life was apparently much better with one language!

As I write this in 2009, it is hard to say whether policy will change under the Obama presidency, but judging by comments made during his election campaign, his views are not sympathetic to the English Only Movement:

> I don't understand when people are going around worrying about we need to have English Only. They want to pass a law: we want English Only. Now I agree that immigrants should learn English. But understand this. Instead of worrying about whether immigrants can learn English—they'll learn English—you need to make sure your child can speak Spanish. You should be thinking about how can your child become bilingual.
> (Barack Obama, campaign speech 2008[4])

In Britain and Ireland, English Only, though not under that name, has an even longer history. Cromwell's Irish campaigns in the 1650s, which associated the speaking of Irish with the Roman Catholicism and nationalism they sought to suppress, not only reduced the population of Ireland by as much as one half, but also contributed to the ongoing decline of the Irish language (Barnard 1975: 170–180; O'Connell 2001). In Scotland, less than one hundred years later, the English redoubled their persecution of Scottish Gaelic in the aftermath of the 1745 rebellion, making its use a criminal offence, and all but wiping it out. Active promotion of Welsh in Wales in recent times on the other hand has contributed to a reversal of its decline. Meanwhile, more recently arrived languages, despite the large numbers of speakers[5] and the provision for translations and use in many situations, are neglected in the British educational system, where language teaching concentrates almost exclusively on European foreign languages (mostly French and German) with no attempt to incorporate larger minority languages into the curriculum. Legislation in 2003 made proficiency in English[6], together with knowledge of a narrowly conceived 'British culture' (both assessed by tests) a condition of new citizenship. Former Home Secretary David Blunkett appeared to extend this government demand to speak English even into the homes of those who are already British citizens:

> speaking English enables parents to converse with their children in English, as well as in their historic mother tongue, at home and to participate in wider modern culture. It helps overcome the schizophrenia which bedevils generational relationships. In as many as 30% of Asian British households, according to the recent citizenship survey, English is not spoken at home.
> (Blunkett 2002)

There is then, in the UK as in the USA, some reason to characterize the ascendancy of English as promoted at the cost of other languages spoken in those countries.

The objection may be raised that as the USA and UK are what Kachru (1985) refers to as 'Inner Circle' English-speaking countries, i.e. 'the traditional cultural and linguistic bases of English' with predominantly English native-speaking populations[7], it is therefore quite reasonable for English to be maintained in both as the language of national identity and unity, *pace* Theodore Roosevelt and David Blunkett. This view however ignores both the extent of immigration into the two countries, its effect upon the linguistic profiles of their populations[8], and the frequently chauvinistic nature of English Only sentiments. Such negative attitudes to linguistic diversity and the belief, as in the Tower of Babel story, that multilingualism is a curse, are by no means confined to right-wing elements in the English-speaking world, or to the promotion of English. The imposition of one language at the expense of others, often through violence and discrimination or the deprivation of rights, is a depressingly recurring phenomenon in human history (Shohamy 2006: 132). In fascist Spain, to give but one example, Franco promoted the use of Spanish at the expense of other peninsular languages such as Basque, Catalan, and Galician, forbidding their use in documents, school lessons, and signs, and at one time or another, almost all the major European powers, as well as many other nations, have pursued a similar policy to all but one of the languages within their borders.

Globalization

Increased mass migration is one aspect of globalization, though the extent to which it is cause or consequence is open to debate. Globalization has been defined many times and in a variety of ways, but a useful definition for our purposes here is:

> the observable ongoing process of the increasing and ever-more intensive interconnectedness of communications, events, activities and relationships taking place at the local, national or international level. (Block 2006: 3)

Although much of the literature on globalization focuses upon its economic and communications–technology aspects, it is also a linguistic phenomenon. Indeed if one adopts Bourdieu's (1991) notion of 'linguistic capital', or of language knowledge as a commodity which can be traded (for example by publishers, teachers, translators), then the linguistic aspects of globalization are part of, rather than distinct from, the economic ones. Translation, we might note (picking up a word from Block's definition) is of its nature to do with 'interconnectedness'. It relates languages to each other, rather than leaving them to operate in separate compartments, and is thus very much in tune with globalization. Indeed it is, and always has been, a major catalyst of global communication.

In language use, as in all its other aspects, globalization is subject to different and sometimes contrary interpretations. Some see it as a euphemism for Americanization (Ritzer 1998) and/or a general homogenizing force, others as an impetus to heterogeneity, and others still as a more complex interaction between global and local perspectives. Robertson (1995) coined the term *glocalization* 'to make the point that globalization entails a synergetic relation between the global and local as opposed to the dominance of the latter over the former' (Block and Cameron 2002a: 3). Yet however conceived, the impact of the globalization process is clearly of importance in any consideration of the contemporary linguistic landscape, and developments in language teaching and learning. Not surprisingly then, the 2000s have seen a significant applied linguistic interest in globalization and its linguistic consequences (Block and Cameron 2002b; Dörnyei, Csizér and Németh 2006; Rubdy and Saraceni, 2006; Edge 2006; Fairclough 2006; Pennycook 2007; McElhinny 2008; Rubdy and Tan 2008).

Extent of multilingualism

Although often marginalized in both linguistics and political discourse, bilingualism and multilingualism have always been important and widespread aspects of individual and societal language use. The extent of contemporary migration and globalization have made them more so however, especially where there has been extensive immigration into societies which were largely monolingual in the past. Crystal (1997) estimates that monolingualism is now almost certainly a minority phenomenon in the world, and that bilingualism or multilingualism is the commoner case, both for individuals and societies. Indeed, it can be argued that the notion of a monolingual society is now, in much of the world, something of a political myth rather than a linguistic reality.

Even in those relatively monolingual European nation states where one language has traditionally been closely identified with national identity, and where minority languages have been often either ignored or suppressed, the situation is now radically different. The aftermath of empire has left the former colonizers, such as Britain, France, and the Netherlands, among the most multilingual and multicultural of nations. A survey in 2000, for example, revealed that 350 languages were spoken in London schools (Baker and Eversley 2000). Similar situations pertain in many other 'English speaking' cities of the 'inner circle' countries—such as Sydney and New York.

Code-switching and code-mixing

The code-switching and code-mixing—and translation—which arises from such multilingual environments happens in all contexts, from the most personal to the most public, from the inner speech of bilinguals to the world stages of media and politics. There are needs to switch and negotiate between languages in many immigrant families, where the oldest generation often has least command of the ambient language, the youngest generation least command of the heritage language, and the middle generation is balanced between the two. The same is true in mixed-language marriages, where there is not only often code mixing in communication between the partners (even if only in the use of an occasional word in relationships where one language dominates), but also often a substantial need for translation in encounters between monolingual relatives and friends. Similar needs arise in educational contexts. In some London schools, for example, new arrivals whose English is weak are teamed up with a fellow pupil acting as a bilingual 'buddy', who will interpret and explain until they can use English proficiently for themselves. There is also a good deal of more playful and socially motivated use by pupils of each other's languages, which Rampton (2005) has termed 'crossing'. In workplaces, code-switching is common in any workforce where employees share a language other than the ambient one. More formally, the work of many employees in the world, such as bilingual secretaries, is premised upon their ability to use and move between more than one language. In more public arenas, there is interpreting and translation, and the use of bilingual or multilingual documents, packaging, or announcements. A European driving licence, for example, proclaims its identity in nine languages; food ingredients are commonly given in more than one language; and flight information is often in English and one or more other languages. In mass media, various strategies are used to make productions in one language comprehensible to speakers of another, including subtitling or dubbing of foreign-language films. Code-mixing is common—albeit for more complex reasons than comprehensibility—in international advertisements (Bhatia 1992; Tanaka 1994; G. Cook 2001b: 89–90; Kelly-Holmes 2004; Smith 2006).

Identity

Closely implicated in globalization are issues of identity, for the obvious reason that migration and increased international contact, and the encounters between speakers of the languages they entail, may cause those involved to alter their conceptions of their own identity or how it relates to that of others. For this reason the 2000s have seen a great deal of applied linguistic work on this topic (Norton 2000; Kanno 2003; De Fina 2003; Pavlenko and Blackledge 2004; Joseph 2004; Benwell and Stokoe 2006; De Fina et al. 2006; Omoniyi and White 2006; Block 2006, 2007; Riley 2007; Lin 2008; Caldas-Coulthard and Iedema 2008; Dörnyei and Ushioda 2009).

In both liberal and Marxist traditions of research, social and linguistic action and identity is explained and described from the perspective of the larger social systems it exemplifies (Rampton 2000). In keeping with this, sociolinguistics has traditionally understood identity in terms of larger categories, such as class, gender, ethnicity, age, and, more recently, sexual orientation. If we maintain this perspective, then new categories might be added to this list reflecting the new importance of international movement and communication. We might want, for example, to consider and distinguish categories such as 'immigrant', 'migrant', 'ex-patriot'.

Alternatively, however, it may be that globalization calls for new ways of understanding and depicting identity, rather than simply the addition of new categories added to a list. (Or indeed it might be that the conception of identity in any historical context might benefit from a reformulation.) In many recent studies of identity, such an alternative is provided by post-modernist framing of identities as socially constructed narratives that individuals negotiate and project in what they say, do, own, and wear. There is a:

> sense that we 'assemble' ourselves from a plethora of changing options, deciding what is right and wrong for ourselves.
> (Rampton 2000)

Where there is such online on-going self-construction, choice of language (by those who have more than one in their repertoire) will be an important element of communication. Kramsch and Whiteside (2008), approaching such issues from an ecological and explicitly post-modernist perspective, examine the language choices available in an encounter in San Francisco between two Yucatecan immigrants from Mexico to California, the owner of a Vietnamese bakery, and an Anglo-American researcher. They show how the language choices available at various points (English, Mayan, Spanish, and Vietnamese) are influenced not only by speakers' ability in one language or another, or the imperative to communicate information effectively, but also by an awareness of the symbolic value of choosing one language over another at a particular point. This they term 'symbolic competence' (following Kramsch 2006). Switches between languages are influenced by a complex interplay of factors which are not only internal to the dynamic of the interaction, but which also evoke the history and power relations of these languages.

In a not dissimilar way Pennycook (2007: 118) in his work on the language of hip hop, whose transcultural international presence he presents as working against the traditional segregation of languages and cultures, sees its frequent code-mixing as less to do with the 'interpretable meaning of the lyrics' than as 'political statement':

> Choices in language use are deeply embedded in local conditions, from the economy and the local music industry structure (limited recording facilities militate against local practices and languages) to the historical background to language policies, language ideologies, aesthetics, and other local and regional social and cultural concerns.
> (Pennycook 2007: 137)

Own-language use in the classroom

Changes in perception of bilingualism and code-switching and an awareness of its political and personal importance in the maintenance and creation of identity is at least one of the factors behind a growing interest in both the ELT and the applied linguistics literature in the use of students' own languages in the language classroom, and in teachers' policy towards that use. Many recent studies and materials have, with varying degrees of caution or enthusiasm, been both more supportive of code-switching, and critical of the direct-method dogma which precludes it. As already pointed out, these are not in themselves arguments for translation as such, though some studies and materials do refer to it, but they move us in the direction of translation, and provide a much more supportive environment for it.

Some distinctions need to be made, however, between the arguments in such studies, as they are not all of the same kind. Not all draw upon issues of identity and a new linguistic world order to make their case. Nor by any stretch of the academic imagination could they all be classified as post-modern. A significant paper by V. Cook (2001a), for example, to which we shall return later, argues from SLA and practical pedagogic perspectives for 'a re-examination of the time-honoured view that the first language should be avoided'.

Other arguments in favour of own-language use relate more readily to the kinds of changes sketched out in the opening of this chapter, as they concern the ubiquity and inevitability of code-switching, and its positive effects on student identity and emotion. Studies in a wide range of contexts, levels, and languages have reached remarkably similar conclusions. Thus for the teaching of English, Addendorff (1996), writing on South African high schools, Camilleri (1996) on Maltese secondary schools, and Cromdal (2005) on collaborative word processing in a fourth-grade class in Sweden, all found code-switching to promote a sense of class unity and shared identity—factors which have been acknowledged elsewhere in the literature to promote motivation and success (Dörnyei and Murphey 2003). Studies in a variety of contexts also found code-switching to be more frequent than expected—even by teachers ostensibly opposed to it. Arthur (1996) found this in Botswana primary schools, Rolin-Ianziti and Brownlie (2002) in beginner French classes at an Australian university, Kim and Elder (2005) in lessons in four different languages in New Zealand secondary schools, Edstrom (2006) and Polio and Duff (1994) in US university level foreign-language teaching. Mitchell (1988: 28), interviewing language teachers in UK schools, found that using the new language all the time was considered 'too much for lower sets'. Macaro (1997: 96), summarizing several studies, including his own detailed investigations of new and own-language use by secondary school teachers in the UK, concluded that exclusive or near-exclusive use of the new language is rarely encountered in monolingual classes.

A complicating factor is introduced into such studies by the finding of Hobbs et al. (forthcoming) that there is considerable variation in attitude and use of code-switching among teachers from different cultural backgrounds and educational traditions. Their study of teachers of Japanese in a British secondary school found a much more positive attitude towards own-language use among the non-native speaker teachers than the native speaker ones. Regional variation in attitudes is also in evidence in the sources of academic literature in favour of classroom code-switching. The history of bilingual education in Canada, for example, makes it a conducive environment for such views, and many of the most eloquent and persuasive arguments in favour are either written by Canadians and/or are published in Canada (Stern 1992; Auerbach 1993; V. Cook 2001a; Rolin-Ianziti and Brownlie 2002; Edstrom 2006; Cummins 2007).

Many authors go further than merely describing the prevalence of code-switching in language classes and explicitly or implicitly advocate its use, though for a variety of reasons. Nikula's (2007) investigation of content-based classes in Finland saw code-switching as having a positive emotional effect. Ferguson (2003) documents the widespread use of code-switching in English-, French-, and Portuguese-medium classrooms in post-colonial Africa, and argues that it should be more effectively exploited by language planners as a communicative and pedagogic resource. Lin's (1996) study of Cantonese use in Hong Kong secondary English classes sees it as 'the teachers' and students' local pragmatic response to the symbolic domination of English in Hong Kong'. Kumaravadivelu (2003: 250) writes that own-language use can 'offer psychological and social support for minority children and provide a much-needed continuity between the home and school environment'. Fabrício and Santos (2006) illustrate how children in a Brazilian high school are encouraged to discuss mixing English with Portuguese and to see this in its wider social context. Canagarajah (1999), writing of English classes for Tamil speakers in Sri Lanka, notes how teachers and the students switch to their own language to discuss issues relevant to local events, concluding that it helps in 'putting students at ease, conveying teacher's empathy and, in general, creating a less threatening atmosphere' (ibid: 132). Prodromou (2002: 5) comes up with the paradoxical but nevertheless reasonable argument that own-language use provides support to monolingual use of the language being learnt.

> Our strategic objective will continue to be maximum interaction in the target language and the role of the mother tongue will be to enrich the quality and the quantity of that interaction in the classroom, not to restrict or impoverish it.

Even some studies which start out as generally circumspect about own-language use in the classroom come round to it as a result of their research. Edstrom (2006) for example, conducted a detailed analysis of her own use of English while teaching Spanish. Having begun with the preconception that it was pedagogically undesirable, and maintaining throughout that own-language use does not help acquisition, she nevertheless concluded that she had a 'moral obligation' to speak to her students in English sometimes if she were to engage with them on a personal level, observing about one case of an interaction with a student:

> At this point I was truly concerned about his feelings and unconsciously switched to English, the language that, quite frankly, was the most 'real' for all of us... The point is that my concern about my students as individuals, as human beings, at times transcends my concern for L2 acquisition process.

Levine (2003), who studied beliefs about and attitudes towards a range of foreign languages in US universities, began with the hypothesis that 'the amount of TL use overall would correlate positively with student anxiety about it'. To put this more plainly, she thought that a lot of code-switching would make students anxious. However, she found the opposite to be the case. The more their own language was used, the less anxious students felt about the new language. To her credit, Levine—like Edstrom—lets the evidence overturn her initial assumption.

Other studies use their evidence of code-switching in language classes to actively campaign for bilingual teaching. Brooks-Lewis (2009), in her study of adult Mexican learners, found her informants to be overwhelmingly in favour of an English language course which incorporated Spanish, though she does also report some dissent. Fisk-Ong's unpublished survey of teacher attitudes to own-language use and translation in eighteen countries, found her informants divided between extreme opposition and guilty support, concluding that both attitudes were the result of pressure from outside. Thomas (1999) found Slovakian teachers of English to be largely opposed to the monolingual approaches to language teaching promulgated in Anglo-American applied linguistics.

Two of the most convincing arguments in favour of encouraging student first-language use however are not based on specific empirical studies like those discussed above, but on more wide-ranging theoretical approaches to the issue as a whole. The purpose of V. Cook's (2001a) paper 'Using the first language in the classroom' is to suggest:

> that it is time to open a door that has been firmly shut in language teaching for over 100 years, namely the systematic use of the first language (L1) in the classroom.

He first traces the history of monolingual teaching and those few methods which have gone against the trend, questioning the main assumptions, not only of early Direct Method, but also of communicative and task-based teaching, that:

> spoken language is more basic than written, explicit discussion of grammar should be avoided, and language should be practised as a whole rather than as separate parts.

He observes that, in all of these approaches, 'the only time that L1 is mentioned is when advice is given on how to minimize its use'. A good deal of V. Cook's argument is psycholinguistic, criticizing the assumption that teaching should seek to compartmentalize the two languages in students' minds, and the fallacy of seeing (in his terms) L2 learning as a potential repeat of L1. These are followed however by pedagogic arguments, many of which echo the findings of the more empirical research described above, advocating own-language use as a means of explanation, comprehension checking, classroom organization, maintenance of discipline, forming relationships, and testing.

In 'Bilingualization and localized learning', Widdowson (2003: 149–165) deploys a wide range of perspectives—psycholinguistic, pedagogic, and political—to argue strongly for an end to the 'self-inflicted' problem of TESOL's commitment to monolingualism, proposing instead that the learner's own language be used as a resource for:

> the bilingualization process which learners necessarily engage in when they draw on the language they know...for learning the language they do not know.

For Widdowson, the error of monolingual teaching is that it has misunderstood how learners of English engage with their new language, and the purposes for which it is being learnt. To proceed as though the learners' own languages do not exist, attempting to induct learners into a local monolingual native-speaker perspective, is deeply to misunderstand what is happening. Learners will always relate the new language to their own, even if only in their own minds, and if forbidden, will continue to do so as a means of resistance.

Butzkamm and Caldwell's *The Bilingual Reform*

While the studies described above all contribute to the formulation of an argument for the reintroduction of bilingual teaching, they tend to be of two kinds. Either they are studies of a very specific context focusing upon some particular advantage or feature of bilingual classes, or they are theoretical arguments at a level of generality which needs some translation (to use the term metaphorically) if their ideas are to be realized at the level of class-room practice. Both kinds are, in their own way, vital components of a new approach, but they fall short of providing a complete framework.

Such a comprehensive vision of bilingual language teaching is however pro-vided by Butzkamm and Caldwell's landmark book *The Bilingual Reform: A Paradigm Shift in Foreign Language Teaching* (2009). Impressively grounded in a scholarly understanding of the history and theory of the debate between monolingualists and bilingualists, its arguments centre mostly upon the prac-tical realities of the classroom, and each point it makes is illustrated by telling quotations from learners and teachers recounting their own frustrations and triumphs, in a way which carries considerable conviction, especially when contrasted with the somewhat distant tone of much SLA writing.

In addition to providing practical guidance, it also however has elements of a manifesto. The old taboo on mother tongue, it tells us in its opening sentence, 'will be swept away' (op. cit. 13), and it pulls no punches in its pedagogic arguments. Its advocacy of the mother tongue (to use its own term) is not just 'another plea for a flexible and less rigid attitude', but a systematic programme in which mother-tongue use is seen as essential: 'the foundation for all other languages we might want to learn' (ibid.). Nor is it prepared to co-exist peacefully with the old orthodoxy of direct-method native-speakerism.

> Teachers...should themselves be bilingual, i.e. be reasonably fluent speakers of both the target language and the language of their pupils.
> (op. cit. 25)

But the approach is by no means a rehabilitation of bad practices from the past in which (and again these points are all illustrated with engaging exam-ples) mother tongue was used to cover the teacher's own incompetence, as a crutch for weak students, as the main medium of instruction and communi-cation, or as a deadeningly formal approach using only language which had already been taught in the mother tongue. It advocates instead a very high use of the new language (described as a 'language bath'), particularly in sponta-neous communication and classroom management, claiming that:

> paradoxically a targeted yet discreet use of the L1 makes it easier to achieve a foreign language atmosphere in the classroom.
> (op. cit. 33)

Butzkamm and Caldwell's approach then is resolutely focused upon com-munication and meaning, although their understanding of these terms has an important rider. Unlike conventional meaning-focused approaches they stress the distinction used by V. Cook (2001b: 94) between 'decoding' in which a student simply understands the function of what is said, and 'code breaking' in which the student understands how that function is encoded, and can therefore use patterns productively rather than simply on one occasion. In illustration (op. cit. 92[10]), they give the example of a learner of French who understands *S'il vous plaît* only holistically as 'please', in contrast with a learner who also understands the same expression analytically as 'if it you pleases'/ 'if it pleases you'. Only the latter kind of code-breaking understanding can lead to new coinages on the same pattern, such as *si le vin vous plaît* ('If you like the wine'), etc.

They point also to the futility of the belief that conventional teaching can provide enough time to reproduce the exposure necessary for a learner to master the new language in a way comparable with the language acquisition of a native-speaker child. A language cannot be learnt in conventional schooling through:

> mere exposure to the FL learning, because there is simply never enough of it (op. cit. 30)

Mother-tongue use, in short, is the way to compensate for the difference between natural first-language and instructed additional-language acquisition. Although most of the book is about mother-tongue use in general, it is not an argument which quarantines translation in the way described in my opening of this chapter. On the contrary, the topic of translation is present throughout, as well as having a chapter devoted to it explicitly, and we shall return to some of Butzkamm and Caldwell's practical suggestions for TILT in Chapter 7.

Advocacy of TILT

Arguments in which it is TILT, rather than bilingual teaching, which is the main focus of attention remain, however, few and far between. One recent and important exception—which has appeared only as I conclude this book of my own—is *Translation in Second Language Teaching and Learning* (Witte, Harden, and Ramos de Oliveira Harden 2009). In this collection of papers the editors and contributors make a strong case for the relevance and usefulness of TILT in a variety of contexts and for a variety of purposes: Internet communication, language awareness, accuracy and fluency, intercultural competence, and literary understanding. Other arguments specifically for TILT, rather than bilingual language teaching in general, can also be found in earlier work of my own (G. Cook 1991, 1997, 2007b, 2008b).

From own-language rehabilitation to translation

There is then, an array of recent evidence and argument in favour of reincorporating students' own languages into language teaching, and a corresponding disquiet that they were ever excluded. The reasons given are various. Some give political reasons, claiming that first-language use will help to combat linguistic imperialism, especially in the teaching of English, and help students to develop and preserve a bilingual rather than monolingual identity. Others give educational reasons, claiming that own-language use can foster understanding of other cultures and other ways of thinking. Others still point to the needs of learners in multilingual societies and a globalized world, and to the fallacy of supposing that monolingual communication and monolingual individuals are the norm. Then there are those who put forward pedagogical arguments, claiming that own language use enables faster and more efficient explanation, is more motivating and less alienating, and fosters good relationships between teacher and learner. Many bilingual teachers see the exclusion of their students' own language as depriving them of a self-evidently useful tool. Most basic—but perhaps most convincing of all—is the argument that own-language use will occur anyway as a natural teaching and learning strategy, so should be harnessed rather than rejected.

In short, there is a considerable current of opinion in favour of a return to cross-lingual teaching. Calls for the reincorporation of students' own languages do not, however, necessarily entail advocacy of translation, for the obvious reason that while translation is an instance of own-language use, it is by no means the only possible one. Though the step from own-language use to translation might seem small, a deep historical distrust of translation militates against it. Belief in Direct Method is so deeply engrained, and antagonism to translation so intense, that for many this route seems a step too far. Thus cautious revision of monolingual policy often comes with a general hesitancy over translation. Even some of the strongest advocates of own-language use seem to shy away from wholehearted endorsement. V. Cook (op. cit.), for example, though staunch in his defence of first-language use, leaves translation until the very end of his article, admitting that he 'has so far...avoided using the term because of its pejorative overtones'. Though he seems to support it, his statements about it are strangely equivocal. Take for example:

> Once avoidance of the L1 has been relaxed, there is no intrinsic reason
> why translation is wrong, even if it has other snags.

To say that 'there is no intrinsic reason' implies that there is an extrinsic one. The 'other snags' he mentions are not specified. Likewise Stern (1992), in his otherwise balanced comparison of cross-lingual and intra-lingual teaching, is extremely cautious about translation, allowing it only *from* the language being learnt *into* the students' own language, and constantly qualifying any remarks in its favour with caveats about its past use 'to excess' (op. cit. 293). In weighing up the merits of the two approaches, he is also careful to defend intra-lingual teaching for at least part of any syllabus, stating 'axiomatically [that] if any degree of L2 proficiency is to be attained, an intralingual strategy must be used.' (op. cit. 285)

So we should not assume that support for own-language use is the same as support for translation, nor should we confuse the two. Many who are actively for the former are against the latter, while others seem not to have considered the possibility that rehabilitation of own-language use may open a gateway for translation.

Although translation is one kind of own-language use, its advocacy is a more specific and more controversial proposal. One has the feeling that for many commentators, while some smattering of translation here and there might be accommodated within a bilingual classroom, a substantial transla-tion component would mark a much more significant break with the past, and still attract the old direct-method witch hunts. It is because of this hesi-tancy, this unwillingness to take a step further, that this chapter is called only 'A climate for revival' rather than 'Revival'.

Notes

1 An official language is one with a special legal status in a nation, and is used for its government, legislation, and administration. The vaguer and more variously used term 'national language' refers to a language considered to be associated with a particular people, nation, or territory.
2 In Louisiana both French and English are official languages, as are both English and Hawai'ian in Hawai'i.
3 A 2006 amendment to an immigration bill recognized English as a 'common and unifying language'. A similar amendment to a subsequent immigration reform bill was passed in 2007. However neither bill has become law.
4 http://www.youtube.com/watch?v=qiGhntWrLxs (accessed 21/02/2009)
5 There are no official figures concerning use of different languages in the British population as no question on this topic has been included in the national census. However, one study in 2000 reports six languages (Arabic, Bengali/Sylheti, Gujarati, Hindi/Urdu, Panjabi, and Turkish) to be the home languages of 16.18 per cent of London schoolchildren, with 33 languages the home language of a further 15.96 per cent, leaving 67.86 per cent for whom English is the home language (Baker and Mohieldeen 2000: 5).
6 Or Welsh or Scots Gaelic.
7 Others are Australia, Anglophone Canada, the Anglophone Caribbean countries, Ireland, and New Zealand.
8 Indeed the impact of this mass migration on linguistic demography is one of the reasons that many scholars (Canagarajah 1999; Cooke and Simpson 2008: 3; Park and Wee 2009) now find Kachru's (1985) classification unsatisfactory.
9 See also Butzkamm (2001).
10 For a counter argument to this standard view, see Campbell 1998.

4

What is translation?

Rationale for the chapter

One term in the discussion so far has been taken for granted, though its meaning is by no means straightforward. This is the word 'translation' itself, whether conceived as a process (what happens when someone translates) or as a product (a text in one language which counts as a translation of a text in another). Though central to the argument about TILT, translation is by no means straightforward or easy to define, and perhaps for this reason, like many important terms, it is often used without definition. Its meaning is slippery, but needs to be grasped, and this is what I shall attempt to do here.

The first three chapters of this book have surveyed the history of TILT; the next part will consider arguments and evidence in its favour. Both are directly concerned, then, with the pedagogic use of translation. This chapter, sandwiched between the two, may seem to take a step away from these pedagogic concerns. The idea is, however, that understanding the nature of translation, and the problems it involves, is essential not only to an understanding of TILT, but useful for language learners themselves.

The fashion in 20th century language teaching has been to keep formal academic knowledge of how languages work distinct from the processes of language learning, as though the insights of linguistics are somehow not relevant to learners. What students need (it is argued rather condescendingly), is not academic knowledge about a language but an ability to use it, as though the two could be kept neatly compartmentalized. The prevalence of this rather artificial dichotomy is one reason why the approach of this chapter may seem to some readers at odds with a discussion of efficient language teaching and learning. The view here however is that the description and analysis of translation has a great deal to contribute to successful language learning and use, and this in turn needs both a theoretical framework and some kind of metalanguage. This is not to say that the full details of this framework and metalanguage are needed by every learner. Like TILT itself, they need to be used judiciously. But some kind of descriptive apparatus and some degree of conscious reflection will be needed—by all but the youngest learners—if translation problems are to be discussed.

For students, understanding and discussion of translation problems gives a unique insight into how the new language works and how it resembles or differs from their own. It has the potential to fix these language characteristics and differences in their minds, enabling them to use the new language, whether on its own or when translating, with more confidence and success. Only through conscious awareness of differences and difficulties, moreover, can students become good translators themselves, making judicious choices between possible translations in the light of contextual factors, and participant purposes and needs. As already argued, the two roles of translation—as means and end—need not be kept apart, as they have been traditionally. Learning to translate is not a special purpose or an add-on to general learning, but should be an integral part of a major aim of language learning—to operate bilingually as well as monolingually.

For these reasons, translation theory and translation studies are far from irrelevant to language learning, and should not be kept separate from it. Though it is not my intention here to give a comprehensive summary of these immense areas, this chapter is a necessary excursion into their territory.

Definitions of translation

A popular view of translation is that it involves a transfer of meaning from one language to another, and this is reflected in its Latin root *translatum*, a form of the verb *transferre* which means 'to carry across', and is also the origin of the English word 'transfer'. Embedded in this view, perhaps as an inevitable consequence of it, is the notion of translation loss, the fact that in translation not everything can be 'carried across'. Some see this as a kind of treachery. In the words of the punning Italian maxim: *Traduttore, Traditore* (the translator is a traitor). Yet as translation is necessary to communication between languages, and loss is inevitable, this hyperbolic characterization as betrayal seems both unfair and inaccurate.

Loss is of different kinds. It may be that the sound patterns or word order of the original were important, that the connotations of a word and its conventional translation equivalent are different, or that there is a gap in the lexis of one language. Russian for example has no equivalent of the English word 'privacy' (Pavlenko 2005). Then in addition to these linguistic differences, loss may derive from more general factors. Significance changes as a text moves from one cultural context to another. Readers of the translation often lack the background knowledge possessed by readers of the original. If meaning transference is the goal, then all translation is doomed to failure, as no translation is complete.

Pursued further, the notion of meaning transfer also entails a very questionable view of how languages work. It implies that there are representations of meaning independent of their realization in any given language (sometimes referred to as 'mentalese' (Pinker 1994: 55–82), and that an original and its translation are somehow the same because they both encode the same language-neutral mental representation. This in turn implies a strong rejection of any belief in linguistic relativity—the idea that languages influence views of the world by encoding experience in different ways (Whorf 1964, Pavlenko 2005). Yet while it is true that the fact of translation in some ways undermines the strongest version of linguistic relativity—because translation would not be possible at all if languages were not significantly similar both in structure and in world view—there are nevertheless aspects of meaning which are only accessible if a text is approached in its original, for reasons I shall try to explain below. One does not have to subscribe to any extreme form of the linguistic relativity hypothesis to hold this position.

The quest for equivalence

For these and other reasons, most linguists have found the notion of meaning transference unsatisfactory and preferred instead the weaker notion of equivalence, replacing the idea of translation as:

> the transference of meaning from one set of patterned symbols into another
> (Dostert 1955)

with one of translation as:

> the replacement of textual material in one language by equivalent textual material in another language
> (Catford 1965: 20)

This formulation leaves unanswered the million-dollar question of what constitutes equivalence: the mysterious phenomenon that two texts which are regarded as in some sense the same may nevertheless have no single word in common, nor even—in the case of translations between languages with different writing systems—the same symbols. Two texts may be equivalent, but on the surface completely different. The quest for an understanding of the nature of equivalence, understood in the terms of linguistics, is in many ways the starting point of modern translation theory.

So let us look first at some of what has been said in translation theory about the nature of equivalence. From there we shall move on in the later part of this chapter, to more radical recent notions which see translation in an altogether different light.

Linguistics, language-teaching, and translation theory have, over the last hundred years or so, all taken similar paths, each seeming to be the shadow of the other. In very broad terms, the focus of attention in linguistics has moved from an exclusive interest in the 'lower' levels of linguistic forms, to one which is more interested in the use of those forms in action as discourse. This shift echoes and has informed a similar movement in language-teaching theories from a preoccupation with formal accuracy to one with communication, as described in Chapter 2. Translation theory has followed a similar trajectory, with a developing interest in pragmatic and discoursal equivalence from the 1970s onwards. More recently still there has been a further shift towards a concern with translation as an institutionalized and institution-building practice—a development reflected in a change of name for the academic discipline from 'translation theory' to 'translation studies' (Basnett 1980/1991). In this chapter, my aim is to consider each of these developments, characterizing the main points of each approach and their relation to TILT. The language learner might benefit from following a similar trajectory to translation theory and studies—focusing in the early stages mostly on linguistics and semantic equivalence, only later making discoursal equivalence a central concern.

Levels of equivalence

A language can be analysed as existing on a number of hierarchical levels. In most approaches to linguistics, though with some variation between the various schools[1], these are conceived more or less along the following lines: At the 'bottom' is phonology (in the case of spoken language) or graphology (in the case of written language). These realize, at the next level, morphemes (meaningful units) and these in turn combine to form lexical items (words) which in turn combine syntactically to form sentences. Choices of morphology, lexis, and syntax imbue any sentence with semantics (or meaning). Sentences are linked by cohesive devices, and combine into longer texts.

All these properties of language can be considered at a formal level without reference to the ways in which language is used. When considered as an act of communication in context however, any actual use of language has, in addition, a pragmatic meaning. That is to say it has a particular force, and performs some function for those involved. This is influenced not only by the participants' processing of its linguistic forms (the phonology, lexis, grammar, and cohesion) but also by the context, including the immediate situation, by other modes of communication, such as gesture or images, by participants' background and cultural knowledge, their thoughts, emotions, and intentions, and by the type of communicative act (or genre) they consider themselves to be involved in. The entirety of all these factors and levels is discourse.

To avoid confusion, two further terminological points need to be made at this point, concerning the meanings of *utterance* and *sentence*, and *text* and *discourse*. The term *utterance* refers to a stretch of language used by somebody in context to do something. It may or may not be grammatically complete or conform to grammatical norms. *Sentence* on the other hand is reserved for grammatically complete units regarded purely formally without reference to context. They may have been invented or actually occurred. Many utterances, but not all, are also sentences—but not all sentences have been utterances. *Text* and *discourse* are used in different ways by different writers, but I shall use them as follows. By *text* I shall mean any stretch of language considered in isolation from its context. By *discourse* I shall mean any stretch of language, written or spoken, considered in context. *Utterance* is sometimes used to refer to spoken language only, and *text* is sometimes reserved for written communication only, but I shall use these terms to refer to both spoken and written language.

Equivalence of meaning

In the popular view of translation, something in one language is a translation of something in another because they mean the same, not because they sound the same or maintain the same word order. To put this in terms of level equivalences, a general assumption is that the semantic level should take precedence over all others. A translation refers to the same events in the real (or fictional) world as the original. But this simple idea soon runs into trouble. For a number of reasons, it may not be possible to produce something in one language which means exactly the same as something in another. Take for example the short and apparently simple Russian sentence:

Я пришла (*Ia prishla*)

In many circumstances it might validly be translated as:

'I've arrived.'

on the grounds that the two phrases can refer to the same event, and could be uttered in the same circumstances. An interpreter at a meeting, hearing a late arrival who has just come through the door say *Ia prishla* (я пришла), might be right to translate this as 'I've arrived'. Yet what the two phrases tell us about the event is rather different. The first word *Ia* (я) presents no problem. Russian and English both have a word by which a speaker refers to himself/herself[2]—a first person singular pronoun[3]—and both have a form of this pronoun which is used when it is the subject. So *Ia* (я) means no more and no less than 'I'. (Though even with this apparently simple word there are some complications. There are occasions in Russian, but not in English, when it can be dropped. 'You and I' is translated into Russian as *my s toboi* (мы с тобой)—literally 'we with you'.) Nevertheless, *I* for *Ia* (я) is about as close as one can come to an instance of perfect translation.

The next word *prishla* (пришла) however presents some significant problems if we seek to translate 'the meaning' in its entirety. These are not abstruse problems to do with advanced or literary Russian. They are features of everyday use, and familiar early difficulties both for English learners of Russian, and for Russian learners of English. They are the kind of problems any language learner will encounter quite early in their studies—and therefore highly relevant to TILT.

Firstly, Russian has two verbs corresponding to English 'arrive': *priiti* (прийти) which means 'to arrive on foot', and *priekhat* (приехать) which means 'to arrive by transport', and there is no verb anyone can use which could mean both. Confusion between these two Russian verbs is a common source of error for learners of Russian who, insensitive to the distinction, are likely to say that they have just walked from Paris to Moscow, or taken transport from the kitchen to the hall! Secondly Russian verbs must be either in a perfective aspect, indicating that the action is completed, or in an imperfective aspect, referring to an action which is incomplete or repeated[4]. In this case the verb *prishla* (пришла) is perfective, so the action is completed. *Prishla* (пришла) is also in the past. Russian verbs however have only one past form and no equivalent to the contrast in English between past ('I arrived') and present perfect ('I have arrived') which indicates immediacy or continuing relevance. Thirdly, the past form in Russian is marked for the sex of the speaker. *Prishla* (пришла) is a feminine form and indicates that the speaker is female. (A male speaker would say *Ia prishel* (Я пришел).)

Significantly for the learner of Russian all of these features are obligatory. A Russian speaker cannot say 'I've arrived' without indicating whether they came on foot or by transport, whether the action is completed or repeated, and whether they are male or female.

So how, in the light of all this, do we now translate these two little everyday words, *ia prishla*? Any language has the capacity to say all of these things, though it may need to do so rather more long-windedly. To capture all of the above in English for example we should have to say something like:

'I, a female, have come here on foot and am going no further.'

This reproduces the semantic meaning accurately. Yet outside of very exceptional circumstances, this is clearly not a good translation, and if such an approach were used consistently across a text, it would yield a translation many times longer than the original, making the two unequivalent in a different sense. But it is not usually necessary, of course, because many elements of meaning are likely to be evident from the situation or the surrounding text, or may simply not be relevant. The good translator therefore needs to be selective, to see which elements of meaning are important in a particular instance. In the opposite direction however—from English into Russian—the good translator needs to be aware of and to encode all of these elements, taking into account for example whether the person who says 'I've arrived' is male or female. From such examples, a student can learn both specific facts about their new language, but also the general truth that translations are seldom exactly equivalent, that there are difficult choices to be made about what to drop and what to keep. Catford (1965: 39), who also uses this example of *prishla*, neatly summarizes these differences. (See Figure 3 on page 60.)

In his view, the central problem for translation is that it cannot render all the semantic features on one level, let alone the interaction between features on different levels. The best it can do is to seek 'situational equivalence' by encoding in the translation as many of the elements of the original as necessary, depending on whether they are 'situationally relevant'.

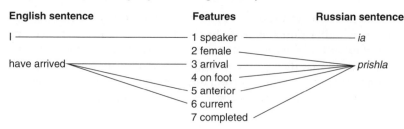

Figure 3 Tabulation of translation equivalence (adapted from Catford 1965: 39)

Deciding on what is 'necessary' or 'relevant' however leaves many unanswered questions. The upshot of Catford's theory of situational equivalence is that translation is a series of choices about what to include and exclude. But this does not particularly help the translator or the student. Describing the linguistics and semantics of the original, though it may be a useful insight into what the choices are, is not in itself a procedure for making such choices. In search of principles for making such choices, translation theory turned to pragmatics.

Pragmatic equivalence

In addition to referring to facts about the world, utterances also perform social actions. Pragmatic theory concentrates on how receivers of messages, by relating what is said to its context, interpret what the sender is trying to do with their words. The literal semantic meaning of an utterance is only one component in this interpretation. Others include participants' background knowledge, the situation, and shared social conventions. If, for example, an army sergeant says 'Your boots are dirty!' to an ordinary soldier on parade, it is likely to be interpreted as an order or a reprimand rather than a conversational remark (Cook 1989: 36–38). The philosophers J. L. Austin (1962) and John Searle (1969, 1975a, 1975b) worked out detailed conditions by which hearers interpret utterances as performing particular speech acts, such as promising, ordering, asking, complimenting, etc. Searle also touched on the implications for translation:

> the standard forms from one language will not always maintain their indirect speech act potential when translated from one language to another. Thus 'Can you hand me that book?' will function as an indirect request in English, but its Czech translation, 'Můžete mi podat tu Knížku' will sound very odd if uttered as a request in Czech.
> (Searle 1975b: 76)

Reproducing the literal meaning of an original in other words does not guarantee that a translation will have the same effect. English uses a question frame *Can you x me y?* to make a polite request, where Czech would use an imperative with *prosím*—the Czech for 'please'.

Often the conflict between form and function in translation arises, as in the example used by Searle, because formulaic phrases or sentence frames have conventional meanings different from their literal meanings. For example an English translation of the Spanish conversational sequence:

- *Gracias*
- *De nada*

might validly be:

- Thank you.
- You're welcome.

on the grounds that the phrases 'you're welcome' and *de nada* have the same function in this context, although their literal meanings are different. In other cases, the literal meaning can be the same but the function different. In English, 'Thank you' often indicates acceptance of an offer, but in French *Merci* is commonly a refusal.

Such functions are formulaic and simply need to be learnt. At other times, more problematically for the learner, the function of an utterance may need interpretation in the light of cultural knowledge. Thus what counts as an apology, insult, promise, order, or invitation may draw upon knowledge of the norms of relationships, hierarchies, privacy, and so forth. The field of cross-cultural pragmatics has been much concerned with such differences, the misunderstandings which arise from them, and how speakers of one language might recognize the intended function, as opposed to just the literal meaning, of an utterance in another language. Wolfson (1989: 119) uses the example of how North Americans close conversations by suggesting that the participants should meet again and have lunch. She tries to assess when it counts as a real invitation to be followed up, as opposed to just a vague expression of friendliness, or a way of drawing a conversation to a close, arguing that in the latter case:

1 time is always left indefinite
2 a response is not required (i.e. there is no yes/no question) and
3 a modal auxiliary such as 'must' is used.

This means that 'Do you want to have lunch tomorrow?' is a real invitation, while 'We must do lunch some time' is not. Travellers' tales abound with examples of such misunderstandings. To pick one example out of many, an Arab friend once told me of arriving at his British host's house feeling extremely thirsty, and hoping that he would be offered a drink. When asked if he was thirsty, however, he followed Arab etiquette and answered 'no', expecting the invitation to be reiterated. He did not get his drink.

Awareness of such well documented misunderstandings has had an influence on language teaching practice, where it has sometimes been deemed necessary to teach culturally appropriate behaviour. This was especially popular in the early days of CLT when it was assumed that learning a language—and particularly learning English—should necessarily involve the acceptance and adoption of the cultural norms of native speakers, causing the language learner's identity to disappear into the new culture. Many of the recommendations of that time now have a rather authoritarian and chauvinistic ring. William Littlewood, introducing the new communicative movement to teachers wrote:

> To a large extent it is a question of a speaker conforming to linguistic (or rather sociolinguistic) convention in order to be unobtrusive. He may choose socially appropriate speech in so far as his repertoire permits, just as he may choose socially appropriate dress in so far as his wardrobe permits.
> (Littlewood 1981)

White told learners of English that in Britain:

> Questions about where a person works and where he or she lives are acceptable. Questions about his or her age and how much he or she earns are not.
> (White 1979)

Rewriting such norms as exercises, Morrow and Johnson were even prepared to have culturally inappropriate behaviour marked as 'wrong' in the same way that 'swummed' might be considered the wrong past of 'swim'.

> **Doing the right thing**
> *How much do you know about the way the British live and behave?*
> *Do this quiz.*
> You're in Britain.
> 1) You're visiting the house of a British friend. It's very beautiful. Do you:
> a) tell him how beautiful it is?
> b) ask how much it cost?
> c) ask if he'll take you round every room?
> (Johnson and Morrow 1979: 5)

The answer given in the back of their course book *Communicate* was a).

Somehow the teaching of language had become unproblematically intertwined with the teaching of culture, although the questions raised by this were legion. Firstly it assumed a single national uniform way of behaving—'British culture' in the examples above—ignoring regional, social class, ethnic, and individual differences and, in the case of English and other widely distributed international languages such as Spanish, those between nations speaking the same language. Secondly it assumed that learners of a language would want to be insiders rather than outsiders, to learn the language to assimilate. Thus the ostensibly liberating communicative movement sought to impose behavioural patterns on students, teaching them not only how to say something, but what to say as well. Ironically in a movement ostensibly preoccupied with dialogue, this vision of communication seems to be one-way only.

Though such approaches still persist, more recent English-language teaching has tended to go in one of two opposite directions. In one, prevalent in the teaching of English to migrants in English-speaking countries, the emphasis is very much on raising learners' awareness of cultural difference, while allowing maintenance of their own identity without demanding conformity (Cooke and Simpson 2008). In the other, associated with the teaching of English as an international language (McKay 2002) or as a *lingua franca* (Jenkins 2000, 2007; Seidlhofer 2002, 2010), there is an attempt to treat the language as culturally neutral, without close association with any of the English-speaking nations.

Understandably translation theorists have long argued that, where there is a conflict between semantic and pragmatic equivalence, the latter should take precedence. Russian linguist Komissarov (1973) devised a neat scheme[5] by which a translator's main aim should be to ensure that the pragmatic function of translation and original is equivalent, and then work down through the levels of language, trying to ensure that there is equivalence at each of them, but abandoning the attempt once a level is reached where there is not. Thus, to use the example above, translating from Spanish to English, *De nada* would be translated only at the pragmatic level as 'You're welcome'. The Spanish expression *Cómo estás?* however, can be translated literally as 'How are you?' as the two phrases are pragmatically as well as semantically equivalent.

In many (if not most) instances this is eminently reasonable, and any other principle could clearly lead to serious misunderstandings. Yet while it may avoid momentary hitches in efficient communication, there are also cases when such a principle can lead to deeper misunderstandings, and there is perhaps an argument, to which we shall return later, for allowing some strangeness or 'foreignness' into the translation to avoid this, thus permitting the audience of a translation to see that cultural norms are not actually as easily comparable as pragmatic translation theory implies. Such, for example, is the case in the translation of phrases reflecting values which may not be shared. The case of whether *in-shâ'-llâh* (إن شاء الله) should be translated as 'God willing' or 'perhaps' in my anecdotal introduction to this book is an example. Of course, as Thomas (1998) observes, such an emphasis on difference in translation may lead to conflict and disagreement rather than harmony—an issue we shall return to in Chapter 6 when considering the educational benefits of TILT.

Komissarov's scheme, which is similar to many in subsequent western translation theory (Koller 1979/1989: 211–216; Bell 1991: 46) is moreover, of course, an academic model of equivalence, and not a representation of what translators actually do. (Given pressures of time, many would find so laboriously systematic a process quite unrealistic.) Nevertheless it is true that the translator must decide whether to be pulled towards the pragmatic or the linguistic poles of equivalence, judging each case on its merits. There is a strong case for allowing at least some elements of the language and culture they reflect to remain and but this is an evaluative, ethical, and aesthetic decision rather than merely mechanical one.

Functional and discoursal equivalence

The points so far about linguistic, semantic, and pragmatic equivalence have been made with reference to short examples—reminiscent perhaps of the single sentences used in traditional Grammar Translation exercises to encapsulate a single point. Actual translation however is much more likely to tackle extended texts, and even the translation of a single utterance will take place in a communicative context where meaning is affected by what is said and written before and after it as well as the extra-linguistic context. Consideration of such extended discourse brings with it problems and possibilities which are not evident in a single utterance. Current translation theory has focused upon such discourse issues, making particular use of the systemic-functional linguistics of Michael Halliday (Halliday 2007), paying particular attention to the discourse level and how socio-cultural values and power relations are manifest in lexico-grammatical choices (Hatim and Mason 1990). Attention has focused in particular upon the overall purpose of the source text with reference to Halliday's three macro-functions: the text's encoding of a view of the world (its ideational function), of the relation between speakers (its interpersonal function), and how parts relate to each other to create an overall effect of coherence (its textual function). In pursuit of this functional view, House (1977, 1997), using Halliday's three components of register, advocates systematic analysis of the source text's field (or ideational meaning), tenor (or interpersonal meaning), and mode (the choices which are made between and within speech and writing, monologue and dialogue, and spontaneous or scripted language use). She recommends the assessment of a translation by the degree of correspondence it achieves to the original in each of these dimensions. Baker (1992) also uses Hallidayan and pragmatics concepts, focusing in particular upon the relationship between a text's coherence, its presuppositions (the assumptions it makes about shared extra-linguistic knowledge), and its implicatures (what is implied but not explicitly stated).

In all of these approaches, particular attention is paid to identification of genre of the original text, conceived as a particular type of communicative event (such as sermon, recipe, poem, speech, interview, etc.) which conforms to particular sociocultural conventions and is realized by particular grammatical and lexical units[6], and the choice of appropriate genre conventions for the translation. This becomes particularly important in cases where genres may not correspond in a simple way. Cross-cultural communication is beset by problems in this respect. The boundary between sermon and political speech for example may be different in Iran and in the USA. What may be allowed licence as a work of art in one society, may be seen as blasphemous or obscene in another.

Equivalent effect

The explicit introduction of pragmatics and functional theories into discussions of equivalence, evokes an early formulation by the classical and biblical scholar and translator, E. V. Rieu, about what makes a good translation. In his view:

> that translation is the best which comes nearest to creating in its audience the same impression as was made by the original in its contemporaries.
> (Rieu 1953: 555)

This elevates what pragmatic theorists call *perlocution*—the overall effect of a text—to the main criterion of equivalence. Known as the 'equivalent effect principle' (Newmark 1981), this doctrine however brings with it all sorts of complications.

Firstly and most obviously is the problem of identifying the audience. Rieu's view was that the relevant audience should be 'the contemporaries' of the original, i.e. those who read it when it was first written. This implies that these contemporaries are homogeneous, and ignores the fact that a text may be read or heard in many different times and places and by many different people, for each of whom it may have a different effect. Even if we establish one individual reader as 'the audience', their interpretation may vary with mood and experience, and where they are reading (home, train, prison, hospital).

Secondly there is the problem of what to do if a literal translation may have a different—even an opposite—effect on readers from that of the original. Take the first line of Shakespeare's Sonnet 18, for example:

> Shall I compare thee to a summer's day?

Translator François Guizot (1821) rendered this into French as:

> *Te comparerai-je à un jour d'été?*

Though there are many matters arising here, even in this apparently straightforward translation, the comparison of the lover to a summer's day is not one of them. In France as in England, summer weather is seen in a positive light. But what for the translator of this line into Arabic? Does the Arabic word for summer الصيف *assayf* have an equivalent effect? Jibraa's translation (1986: 30) leaves the reference to summer untouched:

كيف أقارنك بيوم صائف؟

hal lii an aqrinaka biywmin Saa'if
[Am I to compare you to a summery day?]

As Al-Balushi (2007) comments on this translation:

> Perhaps the most difficult pragmatic issue in this poem is the associations the summer has in hot countries. A summer's day has associations of

warmth, mellowing and pleasantness in Britain. But the reverse is true as regards hot countries; it has association of unpleasant hotness.

Is the translator then to change 'summer' to 'winter', or to rely on Arabic readers making a leap into a different climate and its connotations?

Thirdly, there is the problem that if creating 'the same impression' on the reader is the measure of success, then a translation will need constantly to adjust itself to new or different readers. In this spirit Nida and Taber (1969), who broadly accepted the equivalent effect principle, advocated assessing the success of a translation by questioning the audience for which it was intended in 'a kind of market research' and then altering the translation accordingly. They also advocated different translations of the same text for different (for example, educated or uneducated) audiences.

Cultural equivalence

The debate over such issues among translation theorists was considerably influenced if not skewed by the fact that much of it had developed from problems encountered in translating the Bible (the world's most widely translated text[7]) often for very different cultures from those of the West, an enterprise in which several prominent translation theorists, such as Eugene Nida, were engaged. The purpose of Bible translation is evangelical, to attract and hold religious faith, and other criteria of equivalence may for this reason be held in abeyance by those with this purpose. The equivalent effect which is sought is religious inspiration, rather than, for example, insights into the culture or history of Biblical times.

Attempts to create equivalent effect of this kind can lead to so-called 'cultural translation' in which realia from the original are transmuted into those of the time and place where the translation is to be read. Such updating has a long history. The 1611 Authorized Version of the Bible turns the wineskins of Biblical times into the bottles of the 17th century:

> Neither do men put new wine into old bottles: else the bottles break, and the wine runneth out, and the bottles perish: but they put new wine into new bottles, and both are preserved. (Matthew 9: 17)

But things can be taken much further than that. Clarence Jordan's *The Cotton Patch Version of the Bible* (Jordan 1970) for example is written in a dialect from the region around Atlanta, Georgia. Local place names and modern-day equivalents of clothes, food. etc. are substituted for Biblical ones. Here the verse about new wine and old bottles becomes:[8]

> Nor do people put new tubes in old, bald tires. If they do the tires will blow out, and the tubes will be ruined and the tires will be torn up. But they put new tubes in new tires and both give good mileage.

The description of John the Baptist which in the Authorized Version had read:

And the same John had his raiment of camel's hair, and a leathern girdle
about his loins; and his meat was locusts and wild honey.
Then went out to him Jerusalem, and all Judaea, and all the region round
about Jordan,
And were baptized of him in Jordan, confessing their sins.
(Matthew 3: 4–6)

becomes:

This guy John was dressed in blue jeans and a leather jacket, and he
was living on corn bread and collard greens. Folks were coming to
him from Atlanta and all over north Georgia and the backwater of the
Chattahoochee. And as they owned up to their crooked ways, he dipped
them in the Chattahoochee.

Inevitably when such liberties are taken however, the views of the translator are particularly in evidence. Jordan, writing in the southern states at the
time of the civil rights movement, made the radical decision to use the words
'white man' for 'Jew' and 'negro' for 'gentile', and to have Jesus 'lynched'
rather than 'crucified'.

Despite its vitality and originality, and its well meaning intention to make
potentially alien stories come alive for a modern audience, cultural translation of this kind has some clear disadvantages. It can limit the relevance of
a translation to one time and place, and it prejudges a reader's intentions,
blocking access to some aspects of the original. *The Cotton Patch Bible* is
of no use to a reader interested in finding out about the clothes and food of
Biblical times. On the other hand, the fact that the updating is so extreme
and uncompromising means that the reader is likely to be well aware of the
changes which have been introduced. The changes are—to use terms to be
explained below—overt rather than covert.

Free versus literal equivalence

Translations taking equivalent effect principle to such extremes evoke a much
older debate over the relative merits of 'faithful' and 'free' translation.

Throughout literary history some translators have been uncompromising
in their advocacy of free translation. Thus Cicero, writing in 46 BC, prais-
ing his own translation skills and voicing the origin of the phrase 'word for
word' (*verbum pro verbo*), seems to move in this direction, when he tells us
that:

*nec converti ut interpres, sed ut orator, sententiis isdem et earum formis
tamquam figuris, verbis ad nostram consuetudinem aptis. In quibis non
verbum pro verbo necesse habui reddere, sed genus omne verborum
vimque servavi. Non enim ea me adnumerare lectori putavi oportere,
sed tamquam appendere.*

[And I did not translate them as an interpreter but as an orator, keeping the same ideas and the forms, or as one might say the figures of thought, but in language which conforms to our usage. And in so doing, I did not hold it necessary to render word for word, but I preserved the general style and force of the language. For I did not think I ought to count them out to the reader like coins, but to pay them by weight as it were.]
(quoted in Copeland 1995: 33[9])

Many centuries later, Edward FitzGerald, the popularity of whose own translation of 'The Rubaiyat of Omar Khayyam' (1859) has withstood the many complaints about its inaccuracy, epigrammatically defended 'free' translation by saying:

I am persuaded that...the Translator...must recast the original into his own likeness...the live dog better than the dead Lion.
(quoted by Morgan 1959: 277)

Closer to our own times a similar belief was advanced by American poet Robert Lowell:

I have been reckless with literal meaning and labored hard to get the tone. Most often this has been a tone, for *the* tone is something that will always more or less escape transference to another language and cultural moment. I have tried to write live English.
(Lowell 1962: xi)

Not everyone however is happy with such a cavalier approach to other languages and cultures. Copeland (1995) for example suggests that the general tendency away from linguistic towards pragmatic equivalence is a chauvinistic one which seeks to represent in familiar terms what ought to be recognized and valued as different. And some literary translators agree. A similar sentiment led Vladimir Nabokov to criticize caustically those translators:

offering a free version of the original with omissions and additions prompted by the exigencies of form, the conventions attributed by the consumer, and the translator's ignorance. Some paraphrases may possess the charm of stylish diction and idiomatic conciseness, but no scholar should succumb to stylishness and reader be fooled by it.

claiming that:

rendering, as closely as the associative and syntactical capacities of another language allow, the exact contextual meaning of the original. Only this is true translation.
(Nabokov 1964: viii)

There may be aspects of the literal meaning which, while they may not be relevant to the immediate communicative purpose, situation, or utilitarian demand for information, do nevertheless provide insight into the mores of that language's speakers. It is significant in other words that Arabic invokes God in so many phrases, that Chinese distinguishes between relationships that English does not, that Japanese has so many forms of address, and so forth.

In this light, contrary to current fashions—there is an argument to be made for literal translation and a negative one for looser translations seeking only to reproduce communicative effect. For if we seek only to translate into our own terms—turning *in-shâ'-llâh* into 'perhaps'—then we place a barrier to understanding differences, and close our own language to influence by another. It is perhaps no coincidence that an advocacy of free communicative translation, from Cicero through Edward FitzGerald to contemporary pragmatics, emanates from within empires seeking to appropriate not only the territories, but also the cultures and languages of others into their own.

Equivalence across levels

The problem for all attempts to deal with translation at different levels— whether linguistic, semantic, or pragmatic is that, rather than meaning being found at one level or another, the levels interact to create meaning, often in unpredicted ways. Truth to one level entails betrayal at another, leaving the translator with the inevitable task of prioritizing one aspect of the original over another. Translation theory, while it describes the problem, offers no clear principles as to what should be sacrificed. It may say that choices have to be made, but not which ones in specific circumstances. This dilemma is most clearly in evidence where there is significance in the choice of a linguistic form—the shape of a letter, the sound of a word—which usually has only an arbitrary and conventional relation to its meaning (de Saussure [1915] 1974) but takes on significance in a particular context (Jakobson 1960). The Russian novel *The Bridge* by Y. Mustafin for example describes how the workers' caravans on a Siberian railway construction site were arranged in the shape of the letter *П*:

> были расположены буквой П
> *byli raspolozheny bukvoi* П

As the Roman alphabet has no letter of the same shape as this Cyrillic character, it is simply not possible to find a graphological equivalent with the same meaning. The translators of the novel opted for:

> 'the caravans were arranged along three sides of a square.'

Similar problems arise where sound patterning such as rhythm and rhyme are important but their maintenance in a translation is likely to lead to departure from the literal meaning of the original. Though this problem is particularly intense in poetry (Lefevere 1975), it is by no means confined to it. Sound patterns are important in literary prose, in rhetoric, advertising, children's stories, and arguably in almost all genres with an emphasis on the interpersonal rather than the dry reporting of facts (G. Cook 2000; Tannen 2007). Take for example the sentence:

> The cat sat on the mat.

famous for its use in a book teaching children to read (Cameron and Jones 1901). At the semantic level of meaning this should be easy enough to translate. In Portuguese for example it would be:

> *O gato se sentou no tapetinho.*

This literal translation obviously fails, however, to capture the key features of the original sentence, that its words are all monosyllables and that three of them rhyme. In such situations, the translator cannot have it both ways. Either keep the sound patterns, and ditch the meaning, or *vice versa*. But things do not stop there. This same sentence has a particular cultural meaning for English speakers, standing for an old-fashioned approach to the teaching of reading. This was clear in a remark made at a university seminar I attended on children's reading books:

> I don't think children's reading books should all be 'the cat sat on the mat' kind of stuff.

Here a very different translation of these words into Portuguese might be in order.

> *Eu acho que livros de leitura para crianças não deveriam ter coisas do tipo 'Ivo viu a uva'.*
> (I think that reading books for children should not have things like *Ivo viu a uva.*)

Ivo viu a uva (literally 'Ivo saw the grape') does not mean 'the cat sat on the mat' but it does occupy the same place in Portuguese discourse and makes use of the same linguistic features of sound patterning and short words. The translator in other words has to choose which level is most important in a particular context.

The choice is not difficult in this example, as the literal meaning of 'The cat sat on the mat' is not as important as its sounds and function. In others cases however, such choices can demand very difficult decisions. In the French film *Entre les Murs*[10] (titled in English *The Class*) a young teacher struggles to teach his rowdy, non-standard French speaking secondary school students the forms of the irregular verb *croire* which include such departures from the regular verb forms as *je croyais* (imperfect) and *je crus* (past simple). However, this poses a problem for the translator writing the subtitles, as the equivalent English verb 'believe' is regular, and would not pose for non-standard English-speaking students the same problem which *croire* poses for these non-standard French speakers. 'Believe' would be a semantic equivalent but not a pragmatic one. The subtitler overcomes the problem by choosing an equivalently irregular English verb 'swim' and translating the non-standard French form as 'swummed' and the standard *croyais* as 'swam' (causing those in the audience who know something of both languages first to gasp at the mistake, and then sigh knowingly as they realize the reason).

A more complex example of level interaction occurs at the opening of Maxim Gorky's autobiographical novel Детство (*My Childhood*). The author remembers the arrival of his grandmother to live with his family when he was still a very small child, and a conversation he had with her. The opening could be translated as follows:

–'Where have you walked in from?' I asked her.
–'From higher up the river,' she answered, 'from Nizhny. And I didn't walk here, I came by boat. You don't walk on water, silly!'
–'Why am I silly?'
–'Because you're a silly Billy,' she said, laughing too.

The original Russian captures the confusion of a small child with an imperfect knowledge of his own language and surroundings, and the playful repartee between grandmother and grandchild, underpinned by joy in each other's company. As such it rests, like a good deal of playful human communication, on two aspects of the formal linguistic system: coincidences and ambiguities of meaning, and coincidences and patterning of sound. The general phenomena of child misunderstandings and merry banter are universal, but the particularities of their realization in this Russian scene are arguably untranslatable. The example—which is quite a famous one in the teaching and translation of Russian—is worth expounding in some detail.

Working through this example also illustrates a way of presenting translations through a series of changing interlinear renderings (which could be useful in TILT), including one from one way of writing to another—in this case the Cyrillic to the Roman alphabets[11]. The original Russian reads as follows:

– Ты откуда пришла?—спросил я её.

Она ответила:—С верху, из Нижнего, да не пришла, а приехала!

По воде-то не ходят, шиш!

– А отчего я шиш?

– Оттого, что шумишь,—сказала она, тоже смеясь.

Transliterated, each word can be related, as a way of revealing the problems, to an English equivalent as follows. (Brackets indicate that more than one word in one language is used to translate a single word in the other. Forward slashes indicate ambiguities.)

Ты	откуда	пришла	спросил	я	её.
Ti	*otkuda*	*prishla*	*sprosil*	*ia*	*ee*
You	(from where)	came?	asked	I	(to her)

Она	ответила	С верху		из	Нижнего
Ona	*otvetila*	*S verkhu*		*iz*	*Nizhnego*
She	answered	From (above/up-river)		from	below/Nizhni)

Да	не	пришла	а	приехала!
Da	*ne*	*prishla*	*a*	*priekhala*
Yes	not	(came on foot)	but	(came by transport)

По	воде-то	не	ходят	шиш
Po	*vode-to*	*ne*	*khodiat*	*shish*
On	water	not	(they go on foot)	(nothing)

А	отчего	я	шиш
A	*otchego*	*ia*	*shish*
But	why	I	('shish')

Оттого	что	шумишь—	сказала	она	тоже	смеясь
Ottogo	*chto*	*shumish'*	*skazala*	*ona*	*tozhe*	*smeias'*
Because	you	(make a noise)	said	she	also	laughing

The first misunderstanding arises when the grandmother says she has come from up-river, using a phrase which can also mean 'from upstairs', and then adds that she has come from the town of *Nizhni* (*Нижний*) (short for *Nizhni Novgorod*) (*Нижний Новгород*) which literally means 'Lower', and is interpreted as such by the child. From the point of view of the child, who has presumably not heard of the town before, this creates a complete contradiction. The grandmother says she has come from above, but also from below. She then goes on—using the lexical distinction we have already encountered—to point out that she has not walked but come by transport, presumably on a river boat. Then affectionately she calls her grandson *shish* (*шиш*), a non-sensical term which literally refers to a rude gesture made with the thumb between the fingers, and when he asks her why, she appeals to the 'logic' of rhyme: you are a *shish* (*шиш*) because you *shumish'* (*шумишь*), literally 'make a noise'.

How is a translator to cope with this intense combination of linguistic coincidence, ambiguous meaning, and interpersonal banter? The answer is surely only by losing some of the double meanings and treating them as single, by finding similar but different coincidences in English ('silly Billy' in my translation above), or by abandoning the attempt and explaining in a note. None of these is satisfactory. But pedagogically such examples have enormous potential. The task for students need not be to translate them—that might asking too much—but rather to understand why translation is so difficult, indeed sometimes impossible, and in drawing attention to the reasons, in order to highlight the unique features of each language, to fix them in the mind, and to illustrate the need to read the original rather than a translation. Attention is on neither the 'first place' of the student's own language nor the 'second place' of the new language but on a 'third place' of the interaction between the two (Kramsch 1993: 233–258). What is so striking and attractive about this example is that it simultaneously draws attention to something which is universal—the confusion of a child exploring his own language—and to features unique to that one language. It is sometimes suggested, usually without evidence, that students find the problems of translation and the explicit comparison of languages boring and tedious. This seems pessimistic and rather patronizing. It is just as likely that those who are interested in the language they are learning would find an example such as this one both inspiring and instructive.

Levels of equivalence and learners

We have traced the development of translation theory from concerns with semantic equivalence to those at the level of pragmatics and discourse. And the issue of equivalence is undoubtedly one of relevance to learners as well as translators:

> both are confronted with the task of 'making sense', the translator for a particular audience, the second/foreign language learner for him- or herself. Thus, in a different form and shape and certainly on a different level, the question of 'equivalence' of whatever nature is a problem for both.
> (Witte, Harden, and Ramos de Oliveira Harden 2009: 11)

Not all types of translation equivalence are equally relevant to all learners, however. As hinted earlier, it may be that learners' encounters with translation should follow a similar trajectory to translation theory. There is a pedagogic argument, to which we shall return in Chapter 7, for keeping beginners' attention focused mainly upon semantic equivalence (with some consideration for pragmatic equivalence where this diverges dramatically), leaving attention to issues such as functional and discoursal equivalence to increase through the intermediate stages, becoming a major focus of attention for advanced students. In this way, strategies for coping with advanced translation problems will be firmly based on an understanding of literal semantic equivalence, rather than used as an avoidance strategy. It will also be harder for the teacher to diagnose gaps in student knowledge. As Butzkamm and Caldwell argue, there is a pedagogic case for attention to semantic equivalence, even where ultimately the best translation will be a pragmatic one. This is true even in the case of fixed formulaic expressions and idioms. There is a world of difference between the student who translates *de nada* as 'you're welcome' but knows that it literally means 'of nothing', and the student who translates it in the same way, but is unaware of this literal meaning. We shall return to some of the evidence for the advantages of such awareness in Chapter 5, when we turn to research on translation and acquisition, and in Chapter 7, when we examine pedagogic uses of translation.

At the heart of this difference lies the issue of what makes a good translation in the world at large, and how it differs from what is a helpful use of translation in the classroom—the differences between translation as a process and a product (Witte 2009), between translation as an end of learning, and translation as a means. Where the focus is upon good translation in the world at large, there is good reason to explore options beyond semantic equivalence at the level of sentence or utterance. Where the focus is on developing student understanding of the new language—i.e. translation as a means—then there is good reason to ensure students understand semantic equivalence first before moving on to other problems. As argued earlier, however, there need be no rigid barrier between means and end. As learning progresses, translation as a means with its early focus on the literal can transform into translation as an end with its focus on discourse.

Beyond equivalence: making the issues overt

The overemphasis in teaching upon the final product of translation rather than the translating process and the ways it can be developed is also inherent in the translation theories focusing on equivalence which we examined above. What these theories have in common is a tendency to reduce the visibility of translation, hiding away both the process itself, and the presence and role of the translator. Their interest is in the finished product rather than an ongoing process, the noun *translation* rather than the verb *translating*. Whatever difficult choices have been made between the myriad options available, they have happened behind the scenes, resolved before the finished product is made available to its audience, almost as though the process of arriving at that product had never taken place. Those receiving this product, it is implied, should not want to know about its genesis. The physical layout of conference halls with simultaneous interpreting facilities is emblematic of this attitude. The interpreters sit in darkened booths around the periphery, out of the sight of those for whom they are interpreting, and relay their words through microphone to headphone. The implicit assumption of such an arrangement is that a good interpretation and a good interpreter are those of which the recipient is as unaware as possible. There is certainly no scope for bringing any translation problems or alternative solutions of them to the attention of the recipients. Issues of equivalence remain literally behind closed doors.

Although this preference for keeping translators in the shadows is still the received wisdom among those employing them, recent academic approaches have advocated bringing both the process of translation and the role of the translator into the spotlight. A vivid example, and a challenge to the status quo, is provided by Jieun Lee (2009) in a study of consecutive interpreting from Korean into English in an Australian courtroom. She explains how certain characteristics of Korean grammar (such as the frequency of ellipsis, the lack of definiteness markers, and the absence of subject–verb agreement for person, gender, or number) often make contradictory English translations possible. She gives numerous examples of instances where rival interpretations are valid, and where making the right choice is crucial to the witness' evidence being correctly understood. For example, in a trial involving serious charges of assault, kidnapping, and robbery, a key statement by a witness:

어 이혼한 딸의 옷을 전해준다고 했습니다.
e ihonhan ttaluy osul cenhaycwuntako haysssupnita.
[filler] divorced daughter's clothes [-object] to pass-give [pro-verb] do
(past)
(Ø said Ø pass/give divorced daughter's, daughter's clothing)

contains so many ellipses (Ø), and was moreover so unclearly spoken, that in context it could validly have been translated in four ways as:

a) Kim said he wanted to meet my husband to receive the clothing of a divorced daughter from him.
b) Kim said he wanted to meet my husband to give him the clothing of a divorced daughter.
c) My husband said he wanted to meet him to receive the clothing of a divorced daughter from him.
d) My husband said he wanted to meet him to give him the clothing of a divorced daughter.

Although such heavily ellipted utterances may often be disambiguated through familiarity with the context and the preceding discourse, this is not always possible for interpreters who, as Jieun Lee points out, are moved around from courtroom to courtroom, and are therefore not always aware, as judge, counsel, and jury are, of what has gone before. An obvious strategy for the interpreter would be to seek clarification from the witness—and this is sometimes done surreptitiously while talking to the witness in their own language—or explain the problem to the judge. Yet, disturbingly, when one interpreter did try to adopt this latter strategy and explain the difficulty to the court, they were ordered dismissively by the judge to:

Just translate!

A further disincentive is that the translator who does try to explain is likely to be regarded as incompetent. In Jieun Lee's study 'most of the interpreters interviewed were…reluctant to interrupt procedures for clarification' (ibid.).

In the light of such concerns, the old debate about 'equivalence' and the quest for objective principles to achieve this elusive quality have been superseded by a new focus on the translator, what they do, and why. Rather than agonize over what is equivalent, some theorists have argued for turning the question on its head—beginning with 'postulate equivalence' (Tourey 1980), i.e. the fact that two texts in two different languages are accepted as equivalent, and then asking what type of equivalence it is, what procedures underpin it, and how it came about. In this approach 'Equivalence becomes a negotiable entity, with translators doing the negotiation' (Kenny 2009) and this leads in turn to a greater emphasis on studies of translators rather than of translations (Pym 1992). Hu (2004) suggests a shift from 'translation studies' to 'translator studies' in which the focus of attention is on neither the source nor the target, but on the individual imprints made by translators on their work. Research enterprises following this lead involve such practices as asking translators to comment on their own work either as they are doing it (think-aloud protocols) or after the event (retrospective protocols)—though both of these procedures have occasioned heated academic debate as to their validity, given that they may either distort the process or not accurately reflect it. This new academic focus coincides with a greater popular interest in translators 'as metaphors for varied aspects of life in a world increasingly marked by migration of all sorts' (Maier 2007: 7). Wars such as those in Iraq and Afghanistan have brought translators and translator casualties to public attention[12]. Recent years have seen a number of novels, biographies, news reports[13], and even a Hollywood film[14] focusing on the role of translators and interpreters in the globalized world.

Overt versus covert translation, foreignization versus domestication

This new focus of interest, and the challenge posed by such studies as Jieun Lee's, evoke a long-standing distinction between translations which are clearly translations and maintain a sense of otherness, and those which try to hide this nature and present themselves as 'normal' texts within the language they use. Although this distinction has a long history, going back in the early 20th century to philosophers Walter Benjamin and Ortega y Gasset, in the 19th century to the Romantic theorist Schleiermacher (Munday 2001: 27–29; Pym 2009), and indeed further back in history to the distinction between free and literal translation discussed above, it has been revived in recent translation theory with a new terminology. House (1997) makes a clear and useful distinction between 'overt' and 'covert' translations. Venuti (1986, 1995) talks of visible and invisible translators, arguing that the latter have been the norm in Anglo-American ideas of translation since Dryden's comments on translation in his preface to Ovid in the late 17th century.

> A translated text, whether prose or poetry, fiction or non-fiction, is judged acceptable by most publishers, reviewers and readers when it reads fluently, when the absence of any linguistic or stylistic peculiarities make it seem transparent, giving the appearance that it reflects the foreign writer's personality or intention or the essential meaning of the foreign text—the appearance, in other words, that the translation is not in fact a translation, but the 'original'.
> (Venuti 1995: 1)

He goes on to point out that translators' and interpreters' own practice of translating fluently as though there were no problems involved aggravates this ideology. Related to this are his notions that a translation adopts either a strategy of 'domestication'—'an ethnocentric reduction of the foreign text to target-language cultural values'—or 'foreignization'—'an ethnodeviant pressure on values to register the linguistic and cultural differences of the foreign text, sending the reader abroad' (1995: 20).

Venuti very much favours the latter of these strategies, and many other theorists have been of the same opinion. Others however have pointed to the assimilationist and colonizing effects of foreignization. The danger was felt long before the notion was explicitly formulated. As long ago as 1904, Fulda (cited in Morgan 1959: 279) characterized bad translation as being either a form of colonization or having the effect of turning an eloquent poet into an inarticulate foreign immigrant. In similar vein, Liu Yameng (2007) argues that the adoption of quirky language or alternative styles to mark translations as foreign may also serve to keep important foreign works marginal within the dominant cultures for which they are translated. He sees this as part of a general 'Northerncentredness' in global patterns of translation, whereby the rich and powerful Northern nations select for translation from the poorer South only those works and writers which reinforce and confirm their own values—or can be translated to appear to do so.

Intervention

The notions of foreignizing or domesticating a text, making it overt or covert, suggests that translators must choose one of two voices. They may seek to keep the voice of the original (i.e. be overt and foreignizing) or try to adopt the voice of the culture and language they are translating it into (i.e. be covert and domesticating). There is however a third possible voice—the translator's own.

Once the translator and the act of translation are made apparent and objectivity is no longer seen as possible or necessary, then the issue arises as to how much of a personal imprint the translator should leave, how far they should seek to intervene in the process of which they are themselves an essential part. The issue has always been most apparent in matters of political allegiance and ideology. The traditional notion, with good reason behind it, is that the translator should reproduce the original as 'faithfully' as possible (though this is not a straightforward notion, as we have seen) so that readers of the translation may as far as possible make their own judgments on the original and its producers. To do otherwise seems obviously wrong and self-defeating. To remove the anti-Semitism from Hitler's *Mein Kampf* would give a seriously misleading view of Nazism and make readers less critical of it than they might otherwise be, and no one, as far as I know, seriously advocates such an irresponsible political bowdlerizing. Yet there is perhaps a case for resisting what is perceived as the role of translation in perpetuating institutionalized ideology—and many translators deeply embedded within institutions—where 'translation practices can also serve to strengthen the institutional voice by abiding with and propagating the 'habitualized' discourses promoted by organizational agendas' (Baker and Pérez-González forthcoming). If one considers the cases of sexist language, for example, the issue might be framed in terms of how far the feminist translator should reproduce in the translation manifestations of sexism in the original. Luise von Flotow (1997) argues that the translator should take responsibility for the texts they produce, seek to combat the spread of views they oppose, but overtly indicate changes they have made in so doing:

> translators and translation critics working within the ethics of
> feminist thought [should not] 'hide behind the inverted commas'
> of translation ... [but] declare their responsibility and positionality
> towards the text and the community it is destined for ... [avoiding] the
> dissemination of culturally and politically questionable material about
> women or feminism.
> (von Flotow 1997: 96–97)

Translation has always had political overtones and there is certainly nothing new in its role and use in propaganda. Liu Yameng (2007) gives the example of a change in the British translation of the Chinese character *yi* (夷) used by the Qing government of China in the early 19th century to refer to Europeans. The original translation by the British of the combination *yi* + *ren* (夷人) as 'foreigner' was ominously replaced at some point in the early 19th century by a translation of the same combination as 'barbarian', leading British readers of translations using this term to believe that the Chinese regarded Europeans and inferior and uncultured. This belief was then used as a *casus belli* for Britain's infamous Opium War of 1839 in which China was forced to allow free trade including the import of opium.

Such political translation issues are a perennial source of contention. Baker (2007) for example, in criticism of English-language reporting of the Israeli Palestinian conflict, challenges the validity of the translation of the Arabic word *shaheed* (شهيد) into English as 'martyr', seeing it as both inaccurate and inflammatory, because:

> In Arabic, *shaheed* is generally used to refer to anyone who is killed
> violently, especially in war, whether they choose to be involved in that war
> or not, and irrespective of their religion. It therefore does not have the
> overtones of militancy and extremism that the term martyr has come to
> acquire in English, in connection with the Arab and Islamic world.

She goes on to give illustrative examples of alternative translations with very different overtones. A documentary about an Israeli attack on the Jenin Palestinian refugee camp in 2002 for example preferred to translate the Arabic

السه بندوّر شهدا من تحت الأرض

lissa bindawar shuhada min taht elard

as:

We are still pulling victims out of the rubble.

rather than:

We are still pulling martyrs from underneath the ground.

The translator and the learner

While the problems of translation have remained constant throughout history, perceptions of these problems and how best to deal with them have, in recent years, undergone some considerable change. The role of translation and the translator is being brought out of the shadows, and can be seen as emblematic of times when, with increased mobility and international communication, the process of contact between communities and languages becomes for many people as important as their separate static identities. In this world, the translator should no longer inhabit an unacknowledged no-man's land between 'source language' and 'target language'. The spaces in between are becoming bigger than those on either side of them. Those nations of the world that consider their identities to be tied to one language have much to learn from these intermediate territories.

Translation mediates between monolithic cultural and linguistic blocks. Given the impossibilities of absolute or objective equivalence and therefore of a simple transmission of a message from one culture or language to another (the traditional view of translation with which this chapter began) it can give language learners unique insights into their encounters with new languages. This should make it a key and high-profile constituent of language learning. Yet although it has always been a natural and obvious means and end of language learning and teaching, in the 'cutting edge' applied linguistic theories of the last century, as we have seen in Chapter 2, it has consistently been pushed to one side. As in the wider world, the act and process of translation has been treated in the classroom as though it did not exist. Though it is perhaps assumed that a person who has successfully learnt a new language will at the end of their studies not only be able to speak and write the new language but also to translate in and out of it, quite how this is to be achieved has, in these same theories, been left out of account. The extent of this neglect, and the reasons and means for bringing it to an end, are the subject of Part Two.

Notes

1 There are inevitably complications to this simplified scheme as I have set it out above, and various schools of linguistics would take issue with one aspect or

another of my summary. Comparative linguists would point out that the relation between graphology and morphology varies between different writing systems. Systemic functionalists would prefer to treat morphology, syntax, and lexis as a single system of 'lexicogrammar' on the grounds that lexis is 'the most delicate grammar' (Halliday 1976: 69). Building upon this, corpus linguistics further questions the distinction between lexis and grammar (Sinclair 1991, 2004) arguing that a word is not just slotted into a grammatical structure depending on which part of speech it is, but has tendencies to co-occur with other words in collocations, or to favour particular grammatical structures in colligations. Moving upwards, some schools of thought do not use a semantics/ pragmatics distinction at all on the grounds that all meaning is negotiated and context dependent. Definitions of genre also vary (Martin 1985; Swales 1990), and the superordinate term 'discourse' is notoriously used in a variety of ways (Pennycook 1994), sometimes as more or less synonymous with texts of more than one sentence, sometimes referring to acts of communication in their entirety, and sometimes as a countable noun (discourses) to talk about how institutionalized ideologies are (partly) expressed through uses of language.

2   This is not so straightforward in all languages. Some languages inflect the first person for gender (Fillmore 1992), some use forms which vary with social rank. Dixon (1980: 247) describes the Australian language Adnyamadhanha as having ten first person inclusive dual (you and I) pronouns.

3   In Russian this word has four forms depending on its grammatical function. Russian has six cases, but for *Ia* (я) the accusative and genitive forms are the same, as are the dative and prepositional forms: Nominative = *Ia* (я), Accusative and Genitive = *menia* (меня), Dative = *Mne* (мне), Instrumental and Prepositional = *Mnoi* (мной).

4   In the case of verbs of motion such as *priiti* (прийти), the imperfective signifies repetition rather than incompletion.

5   Komissarov's five levels are of:

  1   linguistic signs (*iazykovykh znakov*) (языковых знаков)
  2   collocation (*vyskazyvaniia*) (высказывания)
  3   information (*soobshcheniia*) (сообщения)
  4   situation (*opisaniia situatsii*) (описания ситуации)
  5   communicative aim (*tseli kommunikatsii*) (цели коммуникации).

6   For a view of genre with less emphasis than the Hallidayan model on characterization of genres by linguistic features, see Swales 1990.

7   According to the United Bible Society, The New Testament is available in 1168 languages, and portions of the Bible in 2,454 languages. http://www.ubs-translations.org/about_us/#c165 (accessed 19 April 2009).

8   Jordan did however work from the original Greek, not from older English versions, though he must have been aware of them.

9   The name of the translator is not given.

10   *Entre les Murs* (2008), directed by Laurent Cantet and adapted by François Bégaudeau (who also plays the teacher) from his own book about his teaching experience.

11   Apart from the obvious feature of being written in a different alphabet this also reveals one of the many difference between Russian and English punctuation—that dialogue is marked off by dashes rather than inverted commas—which are

almost always neglected in the teaching of either language to speakers of the other.

12 Statistics released by the US Ministry of Labor indicate that between the invasion of Iraq in 2003 and August 2006, 199 translators were killed and 491 injured, many of them specifically because of their work. These statistics do not include translators and interpreters working for the British (or any other) army in the region, nor those working for journalists and foreign correspondents (Chaterjee 2006). See also http://ipsnews.net/news.asp?idnews=34319 (accessed 17 September 2009).

13 For details of some of these, see Maier 2007.

14 *The Interpreter* (2005), directed by Sydney Pollack, starring Sean Penn and Nicole Kidman.

PART TWO
Arguments

'Translation has been too long in exile, for all kinds of reasons which . . . have little to do with any considered pedagogic principle. It is time it was given a fair and informed appraisal.'
(Widdowson 2003: 160)

5

Evidence-based arguments

Values and technologies

Educational decisions can be driven by a variety of criteria. They may seek to pass on information and values from one generation to another, to reconstruct society in new ways, to develop and fulfil individual students, or to answer a society's economic and political needs (Skilbeck 1982; Clark 1987). A good deal of educational debate concerns which of these different criteria should be prioritized, and then if that is resolved, how exactly should an agreed aim be interpreted: which values should be passed on, how should society be changed, and what constitutes individual fulfilment? There are thus two levels of debate, corresponding in some terminologies to the difference between 'curriculum' and 'syllabus' (Nunan 1988: 3; Johnson 1998: 93). The first is concerned with values and outcomes, and seeks to decide what education is trying to achieve. The second takes objectives for granted and is concerned with their efficient delivery. In broad terms, the language-teaching literature has tended to operate at this second level. Although there is a lot that can be said about why language learning is desirable, or what exactly we are seeking to achieve through it, a good deal of work proceeds as though broad aims were already agreed, and focuses upon the most efficient ways of achieving them. Another way of putting this is to say that language teaching has been perceived as a technology within a framework of agreed values (rather as medical technology is developed without questioning the assumption that life and health should be preserved), or, to use a more negative example, weaponry is developed in the belief that armies should have a capacity for attack and defence. As with the development of these other technologies, the concern is often with improving delivery rather than questioning underlying values.

TILT is intimately bound up with this distinction between evaluative and technological discussion. For although there is a case to be made for it as a technology, many arguments for its reintroduction are value-oriented, and involve a reconsideration of the overall aims of language learning. This book attempts to make a case on both levels. This chapter is concerned with the technological level—what the evidence against TILT is within the context of assumed purposes. The next chapter, on educational arguments, examines the values underlying these assumptions.

In keeping with the technological spirit of the times, 'scientific' influences have been a prominent driving force behind most dominant approaches to language teaching and learning over the last hundred years. In this 'scientific turn', a succession of influential movements—from audiolingualism through graded structures and notional functional syllabuses to task-based instruction, the lexical syllabus (Willis 1990), and 'psychology for language teachers' (Williams and Burden 1997)—have all appealed to the latest scientific findings about learning, language, and language acquisition. By a 'scientific' influence (and the reason for my scare quotes will I hope become apparent) I mean one which claims both to be based on rigorous examination of experimental or observational evidence and/or the latest theory, and to be able to make predictions about the relation between language-learning conditions and success (Spolsky 1989), and on that basis to propose new and more efficient ways of teaching and learning a language.

There is always the possibility that such scientific investigation will simply confirm common sense and traditional practice. Yet for findings to make an impact and effect change, they need to be in some way surprising. They need to overturn popular wisdom as the natural sciences have done, showing the earth to be round, humans to be related to other apes, or time to be relative to space. Many of the ideas of scientific 20th century language teaching theory have been of this surprising kind. They purport to reveal 'facts' about language learning which are not intuitively obvious to teachers and learners, and indeed often run counter to received common-sense wisdom. Enquiry into the cognitive processes involved in language learning has been a particularly rich source of such surprises, precisely because it delves below the threshold of consciousness, and reveals things which are counter-intuitive and not easily available to conscious reflection. A common refrain in such research findings has been that while teachers or learners may think that a particular activity or learning strategy is working, the scientific evidence shows them to be wrong. Thus, apparently obvious and effective ways of teaching and learning have been represented as misguided. This leads to a continual turnover of ideas in a self-perpetuating process of action and reaction. Once an idea catches on and becomes widely accepted, it too becomes susceptible to being overthrown by new scientific findings. For language teachers this novelty-promoting process can prove unsettling. After even a short time in the profession, they may have encountered opposite 'truths', so leading to a general disenchantment with academic theorizing (G. Cook 2009). (This book is open to the charge of belonging to this process too.)

As we have seen, translation was an early casualty of the scientific turn. The work of the Reform Movement can be seen as 'applied linguistics'—although the term did not then exist—in which the findings of 'linguistic science' were used to exert a one-way influence on the practice of language teaching[1]. It deployed arguments from the scientific linguistics, psychology, and phonetics of its time, and saw these as the driving forces behind the adoption of Direct Method, rather than the demographic, political, and commercial factors analysed in Chapter 1.

From the 1970s, however, the dominant 'scientific' influence on language teaching and learning has been SLA theory, seen by many as the pre-eminent informing authority for effective and successful teaching and learning (and at some points and in some quarters considered almost co-terminous with applied linguistics). In its early heyday, SLA was invoked to support many counter-intuitive ideas—for example that error correction and conscious learning of rules were of no use, that the order of acquisition was immune to instruction, and that a language could be acquired through exposure to meaningful input (Krashen 1982, 1985). Once such ideas had become established, they were then overturned by new SLA research, re-advocating many of the activities which had previously been rejected.

So specific ideas change. The excesses of Direct Method and Krashen's belief in natural acquisition are no longer supported by the latest research. But the underlying notion remains that scientific findings can and should determine language teaching and learning, and that progress will follow the right theory. Brian MacWhinney, writing in 2006, neatly summarizes this doctrine when he sets out his criteria for evaluating the articles in a special issue of the journal *Applied Linguistics* devoted to a new emergentist theory in SLA (N. Ellis and Larsen-Freeman 2006). His yardstick is:

> How well do these analyses succeed in generating precise predictions for patterns in language learning? Can we use these predictions to improve language learning?
> (MacWhinney 2006: 734)

This is a useful quotation for my purposes as it encapsulates two key presuppositions of the scientific turn: that precision and prediction are possible, and that defining 'improvement' is unproblematic. Claims made under this rubric can be contested in two different ways. Either one can accept the premises but argue that specific predictions are wrong, or one can argue with the premises themselves. In this chapter I want to pursue both lines of attack: firstly by challenging the evidence and reasoning of supposedly 'scientific' ideas which have been advanced against TILT, and secondly by challenging the notion that anything as value-laden as the concept of 'improvement' can ever be scientific.

The process by which scientific research first overturns popular wisdom, then revises it in the light of later research, can be seen very clearly in the history of attitudes to the relation of learners' own languages to new ones. But it is an unfinished history with a strangely abrupt ending. For just at the point when the trajectory of ideas should have led to investigation of the effects of TILT, the scientific principle seems to have failed, and for some reason the research has not been done. In SLA in particular, the notion that translation is not helpful to acquisition seems to have become so firmly established that it has hardly been investigated at all.

SLA assumptions

So let us consider what the SLA assumptions about TILT have been, and what arguments and evidence there is for them. Translation is often considered to be detrimental both to fluency in communication and to the learner's development of a new language.

A common objection to TILT is that it obstructs development of an ability to use the language automatically. The process of translation is seen as a slow and laborious one, focused more upon accuracy than fluency, making it somehow impossible ever to escape this impediment. The person who has learnt through translation will forever be locked into this laborious process, always condemned to start production and finish comprehension in their own language, and unable—to use a popular formulation—'to think in the language' they have learnt. Related to this is the popular idea that translation promotes 'interference' and 'transfer' from a student's own language. There are, of course, good reasons for this view. As Mitchell and Myles point out:

> Everyday observation tells us that learners' performance in a second language is influenced by the language, or languages, they already know. This is routinely obvious from learners' 'foreign accent', i.e. pronunciation which bears traces of the phonology of their own language. It is also obvious when learners make certain characteristic mistakes, e.g. when a native-speaker of English says something in French like *je suis douze*, an utterance parallel to the English 'I am twelve'. (The correct French expression would of course be *j'ai douze ans* = I have twelve years.)
> Mitchell and Myles 2004: 19

Transfer of this kind was a key issue for research in the behaviourist paradigm which dominated ideas about language learning in the 1950s. 'Negative transfer' was when learners wrongly assumed a feature of the new language to be the same as in their own (as in the example above); 'positive transfer' occurred when the two languages do things in the same way so the assumption of similarity works (the order of number and noun in *douze enfants/ twelve children* is the same in English and French). As discussed in Chapter 2, Contrastive Analysis of languages was used both to predict learner errors and to select items to teach (Lado 1957). The idea was that by focusing on the differences between the learners' own language and the new one, the teacher could tackle the majority of their difficulties.

From the late 1960s, the new post-behaviourist study of SLA quickly overturned these assumptions, although in doing so it had also to caricature and simplify what contrastive analysts such as Lado had actually said (Swan

2007). Corder's work on learner errors (1967) and Selinker's (1972) theory of 'interlanguage' distinguished between 'errors' as part of a positive process of gradual approximation to the new language system and 'mistakes' as less important unsystematic performance errors[2]. For both writers, so-called 'negative' transfer was relegated to being only one source of error. Block, writing thirty years later, summarizes the kind of evidence used to support this view as follows:

> Not only did learners fail to exhibit the errors predicted by negative
> transfer but many cases of positive transfer did not materialize' (Newmeyer
> and Weinberger 1988: 35). As regards negative transfer it was predicted
> that a L1 speaker of Spanish, a language with preverbal pronouns ('el gato
> los comió'), would produce utterances such as 'the cat them ate' instead
> of 'the cat ate them'. However, Spanish speakers do not normally produce
> such utterances. As regards positive transfer, an L1 Spanish speaker would
> be expected to have no problem producing simple utterances such as 'John
> is not here' in English; yet Spanish-speaking students are often observed to
> produce copula-dropping utterances such as 'John not here'.
> (Block 2003: 15)

Building on the work of Corder (1973) and Selinker (1972), Dulay and Burt (1973, 1974, 1975) took this view of errors further, claiming that interference errors were far less prevalent than those deriving from a universal natural developmental order, similar to that found in child language acquisition, where infants acquire the morphemes of their first language in a fixed sequence (Brown 1973). In the highly influential work of Stephen Krashen (already encountered from a different perspective in Chapter 3) this last claim crystallized into the hypotheses[3] (echoing Corder's earlier notion of an 'inbuilt syllabus') that learners follow 'a natural order of acquisition', and that a new language can be acquired without conscious learning through exposure to 'comprehensible input' (Krashen 1985). Under the influence of these ideas, details of the learner's own language ceased to be regarded as important, and the dominant notion that a monolingual environment is best for successful language acquisition was reinforced.

The general flaws in Krashen's reasoning and evidence were soon convincingly exposed (Gregg 1984; McLaughlin 1987; Widdowson 1990a *inter alia*) and subsequent SLA research replaced the notion of wholly subconscious acquisition with the more reasonable idea that there are benefits in the promotion of student noticing (Schmidt 1990) and in an incidental focus on form (Long 1991), i.e. the use of explicit teacher comment on elements of language structure as they arise in activities that are otherwise meaning centred, as already discussed in Chapter 2.

This is the point in SLA history when one might have expected research into the possible role of translation in language acquisition to have opened up. For the act of translation is surely a real-world task in which incidental focus on form and the explicit noticing of features in the new language inevitably occur. Yet somehow this line of enquiry never materialized. Källkvist (2008), attempting to survey a near non-existent literature on the topic nearly twenty years later, comes to the following wistful conclusion:

> Unfortunately, empirical work on the effect of translation exercises on L2 learners' morphosyntax is scant.

This is a massive understatement.[4] Apart from earlier work of her own (Källkvist 2004), this study of Källkvist's is unique in taking an SLA experimental approach to whether the use of translation might aid acquisition of grammar. It also reveals, incidentally, a great deal about SLA and misunderstandings of pedagogic translation. It begins with the mistaken premise that 'translation as a pedagogical tool' necessarily

> represents a focus on formS activity since target structures have been selected in advance for deliberate attention in the L2 classroom.

This assumes that artificially constructed exercises reminiscent of Grammar–Translation are the only possible vehicle for translation use, and ignores the possibility of translation as a communicative activity, or the selection of translation tasks without pre-selection of structures. Källkvist next acknowledges that 'translation remains part of language instruction in many… parts of the world', but sees this widespread use as only 'relevant for careers in teaching or translation and interpreting'. Translation is simply assumed to be of no use or interest to the majority of learners. (One wonders how she would explain the Chinese tertiary English curriculum requirement that all learners of English should be able to translate (He 2000).) Källkvist's survey of the SLA literature which follows finds virtually nothing on translation, as already remarked. It does however acknowledge that outside SLA the situation is very different.

> … an entirely different view [of the usefulness of TILT] comes to the fore in publications written by translation studies scholars and language educators who express an overwhelmingly positive view of the merits of translation-related activities for language learning.[5]

With an air of desperation Källkvist concludes that within SLA there are a number of studies[6] which, while they do not concern translation directly, 'suggest that explicit contrastive information coupled with error correction enhances the learning of certain grammatical structures'. She also refers to evidence from cognitive psychology—to which we shall return shortly—that the elaborate processing required to deal with translation may aid retention in memory.

Källkvist's article is an example of the fact that SLA has traditionally been mainly focused, as many of its critics have pointed out, on grammar, treating other areas of language, such as vocabulary and pronunciation, as poor relations. In the fast-growing study of vocabulary acquisition, however, the situation is very similar, and research into translation as a means of learning is also almost non-existent. Laufer and Girsai (2008), making 'a case for contrastive analysis and translation' uncover only two studies which involve translation as a strategy in vocabulary teaching (Snellings et al. 2002; Horst et al. 2005) and conclude that:

> To our knowledge, no research has examined the value of contrastive FFI [Form Focused Instruction] of vocabulary, such as interlingual comparisons with learner's L1, or translation.

Following this with an understatement remarkably reminiscent of Källkvist's on research into grammar, they comment that in vocabulary acquisition:

> Lack of contrastive FFI studies is rather surprising.

Laufer and Girsai's own study comes up with results which are far less equivocal or task-relative than Källkvist's for grammar. Keeping variables as constant as possible, they taught the same vocabulary to three groups using three different types of instruction—meaning-focused, form focused without translation, and through contrastive analysis and translation. They then tested the groups for both active and passive recall of the words encountered. Their results were that 'The CAT (contrastive analysis and translation) group significantly outperformed the other two groups on all tests'.

Taken together, these two studies suggest that the SLA blind spot about translation derives from fixed but mistaken ideas and an inability of SLA researchers to follow promising leads both outside their own field and within it.

Why did this happen? Why, in a scientific paradigm which should have taken nothing for granted and comprehensively investigated all possible avenues of activity, was such an obvious line of enquiry ignored? Why was the notion that translation interfered with successful acquisition never questioned? Were the effects of translating just deemed too self-evident to merit investigation? Or were there perhaps, in this continuing neglect of translation, other *non*-scientific factors at work—as was the case in the Reform Movement's earlier dismissal of it? Thus, while SLA never balked at challenging other cherished beliefs—the efficacy of instruction, graded syllabuses, and the learning of rules—the rightness of monolingual teaching was never scrutinized.

Evidence outside SLA

Before attempting to answer these questions at the end of this chapter, let us consider further some of the common assumptions about the effects of translation, and the evidence which might be mustered, in the absence of SLA studies, for and against them. To do this, we might note that there are two possible dimensions to the claim that translation induces detrimental effects. Firstly, it may mean that these effects occur during communication, when someone produces utterances by first thinking of them in the one language, and then translating them into the other. Secondly, it may mean that learning through translation causes long-term damage to a speaker's systematization of a language, making it so fossilized that the errors it has induced cannot be shaken off, even if later this speaker progresses to using the new language without translating. Let us keep these two possibilities separate, bearing in mind that they might nevertheless occur together, and that errors caused by translating while communicating might be compounded by fossilized errors caused by having learnt through translation.

Most of the arguments we have considered so far have been concerned with possible long-term effects. Less has been said on the issue of interference in real-time processing. It is often simply assumed to occur, even by some of those who have spoken against the assumption that intralingual teaching is always best. Stern (1992: 284) for example writes that:

> if we want to use the L2 to take part in a conversation, listen to a lecture, read a newspaper, or write a letter or report, it is better if we can do that without translating from or into L2.

But no reasons or evidence are given for this claim. Nor are we told in what sense it is 'better' not to translate. It seems to be another of those beliefs which is just too obvious to question. But let us question it here. Is translating during online language processing necessarily 'bad'? And if so, why and in what sense?

Bilingual processing

Here, in the absence of SLA studies, it is worth looking at work in cognitive psychology on bilingual language processing of the kind which Källkvist alluded to in her attempt to find some existing research basis for her study. She refers to Hummel's (1995) notion of elaborateness of processing, and the claim that:

> the translation process should entail just such an increased set of interconnections, resulting in a more elaborate set of memory traces...
> and...the L2 structures should therefore be more resistant to forgetting.

These ideas have also been borne out in work by Bialystok and her colleagues, who have used both behavioural and brain research to examine variation between bilingual and monolingual language processing (Bialystok et al. 2005; Bialystok and Feng 2009). They have found significant differences between the two groups both in the ability to perform certain tasks, and in the areas of the brain which are activated when performing them. Speaking a second language, it is claimed, increases blood flow and oxygen in the working of the brain[7]. Bilinguals showed faster reaction times in some tasks with greater activity in the left prefrontal cortex and anterior cingulate cortex, whereas monolinguals showed faster reaction times in other tasks with greater activation in middle frontal regions. In bilingual processing, Bialystok argues, both systems are activated in all tasks, even those which seem to involve only one language. Differences can be explained with reference to the cognitive control required to manage attention to two language systems (Bialystok 2009). Bilinguals have more frequent cause to use the executive functions of the frontal regions of the brain involved in planning, staying focused, and avoiding distractions. The result is that bilinguals, though they may be slower in some operations, are more successful in choosing between competing stimuli.

The claim that translation slows down communication, though it seems intuitively obvious, is thus rather more complicated than popularly believed. There are a number of everyday observations which support this view too. One is the work of simultaneous interpreters who, by definition, must translate what is said at usual speeds, but do not falter in this task because they are translating. Indeed, so fast is their work that they typically finish a target language utterance at the same time as the source language speaker, and sometimes even in front of them (Chernov 1992), presumably through the operation of subconscious predictive powers based on likely phrasings! In some ways, simultaneous interpreters are—as one described herself to me in conversation—'an exceptional category of language users', whose achievement is beyond the reach of most people. Reference to their skills could perhaps thus be dismissed on the grounds that it is irrelevant to the vast majority of ordinary learners. Nevertheless this achievement cannot be left out of account in any theory of bilingual language processing which aspires to generality, which is what most SLA theories seek. The existence and success of simultaneous interpreters undermines any claim for a detrimental effect of translation on fluency as a universal feature of human language use[8].

It is not scientifically very respectable to leave counter-evidence of this kind out of account as 'exceptional' because it does not suit, but let us, for the sake of argument, go along for a moment with the critics of 'translating as we talk', leave aside the case of simultaneous interpreters, and ask what the situation is for less exceptional but nevertheless expert speakers of an additional language. How would one set about investigating whether it is an impediment to fluency? The best procedures might be to ask proficient speakers two questions: whether they do actually translate from their L1 while speaking, and secondly whether they can. The answers to these questions are open to investigation, both through introspection or through asking others, or through the kind of behavioural and brain imaging referred to above; and the answers must for the moment remain open. Although there is a tradition of research into these processes in interpreters (see Lambert and Moser-Mercer 1994; Moser-Mercer 2001), and into their relevance to training (Daro 1990), there is no such tradition of research for 'ordinary' language users. But two hypotheses do seem valid— though they are open to contradiction through investigation. The first is that learners who reach a state of proficiency, even if they have proceeded to production via translation in the early stages of learning, reach a point where translation is no longer necessary. (Indeed, this is something of a circular observation, as proficiency could partly be defined as the ability to reach this state of automaticity.) It is also worth noting that the transition from one process to another (translation to automation) is yet another topic which has not been researched. The second hypothesis is that if we asked such learners to consciously but artificially translate 'in their heads' while producing, this might not slow them down as much as is often supposed. The reader who is proficient in an additional language is invited to conduct this thought experiment upon themselves, perhaps upon what they are reading at this moment.

Whatever the conclusions of reflection or research, there is undoubtedly in the world a large number of fluent users of an additional language, who studied initially through translation. Of course it is possible to claim that their fluency is not the result of these studies, but of subsequent exposure and monolingual practice. Such an argument however is reminiscent of one used in SLA debates in the 1980s around the concepts of 'acquisition' (a subconscious process) and 'learning' (a conscious one) and the discredited claim by Krashen, discussed above, that only the former is effective. Any evidence of success by those who make a conscious effort to master and practise the rules of a language was attributed to a parallel process of acquisition. In the same way, it is possible to dismiss the fluency of those who have studied through translation but also use the language for monolingual communication, by attributing it wholly to the latter. These are truly futile arguments, and hopelessly impervious to any scientific investigation, as claims on either side are unfalsifiable. Any learner will inevitably both learn and acquire, translate and not translate, and it is not feasible to attempt a separation of the effects. They are simplistic dichotomies in any case, with many fuzzy possibilities between the two; actual learning and actual use may well combine both translated and non-translated elements.

Lastly, there is the issue of componential learning, and whether skills which are practised separately can later be integrated. The communicative movement and its successors, such as task-based instruction, assumed that because the goal of language learning is real-world behaviour and real-language use, these skills must be used by learners straight away. Behind this holistic assumption is the SLA assumption, inherited from Chomskyan linguistics, that language knowledge is different from and less amenable to instruction than other human skills. Yet once we question this assumption, as many linguists have, then there is no reason not to question the assumption that only holistic 'deep-end' language learning is effective. Johnson (1996), for example, asks whether skills are best acquired by attempting them holistically from the outset, pointing out that in a good deal of learning, objectives can be obtained indirectly, by doing something different as an intermediate stage on the way. Examples are many. Someone learning to play the piano practises scales and arpeggios; someone preparing for a tennis match may go running to increase overall fitness. In addition, people

may break the target behaviour down into manageable bits to be practised. Someone learning to drive a car does not go out on the motorway
immediately, but practises changing gear, reversing and so on, away from
other traffic. Aspiring footballers may spend hours shooting a ball at a goal.
Such learning is not confined to such artificial cultural activities either, but
seems to come naturally to intelligent mammals (G. Cook 2000: 101–108).
Young animals practise adult skills atomistically in games. Kittens chase and
pounce, antelopes jump in random directions.

This raises big questions. The view that language is a modular faculty
which operates in a different way from other types of knowledge is not necessarily true. If we do not doubt the structured atomization of component
skills in other learning, why should language learning be different? Could
translation not help with monolingual communication later? Could the focus
on components which it may involve not be assimilated later into holistic
language use?

The testimony of experience that translation may aid acquisition has yet to
be overturned. In a sustained argument against task-based instruction, whose
faith in the efficacy of a focus on meaning is in many ways the successor of
Krashen's ideas, Michael Swan makes the following point:

> The claim that acquisition only take place on-line during
> communication . . . is also undermined by the experience of countless
> people who have apparently learned languages successfully by
> 'traditional' methods incompatible with the hypothesis. And, if pushed to
> the limit, it is seriously counter-intuitive. (Suppose I tell you that Japanese
> questions are made by adding the particle 'ka' to the corresponding
> statements, and suppose that a year later you start learning Japanese and
> remember what I told you. Are you really not able to ask questions until
> the rule has been acquired naturalistically in the prescribed way?
> (Swan 2005: 379)

This argument, though here presented to support explicit grammatical explanation, is equally applicable to translation. Indeed this piece of information
about 'ka' can be conceived as one related to how to translate English questions into Japanese—one which simultaneously reveals the difference between
the two languages, and the futility of word for word translation (to which we
shall turn shortly).

Negative and positive views of influence

Although the limited behaviourist idea of first language influence as interference has been replaced in SLA by the more benign term of transfer, which
can be positive as well as negative, and is generally seen as a much broader
phenomenon than just a potential source of errors (Ellis 2008), the whole
question of the influence of one language on another has been seen in SLA
in curiously and unnecessarily defensive terms. The underlying assumption

seems to be that, whether at a societal or individual level, influence should not be allowed to disrupt the *status quo* of the language. It must never cause change or diverge from native norms.

Applied linguistics outside SLA has taken a rather different view, seeing influence as a source of stimulation, variety, and creativity, and a mechanism for language change, in which usage is enriched, rather than impoverished by language contact. Rather than deploring such influence, Rampton (1996, 1999a, 1999b, 2005) has analysed approvingly how British schoolchildren incorporate elements of other languages into their everyday speech in a phenomenon which he calls 'crossing'. Studies of hip-hop lyrics (Pennycook 2007; Sarkar and Winer 2006) have seen their mixing of languages (e.g. *Tout moune qui talk trash kiss mon black ass du nord*[9]) as a revitalizing force.

The influence of one language on another becomes established in some varieties. The lack of words for 'Yes' and 'No' in Irish, for example, has led to a tendency in Irish English to answer a question with 'That's right' or a negative or positive verb (Q: *Did your brother work on the farm as well?* A: *He did not.*) (Hickey 2007: 139–140). Some Jewish speakers of English use constructions from Yiddish, most famously the double negative, sometimes embellished with an extra 'from' as in 'He don't know from nothin', echoing Yiddish *Er veyst nit fun gornit* (Feinsilver 1962). Such crossovers can then permanently influence other varieties. Some Yiddish-influenced constructions have become generally common in colloquial English. Examples include the construction 'It's all right by me' and the elliptical 'What's with...?' (*Vos iz mit..?*) (ibid.).

At a more formal level, religion and poetry are often the vehicles for such penetration too. Greek and Hebrew syntax exerted influence on English through the use of grammatical constructions from those languages in the Authorized Version of the Bible, and Latin and Greek syntax influenced Milton's *Paradise Lost*—both works which, far from being given low marks for interference, are regarded as classics of English prose and poetry respectively. Kachru (1995) sees this penetration of one language by another as a source of literary creativity, contrasting the predilection of writers in his native Kashmir for writing in other languages ('Sanskrit, Persian, Urdu, Hindi and English') with the view of some Western scholars that there is a privileged relation between literary creativity and a writer's native language. In the numerous cases of non-native authors, such as Joseph Conrad or Vladimir Nabokov, both excelling in a new language, it may be that their style is enriched by importing phrasing from their other tongues. Nabokov, significantly, as we have seen, was an adamant champion of allowing 'interference' from the original in a translation:

> to my idea of literalism I sacrificed everything (elegance, euphony, clarity, good taste, modern usage and even grammar) that the dainty mimic prizes higher than truth.
> (Nabokov 1964: x)

More generally there is a widely held belief that literary English has benefited considerably from the influence of writers from former British colonies bringing to it the influence of non-standard and regional forms, many of which reflect the influence of other languages.

All this may seem a long way from the topic of learner errors and how to deal with them, and it does not mean that errors should not be corrected and dealt with. But it does suggest that the fear of any change to a language through its learning by outsiders need not be as extreme as it implicitly is in SLA research. There are also potential benefits.

Word-for-wordism

Related to concerns about transfer and interference is a popular belief that the practice of translation by language learners will lead to their producing, when speaking or writing, word-for-word translations from their own language, which are at best markedly a-typical, or at worst grammatically incorrect. Let us call this putative bad consequence of using translation 'word-for-wordism'. This charge differs from those of transfer and interference in that it refers to instances of the target language which the learner actually produces rather than to its representation and processing in the mind. Transfer and interference in other words are cognitive phenomena, word-for-wordism is a textual phenomenon. (As before, I use the word 'textual' to refer both to written and to spoken language.) Such utterances are used to comic effect in the English speech of Agatha Christie's Belgian detective, Hercule Poirot, who, drawing on his native French, is prone to such phrasing as:

'Tell me if you please Miss.' (*Dites-moi s'il vous plaît mademoiselle.*)
'How do you call yourself?'(*Comment vous appelez-vous?*)
'The doctor he was there, is it not so?' (*Le médecin il était là, n'est-ce pas?*)

The tradition of teaching students to avoid word-for-wordism in translations stems back to classical times and has endured in the teaching of translation and interpreting ever since. (Though it may be advocated as a strategy in tackling problems or drawing attention to differences between languages (Butzkamm 2001; Marlein 2009), it is seldom advocated as good translation in itself.) However, the notion that students who have studied a language through translation will be more prone to such Poirotisms than those who have not is one of the oddest and least substantiated in Direct Method mythology. Since Ancient times, the overwhelming view of theorists, practitioners, and teachers of translation has been that that a 'good' translation is seldom word for word. Horace, in the 1st century BC cautioned translators:

Nec verbum verbo curabis reddere fidus interpres
[Nor will you as faithful interpreter render word for word.]
(quoted in Morgan 1959: 274)

The persistence of this tradition has meant that the teaching of translation, rather than encouraging word-for-wordism, has consistently involved
weaning students away from it, and nurturing in them more global criteria
for equivalence. Thus while word-for-wordist howlers make good material
for jokes at the expense of teaching through translation, this is not to say
that they are advocated by teachers of translation, or ever have been. The
howlers of literalism are more likely to be committed by those who, having
learnt a language through Direct Method without the benefits of training
in tackling translation problems, then come to translation for the first time.
Other students will have long left such errors behind them. But here—as with
almost every interesting possibility in translation teaching—the research has
not been done.

In a similar way, it is well known to all with any experience in translation that equivalence at the level of collocation overrides that at word
level. This has long been a staple of translation classes, and can be well
illustrated—and has indeed been flogged to death—through examples of
metaphorical idioms. In other words, a phrase like 'flogged to death' (which
means that something is repeated too many times) cannot be translated into
French as *fouetté jusqu'à la mort*, German as *zu Tode geprügelt* or Spanish
as *flagelado hasta la muerte*—unless, of course, it refers to someone being
literally whipped until they died. This point, which has a long and rather
tedious history in language teaching and teachers' anecdotes of learner
errors, applies to more than just fixed idioms. As corpus linguistics has
revealed, the extent of the 'phraseological tendency' in actual language use
(Sinclair 1991, 2004; Stubbs 1996, 2001) goes well beyond fixed idioms.
Knowledge and appropriate use of collocation has been revealed as a key
element of language competence, adding weight to the translation theorists'
insistence that word-for-word translation is unlikely to be adequate. Indeed
one might reverse this and say that the potential of a phrase to yield to word-
for-word translation or not is an index of the strength of the collocation
involved.

Word-for-word translation means privileging the lexical and syntactic
levels, translating each word in the same order as it occurs in the original,
with disregard for all other levels, including even the semantic and pragmatic
where they cannot be preserved without disrupting this itemized ordering. Quite why the language learner should wish to do this, or be unable
to progress beyond this practice, especially after translation classes where
the teacher has repeatedly stressed that this practice is not good translation,
is unexplained by those who assert it as an adverse consequence of using
translation in language learning. It is certainly not advocated in translation
textbooks, or held up as a successful technique—another of the myths of
Direct Method-ists. On the contrary, the burden of most translation courses
is to sensitize students to the importance of other levels, predominately those
concerned with meaning and communicative function, training them in techniques for avoiding the bad translation which arises when the focus is upon

the trees of the words rather than the forest of the text. The Hercule Poirots of this world are more likely to be those who have never had the benefit of translation classes but have learnt their language through Direct Method, and are consequently thrown when confronted with the common real-world communicative task of having to put their language knowledge to practical use in translation.

'Improvement'

Let us go back now to MacWhinney's criteria for assessing research, on the grounds that they encapsulate the scientific turn and its programme for language teaching:

> How well do these analyses succeed in generating precise predictions for patterns in language learning? Can we use these predictions to improve language learning?
> (MacWhinney 2006: 734)

So far in this chapter I have been focusing on the first of these questions, contesting arguments that TILT is detrimental to language learning, pointing to the lack of evidence of harm. I have been assessing, in other words, scientific predictions about translation on their own terms. Let us turn now to MacWhinney's second question and challenge its terms, on the grounds that it poses a much more serious problem for those who, like MacWhinney and many SLA researchers, talk as though there were a straightforward and unproblematic relationship between scientific research and the improvement of language learning.

The problem is theoretical rather than evidential. Scientific categories need to be as objective as possible, so the notion of 'improvement' is not suited to scientific purposes. It can be interpreted in too many different ways. It is what philosopher Jamie Whyte calls a 'hooray word', one with which everyone can agree (Whyte 2003: 61–63). Saying we seek 'improvement' is the language-teaching equivalent of a politician saying they are on the side of 'freedom' and 'democracy'. Thus most people want the world to be *free* but when we specify freedom *from what* and freedom *to do what*, then they start to argue. Most people support democracy, but differ on what it involves. 'Improvement' in language learning is similar, and can be variously interpreted. When people say language learning can and should be improved, we should, like a badgering interviewer with a campaigning politician, immediately ask them precisely what they mean. It is surely ironic that MacWhinney should praise 'precision' in one sentence, then use such an imprecise term in the next!

Talk of 'improvement' is teleological. It assumes a known and fixed end-point towards which learners are progressing, without countenancing the possibility that there are different ideas about what that end-point is. It is about how to get there, not where we are going. Yet ideas about success in language learning are highly relative. They vary historically and culturally, and with different ideological and educational standpoints. They reflect values just as much as facts, and there is considerable variation. In SLA research and the communicative approaches into which it has fed, success is implicitly conceived in a particular way, though this is usually taken for granted rather than spelt out, making it hard to engage with. It seems fair to say, however, that the ideal successful language learner is seen as one who has internalized a representation of the language system similar to that of a monolingual, and who has acquired a native-speaker-like ability to use this new language system fluently, accurately, and functionally in monolingual communication without reference to their own language. Improvement is therefore seen as movement towards this goal, even if, as non-native speakers cannot become native speakers by definition (Davies 1995, 2003), it can never be fully attained. This version of success must therefore remain an idealized one, rather than a potential actuality.

Now it might be that, if one accepts this ideal of success, translation might not help learners to achieve it, and might even prove a hindrance. But what if one were to adopt a different model of success, and consequently a different notion of 'improvement'? Then the same evidence that worked against translation might now work in its favour. What, for example, if one were to regard 'success' as including the ability to move back and forth between two languages, to have explicit knowledge of each language and the differences between them, to operate in the new language while not losing one's own-language identity, and to have an impact on the new language, making it one's own, and perhaps introducing to it new phrases and ideas from one's own language? Then the criteria for success might be different, and the student whom SLA researchers had regarded as a failure might suddenly seem to be a success, and *vice versa*. A foreign accent or the use of effective but non-native-like expressions might seem a good thing—while pale and unsuccessful imitation of native-speaker language use might no longer seem so attractive. In this context, what had formerly been regarded as 'interference' and 'negative transfer' might suddenly appear in a positive light—just as openness to foreign-language influence has been regarded positively in some literary works (as discussed above).

As already argued in Chapter 3, the 1990s and 2000s have, for a variety of reasons, already witnessed some shift away from conceiving the successful language learner as one who operates only monolingually in the new language towards an appreciation of bilingual identity. Language learning is beginning to be seen less as a temporary shedding of one identity, and more as a permanent addition to create a new composite persona. As Sridhar and Sridhar (1986: 5) have put it:

> SLA researchers seem to have neglected the fact that the goal of SLA is bilingualism.

Citing this quotation, Pavlenko and Lantolf (2000) suggest that it is the *relationship* between own and new language which lies at the heart of encountering a new language, rather than the new language being regarded in isolation, and that a better metaphor for what happens should be participation rather than acquisition. Translation would seem to be the prime candidate for fostering a sense of that relationship.

The relativity of evidence to values means that a good deal of debate about success becomes circular. Students who are taught to translate are likely be better at translation than those who are not, but this will count for little if they are assessed only for monolingual use of the new language. The influence of the student's own language on the new one will inevitably be seen as 'interference' (a bad thing) in an approach which wants to shift the learner wholly into monolingual use, but not necessarily so in another model. Scientific research, in other words, may be able to relate an outcome to a kind of teaching or learning, but not to say which outcome is better. Källkvist's scientific study, for example, compared the effects of teaching with and without translation to two groups of Swedish university-level students, and came to the unsurprising conclusion that those in the group exposed to translation were better at translation tasks, while those taught intralingually were better at intralingual tasks.

A similar point might be made about speed of processing as a sign of success. It depends whether speed is regarded as always desirable. I have argued above that there is no evidence that translation necessarily slows language production down, and I believe that to be the case. Yet even if there were such evidence, it could not be regarded as an absolute indictment of translation. Speed is not a virtue in all tasks, nor fluency the be-all and end-all it has been held up to be in CLT. Translation might sometimes be useful to learners in formulating what they have to say or write, precisely because it slows them down, allows them to consider carefully what they are saying, and provides them with a resource to be as exact as possible in understanding what they encounter, or formulating what they want to say.

Lurking also in the notion of improvement is a presupposition of progress, that language teaching is more successful now than it was in the past, and will be even more successful in the future. This is a widespread assumption among language-teaching theorists, and indeed is one of the justifications for what they do. In Chapter 2, for example, we saw Long and Robinson's confident claim that traditional approaches

> are often asserted by their advocates to account for classroom language learning success. Attested by the ratios of beginners and false beginners to finishers, however, the same phenomena are more frequently associated with failure.

Such claims are quintessentially unscientific for a number of reasons, some superficial and others fundamental.

Firstly—least seriously—they assume data which simply does not exist. To make such a claim scientifically one would need test results for language learners from all times and places. Human beings have been learning languages at least since classical times, and presumably since prehistoric times. But we cannot say whether Roman legionaries from the borders of the Roman Empire learnt Latin, or barbarian slaves learnt Ancient Greek, more or less successfully than people nowadays learn English, simply because there are no reliable records other than for the very recent past. In fact, as far as we can tell in the absence of data, people have learnt languages successfully or unsuccessfully, using *all* methods and approaches (grammar translation, audiolingualism, graded structures, Suggestopaedia, Silent Way, communicative language teaching, task-based instruction, etc). Of course it may be that, as time passes, we accumulate systematic records of language performance from a substantial period of history and a wide variety of contexts and correlate this evidence with ways of teaching and learning. But we are not in a position to do that as yet. We do not have in our science the equivalent of a fossil record in biology. So all such claims that language learning is improving are purely speculative.

Secondly, such claims assume that language learning accumulates and progresses in the same way that knowledge and understanding do in a science. Thus, for example, each new student of physics reaps the benefit of the trials and errors of everyone who has studied physics before, and does not start from scratch. In language learning, however, arguably this is not the case. Each individual starts the process anew, and their knowledge of the language is individual rather than shared.

But thirdly, and most seriously for their validity, all such claims confuse shifting values with objective measures. When theorists and methodologists look back at earlier approaches to teaching, and criticize them for such 'faults' as elevating writing over speech, accuracy over fluency, knowledge of rules over communication, literary over everyday language, or producing people who could read novels but not order a cup of coffee, they should interpret what was done in the light of the criteria of the time, rather than their own. Perhaps theorists should bear in mind that the definition of a successful language learner is in constant flux, and that teachers in other times and places saw their approach as successful because they had different ends. We might then go on to consider what definition of language-learning success is most appropriate for the needs of our own contemporary world. This definition should not be established as an absolute and eternal truth however, but rather as something temporary and relative, to be rejected in the future, as times and circumstances change again.

Notes

1 This narrow conception of the discipline was later characterized by Widdowson (1984) as 'linguistics applied', and distinguished from what he envisaged as a more dynamic and independent 'applied linguistics' in which the traffic of ideas would be two-way.

2 A distinction which, as it owes a great deal to Chomsky's competence/performance distinction, should presumably stand or fall with it, making it hard to see how those who challenge this Chomskyan dichotomy can still make use of this derivative distinction in SLA.

3 Two of five hypotheses. The others concerned the acquisition-learning distinction, monitoring, and the affective filter.

4 Also confirmed by the following: 'Translation is given little attention by SLA researchers. The only exception is that translation is sometimes used as an elicitation tool to obtain L2 data. As such it is viewed skeptically because it is likely to encourage L1 transfer and thus to overstate the role this plays in L2 acquisition. Translation is seen as an aspect of L2 use rather than L2 acquisition.' (Rod Ellis, personal communication)

5 In support of this claim, Källkvist cites 37 references including Duff 1989, Malmkjær 1995/1996, Hummel 1995, González Davies 2004.

6 Kaneko (1992); Kupferberg and Olshtain (1996); Spada and Lightbown (1999).

7 One interesting claim related to this research is that bilingualism may slow mental deterioration in aging (Bialystok, Criak, and Freedman 2007).

8 This issue is reminiscent of debates over whether general theories of second language acquisition should be influenced by the existence of so-called exceptional language learners: people who, in a very short time and counter to expectation or what is known about the usual course of language learning, become indistinguishable from the native speakers around them (Schneiderman and Desmarais 1988; Ioup et al. 1994).

9 This line, used in the title of Sarkar and Winer 2006, uses elements of Haitian creole, as well as French and English.

6

Educational arguments

As indicated at the beginning of the previous chapter, a standard distinction has been drawn in educational theory between curriculum and syllabus, or—to put it another way—between the underlying rationale for an educational policy and its implementation. Where language teaching is concerned, such matters as whether to teach students other languages additional to their own, which languages these should be, at what age they should be taught, and with what purpose, are all matters of curriculum. Once these issues have been agreed, then decisions have to be taken about implementation, and those are matters of syllabus.

Where language learning is concerned, however, the general if rather vague consensus that it is in some way 'a good thing' to know another language can mean that there is sometimes little debate about why this is the case. In much of the recent language-teaching literature, the focus is upon syllabus-level decisions, with little discussion of the philosophy of education which underpins them. In the school curricula of most countries of the world, for example, it is now simply assumed without much debate that English should be the main foreign language on the curriculum, while in the English-speaking countries, choice of languages is often dictated either by tradition or, where there have been shifts (as in the growth of Chinese and Japanese teaching) it is—by an extension of the argument that makes English the most taught language internationally—that these languages are useful. So in many discussions about language teaching, the original decision to teach an additional language, and which one it should be, has been taken, and is taken for granted. All that remains, it seems, is to decide how best to teach it.

An example of such assumptions, to which we shall return in more detail later in the chapter, is the promotion in many parts of the world (including South Korea, Mexico, parts of the Middle East, and the European Union) of content-based language teaching, in which curriculum subjects are taught through the medium of a new language—almost always English—on the assumption that this simultaneously furthers both student proficiency in that language, and their knowledge of the subject in question. Such a movement takes a great deal for granted, both about language learning and about education and will be worth reconsidering in the light of the educational purposes to be discussed in this chapter.

The two levels of decision making cannot be kept so neatly separate, and much discussion of implementation of any new language teaching programme would benefit from a reconsideration of both the policy and the philosophy behind it. Perhaps one reason for the continued outlawing of translation, and the strange absence of any challenge to this exclusion, is that syllabus decisions have proceeded without reference back to fundamental aims and values. The purpose of this chapter is to go back to the educational arguments, to consider why it is 'a good thing' to learn an additional language in the first place, and to spell out the implications of different educational philosophies for implementation at syllabus level. This will set the scene for the following chapter on the pedagogics of translation.

Curriculum philosophies

Taking the curriculum aims of language teaching for granted has not always been the case however. The 1980s in particular saw some quite intensive introspection. Those who interpreted curriculum theory[1] for language teaching during this period (Allen 1984; Stern 1983; Clark 1987) categorized underlying educational philosophies as falling under three or four broad headings, defining particular education systems and practices by their allegiance to one rationale or another. Terminologies vary, but the ideas are fairly consistent. I shall use the terms in Allen[2] (1984) and interpret them as follows:

1 From a **technological** perspective, education should serve practical purposes, providing individuals and society with needed skills, both general (numeracy, literacy, IT, etc.) and specialized (for example, medical training).
2 From a **social reformist** perspective, education is a means of bringing about desirable social change, developing certain values, beliefs, and behaviours. It might be used, for example, to inculcate good citizenship, a particular religious faith, or a political credo.
3 From a **humanistic** perspective, education should provide personal fulfilment and development for the individual, not only for practical or social reasons, but also as an intrinsic good.
4 From an **academic** perspective, education should preserve, develop, and transmit knowledge and understanding of an academic discipline.

As Clark (1987) points out, each of these perspectives has implications for implementation. Ideas about assessment, content, good teaching practice, and who has the right to effect changes, all vary with the different philosophies. In technological education, for example, preoccupied as it is with selection for specialized training or employment, assessment is necessarily norm-referenced[3]. In social reformism, where the emphasis is upon the attainment of whole-society objectives, assessment is necessarily criterion referenced. So the two approaches differ fundamentally in their ideas about testing. On the other hand, they have elements in common, which distinguish them from both humanistic and academic education. The first two perspectives have a behavioural outcome-oriented emphasis, specifying learning objectives in forms which can be easily manipulated or observed, and both measure success by their 'products' (as students are sometimes called!). Both tend also to be implemented top-down, driven by the demands of government and—in the technological approach—employers. Another similarity between technological and social-reformist education, is that in both the teacher is meant to be a good model for the students. For it is hard to see how a teacher can teach skills or inculcate values which they do not have themselves, such as teaching how to drive a car, for example, if they themselves cannot drive, or how to be a good Christian, if they themselves are atheist. In practice, however, in both technological and social-reformist curricula, there is always a possibility that teachers are being pressed into professing, or at least remaining silent on, social principles that they are not really in sympathy with. Technological and social-reformist approaches, in other words, may be based more on the *assumption* that teachers have certain attitudes, rather than on the fact that they actually have them.

In humanistic education, in contrast with both technological and social-reformist approaches, the emphasis on the individual and the relationship between teacher and students leads to a greater focus on methodology, and on the processes rather than the products of education. Learners are seen as responsible for their own learning, and there is thus a constant negotiation between learners and teachers, who then become facilitators of learning rather than models. Assessment is carried out through self-evaluation by both teachers and students, and renewal and change in the curriculum is 'bottom up', that is to say, it originates in the classroom and spreads 'upwards' through the institution.

An academic focus is different again, though there are elements of similarity with technological education. The emphasis on content has a number of important consequences. Firstly, as the teacher is essentially a guardian and transmitter of knowledge, there will be a great deal of teacher-centred activity, with the teacher talking and the class listening. This means that each member of the class must move at the same pace, and this leads to streaming by level and ability. The need for streaming in turn justifies norm-referenced assessment. The importance of norm-referenced assessment in turn augments the importance of examinations, which take on a determining 'washback' role in curriculum change.

In reality, any actual educational practice is likely to have elements of all four ideas, and what distinguishes one approach from another is a matter of relative emphasis rather than absolute allegiance to one or another. Applied to language teaching (as to any subject) it is not difficult to find approaches which privilege or are driven by one of these perspectives. (This illustrates the point made above, that curriculum issues cannot be kept separate from implementation as syllabus.) The teaching of Language for Special Purposes (LSP), Language for Academic Purposes (LAP), and Language for Occupational Purposes (LOP) are examples of a technological approach, as they are driven by particular behavioural objectives to develop professional skills. An example of 'social-reformist' language teaching can be found in programmes seeking to promote greater mutual understanding between different language groups, such as the French/English immersion programmes in Canadian schools, where English native speakers are schooled in French, and French speakers are schooled in English. The Content and Language Integrated Learning (CLIL[4]) movement now being energetically promoted in the EU is technological, in that it aims to increase the efficiency of the EU by improving the proficiency of its citizens in each others' languages, *and* social reformist, in that it seeks to promote greater integration of its member states. A 'humanistic' focus is exemplified by the learner-centred approaches of the 1980s and 1990s, such as the process syllabus (Breen 1984, 1987; Candlin 1984, 1987). Academic approaches are associated with 'traditional' language teaching which emphasizes formal knowledge of a language system and of a literary canon, presenting the subject as a body of knowledge to be handed down and developed from one generation to the next.

It seems fair to say that this classification of curriculum aims remains fairly stable, and is as valid today as it was in the 1980s. General government statements about educational aims bear traces of one or more of these aims, though with different emphases. The current 'values, aims, and purposes' of the UK national curriculum, for example, are set out as follows:

> Education influences and reflects the values of society, and the kind of society we want to be… Foremost is a belief in education, at home and at school, as a route to the spiritual, moral, social, cultural, physical and mental development, and thus the wellbeing, of the individual. Education is also a route to equality of opportunity for all, a healthy and just democracy, a productive economy, and sustainable development. Education should reflect the enduring values that contribute to these ends.[5]

The 'China Reform and Development Program'[6] which determines a framework for Chinese education, says:

新课程的培养目标应体现时代要求。要使学生具有爱国主义、集体主义精神，热爱社会主义，继承和发扬中华民族的优秀传统和革命传统；具有社会主义民主法制意识，遵守国家法律和社会公德；逐步形成正确的世界观、人生观、价值观；具有社会责任感，努力为人民服务；具有初步的创新精神、实践能力、科学和人文素养以及环境意识；具有适应终身学习的基础知识、基本技能和方法；具有健壮的体魄和良好的心理素质，养成健康的审美情趣和生活方式，成为有理想、有道德、有文化、有纪律的一代新人。

The objectives of this new curriculum should reflect the requirements of the times. Students should:

- be patriotic and collectivist, love socialism, inherit and carry forward the virtues of the Chinese and revolutionary traditions
- be aware of socialist democracy and comply with national law and social morality
- build up correct views of the world, life, and values
- work hard to serve the people
- have a spirit of innovation, practical, scientific, and humanistic qualities, and environmental awareness
- acquire the basic knowledge, techniques, and approaches suitable for life-long learning
- develop physical strength and psychological wellbeing
- form a habit of aesthetic appreciation and a healthy life style.

Through this they will become a new generation with vision, morality, knowledge and discipline.
(China Education and Research Network 2001)[7]

A Brazilian government document referring to language teaching states that:

> *Os temas centrais nesta proposta são a cidadania, a consciência crítica em relação à linguagem e os aspectos sociopolíticos da aprendizagem de Língua Estrangeira.*
> The central themes in this proposal are citizenship, critical awareness in relation to language and the socio-political aspects of foreign language learning.
> (SEF 1998: 13)

and continues:

> *A Língua Estrangeira no ensino fundamental tem um valioso papel construtivo como parte integrante da educação formal. Envolve um complexo processo de reflexão sobre a realidade social, política e econômica, com valor intrínseco importante no processo de capacitação que leva à libertação. Em outras palavras, Língua Estrangeira no ensino fundamental é parte da construção da cidadania.*
> The teaching of foreign languages in secondary schools (from age 10 to 14) as part of the National Curriculum has a valuable constructive role in students' formal education. It should involve a complex process of reflection on social, political and economic issues. These are important values in the process of empowerment, which leads to freedom. Putting it in different words, the teaching of foreign languages is part of the construction of citizenship.
> (ibid. 26)[8]

Such statements as these, with their mix of reasons, underline the complex reality of any actual educational policy and practice, and that the four perspectives outlined in this section are idealizations and, as such, do not capture the actuality of what happens in any particular school, classroom, or course.

We will not find an educational system or lesson which is purely technological, social reformist, humanist, or academic—though the balance between the four is likely to vary, as it does in these three statements. But the headings are useful as a means of categorizing and evaluating educational practices and I shall use them as such in the remainder of this chapter. My argument will be that there is a strong educational justification for TILT from all four perspectives.

TILT as technological education

Let us begin with the practical educational aim of developing skills needed by both individuals and society—a technological perspective.

A traditional assumption in much language teaching has been that translation as a skill in its own right is needed only by the minority of learners going on to be professional translators and interpreters. This means that arguments for and against TILT assess it only as a means rather than an end—and, as we have seen, many people have reached the conclusion that, as such, it is not valid. Yet there are good reasons to question this distinction and its dismissal of translation skills as an outcome needed by only a minority of students. In multilingual, multicultural societies (which nowadays means just about everywhere), and in a world of constant cross-linguistic and cross-cultural global communication, there are reasons to see translation as being widely needed in everyday situations, and not as a specialized activity at all. This is true whether we take translation in the established sense of producing texts and utterances which replace 'textual material in one language by equivalent textual material in another language' (Catford 1965: 20), or in the looser sense of what is done by 'a bilingual mediating agent between monolingual communication participants in two different language communities'—to use the definition of the translator by House (1977: 1). Indeed as we have seen in Chapter 4, translation exists on a broad spectrum between these two poles.

In the contemporary world, translation in both of these senses is a necessary skill and a frequent activity in the personal and professional lives of many individuals, essential for the economic survival of many organizations and for engagement in international affairs. If we conceive of interaction as taking place in a series of concentric circles, with the most intimate relations at the centre, community and professional life in the middle, and international relations at the periphery, then, as already discussed in Chapter 3, we can see this constant need as operating at all levels: in relationships, families, communities, social interaction, travel, jobs, and on the world stage.

Thus in mixed-language relationships and marriages translation will be needed whenever one partner encounters an unknown word in the language of the other. This is the case whether both partners speak both languages, or when only one speaks both languages, or when they use a language which is neither partner's own tongue. Translation will be needed, too, in encounters between relatives from the two sides of the family, who may well know little or nothing of the language of their in-laws. In immigrant families some translation may be needed in communication between grandparents and grandchildren. This is not to say, in all of these cases, that the translation will consist of protracted formal production of extended equivalent language. It may only be the translation of an odd word or some general explanation of something only partially understood—but it is translation nevertheless. This constant need for translation extends into communities where—as within the family—not everyone may know the ambient language. Thus in many schools, for example, as already mentioned in Chapter 3, there is a need for translation for new arrivals, and for their families, and in many multilingual situations this is seen as an everyday activity. To give an example from my own experience, my son who is partly bilingual in Russian, was asked when he was nine years old to act as interpreter at his London primary school for a recently arrived girl from Georgia who spoke no English but some Russian—though her first language was Kurdish. He saw nothing extraordinary in this request however, commenting that his friends who spoke languages which were more frequently needed in the school 'do it all the time'. At a more general level, increased travel, use of the Internet, and the integration of different linguistic communities, means that translation is frequently needed in social situations: to introduce friends to each other, to convey the gist of an email, or for mundane tasks such as reading a menu or a notice. Constant mediation between languages is going on in multilingual settings all the time.

While these personal, domestic, educational, and social needs for translation are undoubtedly both frequent and important, it is to the world of work—usefulness in and for employment—that a technological approach to education assigns the greatest importance. In English language teaching in particular this priority has been reflected in a general emphasis on usefulness, on language to achieve aims and get things done. This is the general thrust of task-based learning, and such terms are often used in its definition. The very word 'task' is a synonym of work, often with connotations of drudgery, and work is often referred to explicitly in definitions (Long 1985: 89; Nunan 1988: 10). More explicitly, the growth of language teaching for specific or occupational purposes has sought to reduce the language being learnt to that which is needed 'on the job' in question, or in the case of CLIL the subject being studied[9].

Arguably, however, there has been something of a mismatch in all such approaches between the purposes for which a language is actually likely to be used at work, and those which are prominent in apparently work-oriented teaching. The problem has been that such approaches implicitly assume the student's primary goal and need is to operate in the new language monolingually, and that the measure of success, therefore, is how well they adopt and melt into the norms of monolingual speakers. Interest in the new culture associated with the new language and a desire to become a part of it are simply taken for granted. However these assumptions are often far from the truth. As Palestinian scholar Edward Said rather bluntly pointed out:

> The reason for the large numbers of students taking English was given frankly by a somewhat disaffected instructor: many of the students proposed to end up working for airlines, or banks, in which English was a worldwide *lingua franca* ... You learned English to use computers, respond to orders, transmit telexes, decipher manifests, and so forth.
> (Said 1994: 369)

In other words, many of those learning English—and other locally dominant languages needed for employment—do not necessarily do so out of any intrinsic interest in the new language or the culture(s) associated with it (though that may develop as a spin-off), but for purely practical work-related needs. If we think further about what these needs actually are, rather than what course designers assume them to be, we find they are at least as likely to be cross-lingual as intra-lingual and therefore to involve translation. Consider the case of someone recruited in, say, China or Russia on the strength of their knowledge of English to a firm whose senior management is largely monolingual. Their use of English is likely to be for mediation between the two languages for those who are more senior but less bilingual than they are. They are expected in other words to facilitate communication between those within their organization who do not know the other language well and those coming from outside the organization who do not know Chinese or Russian. In these circumstances skill in translation is needed for purely practical 'technological' reasons.

At this point it is worth pointing out the symbiotic relationship between the needs of society and individuals and the responsibility which it places upon educators to provide for both. Societies need individuals with certain skills in order to function, and conversely individuals need these same skills in order to gain and succeed in employment. In this respect a technological perspective serves not only society's needs but also those of individuals and, arguably, overlaps with a humanistic perspective, in that employment might legitimately be regarded as a constituent of personal fulfilment and development in life. In these respects, educational practice which neglects to provide needed skills, such as language teaching which fails to provide training in translation, falls short of its obligations to both individuals and society.

The preceding paragraphs have talked of employment as though it were always to do with trade and business. There is also, of course, work related to international communications *per se*. In this area, translation features heavily too: in news reporting, computer programming and mobile technologies, international marketing, film subtitling and dubbing, and in translating books.

The last of the expanding circles of communication in which translation necessarily features is the world of institutional international communication:

in diplomacy, trade and treaty organizations, and negotiations of all kinds. The major international organizations such as the UN, the World Bank, and World Health Organization, employ vast numbers of translators and interpreters. The European Union recognition of 23 working languages also leads to a plethora of translation in different combinations of languages. Its Parliament, Council, and Court of Justice employ around 700 translators each[10], and the Directorate General around 1750[11]. In the institutionalized bureaucracy to which such arrangements give rise, it is all too easy to lose sight of the inspiring truth that translation is a cornerstone of peacemaking and understanding between nations—and that without it conflicts might be even more frequent and more bloody than they are. In the words of Goethe:

> *Denn was man auch von der Unzulänglichkeit des Übersetzens sagen mag, so ist und bleibt es doch eines der wichtigsten und würdigsten Geschäfte in dem allgemeinen Weltverkehr.*
> (von Goethe 1982: 353)
> 'Say what one will of the inadequacy of translation, it remains one of the most important and worthiest concerns in the totality of world affairs.'[12]

TILT as social reform

In the previous section I have argued that good translation, both in a narrow and a broad sense, is a needed and useful skill—personally, socially, professionally, and politically—and is therefore justified within a technological approach to education. In this section I shall argue that it is also amply justified from a social-reformist educational perspective and, moreover, that with TILT there is no conflict between a technological and social reformist approach, as there is in some other areas. (Promoting altruism over competitiveness or non-violence over retaliation for social reformist reasons, for example, may be at odds with the technological self-interest of the state.) TILT can be justified from a utilitarian as well as an ethical standpoint.

A social reformist educational agenda seeks to construct society in ways which those implementing it believe to be for the good. In the education literature, it is usually associated with egalitarian and progressive movements, but there is no reason why this should be so. There are many conflicting views of the 'right' direction for societies to take—so the notion of reform through education can be espoused by very different viewpoints. It could as easily be used to describe the promotion of fascism as democracy, communism as capitalism, atheism as religion. All are right in the eyes of those who believe in them. The defining feature of social reform is that education is being used to promote or preserve values, whatever those values may be. This means that my argument here for a social reformist rationale for TILT must, like any other such programme, first be specific about values. Those values I see TILT as promoting are of a liberal, humanist, and democratic nature.

I shall proceed on the basis that, in encounters between languages and cultures, understanding and awareness of difference, avoidance and resolution of conflict, and equality of opportunity and status, are generally desirable aims, and that TILT is generally supportive of these aims even though it could also, like any other language teaching approach, be used to promote opposite values, and even though there are also cases, to be discussed below, when translation and increased comprehension can exacerbate, rather than calm conflict and disagreement.

Like the administration of education itself, most reformist programmes, have been instituted at a national level. In some cases language teaching has been used to promote *intra*-national understanding. Thus policy in Canada, for example, seeks to promote the learning of French by Anglophone children and English by Francophone children. There have also been language-teaching policies which seek to promote good relations between as well as within nations. There was a belief in Europe between the two world wars for example—unfortunately proved very wrong—that learning each other's languages by the children of the former combatants would help avert future conflict (Titone 1968). Such choices of languages to be taught both express and promote political values—harmony between nations or between communities. But they can also exclude and preserve the *status quo*. It is noticeable in the school curricula of the European nations, for example, that the focus in modern foreign language teaching tends to remain on the national languages of other European nations (English, French, Italian, Spanish, German, etc.) rather than on the languages of sizeable minorities of immigrant descent (Arabic, Hindi, Turkish, Urdu, etc.) or on the indigenous but non-national languages of Europe (Basque, Breton, or Catalan, for example), and that formal educational success in one of the national European languages has much higher status than success in a minority language (however big that language may be in world terms).

CLIL as social reform

CLIL brings a new intensity to this problem of language choice as, although theoretically it may promote any language, in practice it is almost always used to extend the teaching of English. This is overtly so in most content-based language programmes around the world; in Europe the situation is more complex, as other languages are involved too, although English is by far the most commonly chosen. Thus in practice, there is a conflict between the pedagogic claim that *a* language—*any* language—can be learnt through content-based instruction and the political reality of *the* language(s) actually taught. Claims that an initial focus on English is merely a prelude to the development of CLIL in a wider range of languages (Marsh 2002: 76) seem unconvincing and have yet to be demonstrated. Arguments and research showing that CLIL is not detrimental to students' first language development seem similarly weak (ibid.). These are early days to assess its long-term impact, and while individual competence in a student's everyday use of their own language may not suffer in the short term, there may still be long-term detriment to the language as a whole if, say, physics ceases to be taught in Dutch.

Despite its preference for English and a few other languages, CLIL in Europe has received intensive support, in the shape of investment by the EU in research, development, implementation, and endorsement by language-teaching theorists and applied linguists. It is promoted with a mixture of jargon and utopianism:

> Globalisation is moving countries across the World towards a new
> era, the Knowledge Age. This has resulted in sweeping changes in how
> societies, and the educational systems that serve them, operate. In the
> Knowledge Age, creativity, intelligence, and connectivity become key
> resources for success.
> (CLIL Consortium[13])

Although the motives behind it are partly technological—increasing communicative efficiency—it is also, as the evangelical tone of this quotation suggests, classically social reformist, imposed top-down, in this case by a collaboration of government and academia.

The applied linguistic arguments advanced in its favour (Dalton-Puffer 2007: 257–277) draw upon the old SLA view that exposure and negotiation of meaning will be key factors in language learning success—although some acknowledgement is also made of the need for immersion to be supplemented by specifically language instruction (ibid. 261). Advocates broadly subscribe to the notions that 'the requisites of success lie in exposure' and that 'early introduction (4–12 years) is now … advantageous' (Marsh 2002: 9). But this focus of the case for CLIL upon language acquisition too often leaves out of account the social effects of imposing such a 'reform' top down. Even if the language-learning theory behind it were sound, there are many other factors to be taken into account in its implementation. While content-based language teaching may arguably work for teaching a 'second language' in largely bilingual contexts such as Canada, or for new arrivals into a monolingual education system—as in the case of ESL/TESOL programmes in the USA or UK—its use for teaching what was previously regarded as a foreign language raises complex political issues and social tensions. Experience with English-medium programmes elsewhere in the world suggests that it is often met by resistance from teachers whose views run counter to those of the authorities imposing it. These teachers' views may also be at odds with those of some parents who see it as being linked to their children's future educational and career success.

CLIL, in other words, has major implications for language policy, which a focus upon arguments about language acquisition tends to sideline. It seems to overlook the challenges to meaning-focused language pedagogy (of the kind discussed in Chapter 3) which have emerged since the 1980s and perennial educational issues (of the kind being discussed in the present chapter). Its utilitarian rationale virtually ignores the complex impact on diversity and identity which a major shift into Anglophone education (or education in another powerful foreign language) is likely to entail. Claims that its 'global solutions' will be realized in locally various and culturally sensitive ways, and have 'resulted in a range of different models'[14], overlook the fact that its overall effect is to extend Anglophone monolingualism into classrooms and subject areas where previously students' own languages held sway.

While there is surprisingly little academic criticism of CLIL, it does however elicit strong criticism and suspicion of the motives behind it by those asked to implement it, and is seen as detrimental to the maintenance of linguistic diversity and translation. As one blogger[15] writes:

> I've brought up this issue because bilingual education or CLIL (Content and Language Integrated Learning) has become the buzz word in the European Union. Huge funds are spent on projects that experiment with CLIL, which is meant to replace foreign language education. On the one hand this would save the EU a lot of expenses on translations, on the other it would introduce a hegemony of a single European language through the back door. Integration at its worst and at a huge cost.

A teacher in the UAE, writes in an online research paper:

> There is a big difference between treating English as a foreign language and having it as a medium of instruction in Model Schools. If we are teaching our students math and physics which most of the students find them difficult . . . , it would be better to teach them in their mother tongue Arabic rather than English. Why? The answer is simple. When teaching scientific subjects in Arabic, students will understand better because there will be no language barriers that might hinder their comprehension. (Sarsar 2007)

And in South Korea the government's English immersion programme seems to have been halted, partly because of teacher resistance[16].

TILT, social reform, and language equality

Unlike CLIL, TILT is confined to the language classroom, and is focused upon language instruction, though it may use content in that cause. A key difference, however, is that it does by definition maintain the presence of students' own language(s) in their learning—even the learning of a new language—rather than seeking to supplant it/them with another. Like CLIL it is theoretically neutral as to which languages are taught through it—any language can be taught to speakers of any other, using translation.

In practice however, like CLIL or any language-teaching approach, TILT needs to confront the political reality that it is the bigger and more powerful languages which are taught most in the world and the smaller and least powerful ones which are taught least, and this means that for many language learners, the language-teaching situation reflects the inequality of the wider world. They are required to learn other people's language, but cannot expect those other people to reciprocate. The outlawing of translation moreover seems most entrenched in the teaching of the biggest languages, for complex reasons already discussed, including the promotion of native-speaker teachers who do not know the language of those they are teaching. For all these reasons, a discussion of TILT as social reform cannot proceed without an account of which languages are taught as well as how. With globalization and with the growing inequality of power between languages (Crystal 2000b), there is a case to be made for language teaching as a means of social reform at a global as well as a national or regional level. The revival of TILT can make a contribution to such a programme, helping to preserve the identities of the speakers of threatened languages and promoting awareness among speakers of powerful languages of the nature and predicament of others. Let us explore in more detail why this might be so.

Languages may be equal but their speakers do not meet on equal terms. That is to say all languages may be equally complex systems[17], equally capable of performing the same complex functions. They are not however equal in numbers of speakers or geographical distribution, nor in the economic and military power of the countries which use them. Reliable statistics are difficult to come by and date quickly, so estimates vary, but the general picture is clear[18]. While, counting in millions of native speakers, English (at around 350 million) falls behind Putonghua[19] (at around 800 million) and Hindi/Urdu[20] (at around 420 million), the situation with regard to second and foreign language speakers is very different—however we define these elusive terms. As long ago as 1997, Crystal estimated there to be as many as 400 million second language speakers and one hundred million foreign language speakers of English (Crystal 1997: 360–1). Even this figure, which has certainly increased since, would put English in the historically unprecedented position (save perhaps Latin) of having more non-native than native speakers. At the other end of the scale are those much smaller languages—by far the majority of the world's estimated 6000 languages—which are spoken in geographically circumscribed areas by ethnically specific groups with little power on the international stage. For these speakers, when they travel and communicate with speakers of other languages, their correct assumption is that they will need to learn and operate in another language, or to use an interpreter. Conversely, they know that others are unlikely to learn their language, or even to have heard of it. Take for example the contrast between two languages whose names are almost identical but whose power profiles could not be more different: Ingush and English. The former, from the North East Caucasus, has around 180 thousand speakers[21] (Hewitt 1992), the latter—according to the conservative estimates above—around a billion. We might regard the two as at opposite ends of a continuum from very small to very big languages. The situation for speakers of languages at opposite ends of this continuum is very different.

Speakers of the world's largest languages can be confident of the durability, fame, and influence of their languages, of finding communities of fellow native speakers wherever they travel, and that their languages will be widely learnt. English speakers in particular know that English is the pre-eminent international *lingua franca*, the dominant means of communication in science and commerce, and the language of the world's most powerful nation. In the real world outside the classroom then, unequal encounters are inevitable. Despite the best efforts of some language planners to maintain language diversity and enforce equality of opportunity, the reality is very different. Legislation for Wales[22], for example, insists that the Welsh and English languages should be treated equally in the public sector, and, since 2000, the teaching of Welsh up to age 16 has been compulsory in all schools in Wales. This cannot undo the fact, however, that a visitor to contemporary Wales can assume that Welsh people speak English. Similarly in international communication, though other languages may be used and interpreters employed, an increasing number of educated professionals know and understand English, raising the possibility that the practical need for interpreting and translation of English may disappear in the near future—though it will still be needed for the symbolic assertion of identity, and/or to ensure that speakers negotiate on equal terms.

This inevitable inequality in encounters between speakers in the *real* world however need not be perpetuated in the *artificial* world of the classroom. Although much language-teaching theory assumes without question the virtue of making classrooms reflect the real world as much as possible, and there are sometimes good reasons for this, there are also benefits in keeping the two domains separate. Educational institutions can erect a valuable protective cordon, within which some of the injustices of the outside world can be temporarily suspended. Liberal and socialist educationalists aspire to use the enclosed autonomy of schools and colleges to combat the inequalities of the world outside the school, ensuring that every student is treated equally inside, whatever their sex, social class, or ethnicity. The hope is that this greater equality within the walls of the school may in time exert an influence on attitudes outside them. (This is why schools were such a flashpoint in the struggle for Civil Rights in the USA in the 1960s, for example.) In similar spirit, where languages are concerned, differences of population, power, and distribution can be put aside and languages treated as equals inside the classroom, even if they do not meet as such outside. Forbidding the use of students' own languages in the Direct Method teaching of a more powerful language is to reproduce this power differential. It sees language learning as a one-way affair in which teachers can teach the new language without any understanding or encouragement of its relation to the students' own languages.

Translation, however, demands knowledge and understanding of both languages and of the relationship between them. Even when this translation is confined to the classroom, and students go on to communicate monolingually outside, it inculcates a notion of communication across language boundaries as being a two-way affair, in which meaning arises in the interaction between two languages, rather than in one on its own. It promotes a growing awareness of difference and similarity in which there is greater mutual understanding of what these differences and similarities are. In the act of translation languages meet as equals, however different their status and power. For, in translation, knowledge and understanding of both languages and of the relation between them is essential.

It would be facile, however, to assume that increased awareness of difference necessarily leads to greater tolerance and less conflict. Such a belief implies that all cultural values are equally acceptable if understood, and that peaceful coexistence is always possible despite them. It also subscribes to the widespread belief, deriving from traditions of therapy, that the more people talk the more they like each other.

> 'The best way to resolve a disagreement between two people is to get them talking.'
> 'Many arguments would be resolved if people communicated better.'

Citing these two statements from a UK National Communication Survey, Cameron (2000: 161–175) points out that they are by no means necessarily true. While there are times when mutual knowledge may reduce tensions, there are also others when a fuller understanding of other people's behaviour and ideas leads to increased intolerance and resentment. 'Talking things over' may aggravate rather than defuse aggression. Nor is there is a necessary link between articulateness and peacefulness, or conversely between lack of communication and aggression.

Cameron is writing of communication between speakers of the same language, but similar points pertain in cross-linguistic communication too. History provides many instances of communities who have known and understood each other's languages very well but which have been ruthless and intolerant in their relations. Knowledge of another language can, it seems, increase opposition to the dominant ideas among its speakers[23]. Widespread competence in Russian in the countries of the former Soviet Bloc did not abate anti-Soviet sentiments among their populations; many of those who were educated in English in British colonies were strengthened in their opposition to British imperialism by that experience. In addition, languages are often learnt for surveillance and subversion. Thus efficient intelligence services concentrate upon the languages of their enemies. Russian learning thrived in the West during the Cold War, particularly in the military, and received a major impetus after the Soviet launch of the first Sputnik in 1957; after 9/11, the US government belatedly upped its spending on language training both to combat its enemies and to communicate better with its allies (Kramsch 2005). There are also cases where mutual comprehension in what could be regarded as one language is denied to underline differences. Thus Serbo-Croat was treated as one language before the civil war in the former Yugoslavia, but is now regarded as two—Serbian and Croatian—with the bizarre consequence that interpreters are used in some encounters, even though all involved can understand everything being said (Greenberg 2004: 136). Mutual comprehension is in short no guarantee of mutual tolerance and it would be pure sentimental romanticism to suppose that it is (Block 2008).

In an iconoclastic attack on complacent views of intercultural contact as unfailingly benign, Thomas (1998) goes as far as to see translation as provoking disagreement and conflict by laying bare the differences between languages and cultures, frequently making their incompatibility more rather than less salient. Yet he sees as this as positive, a 'healthy clash' which can promote the classical humanist educational values of debate, critical thinking, self-criticism, and self-awareness. Using examples from Arabic and English, and taking a stance based on linguistic relativity, he argues that translation enables:

> a creative reassessment of our theories [which] stimulates a critical
> attitude, enabling participants to liberate themselves from unconscious
> prejudices and from theories embedded in the structure of language
> itself... It is... important to stress the role of the translator in provoking
> cultural conflict, conflict which is positive and creative and which shakes
> our beliefs, enabling us to escape from the prison of language and culture
> by bringing us in to contact, sometimes violently, with views diametrically
> opposed to our own.
> (op. cit.)

Nevertheless the conflict between those who understand each other well (in both the literal or more general sense) are of a different kind from misunderstandings born of ignorance. So while knowledge of a language does not necessarily lead to good feelings towards its speakers, this does not mean that it has no role to play in the development of positive relations. Mutual language understanding that comes through translation may not augment understanding in itself and may even on occasion diminish it, but it can at least lay bare any fundamental differences as a basis for future reconciliation. The example of *in-shâ'-llâh* إن شاء الله with which I began this book is of this kind. An overt and visible translation of this Arabic expression into English would acknowledge its untranslatable nature and the light this throws on the incompatible world views of many of the speakers of the two languages involved. Neither the pragmatic translation 'perhaps' nor the literal 'if God wills' are adequate, so any translation is necessarily only provisional and unsatisfactory. There are fundamental differences between the two cultures, and these are revealed and illustrated by this translation problem. How the two sides cope with this problem is a different matter. Some may intensify their efforts in order aggressively to assert their own values, and to contain or eradicate opposition. Others may take understanding of difference as a cue for moderation and compromise. Translation is not, then, a panacea or guarantee of peace, but it is an important element in a social reformist education which seeks to overcome mutual ignorance and inequality between speakers of two languages.

TILT as humanistic education

With its emphasis upon personal fulfilment for all students, a humanistic approach to education differs from the other three—technological, social-reformist, and academic—in that its measure of success is not imposed upon students from outside, by governments, businesses, or academics. Educators may guide students in certain directions, but ultimately these should fit with students' own values and desires. Of its nature 'personal fulfilment' must come from inside, and cannot be assessed without reference to the student's own perception of whether their experience has been successful. Thus, whereas in the other approaches there is room for disaffection and failure by some individuals without the whole ethos being invalidated, humanistic approaches should strive to be adaptable and diverse enough to please all. Students themselves are the ultimate arbiters of success.

This creates something of a problem for attempts to assess any particular activity or outcome—such as TILT—within a humanistic framework. For it is not an activity or outcome in itself which is good or bad, but its match with the aspirations and inclinations of individuals. Judgments are likely to be as various as students themselves.

Almost all language-teaching movements have implicitly assumed their particular approach to be suitable for all, and have failed to recognize the diversity of individual learning styles and preferences. Ironically, in English language teaching, this has also been true of some 'student-centred' approaches which have ostensibly drawn upon a humanistic ethos. Many have simply assumed without evidence that students will be 'turned off' by traditional activities such as rote learning, repetition, and error correction, preferring instead to concentrate on real-world tasks, group and pair work, negotiation of meaning, etc. In a similar way, the old assumption that students prefer intra-lingual to cross-lingual teaching has not generally been questioned by proponents of ostensibly humanistic approaches[24], and therefore the possible reintroduction of TILT for humanistic reasons has not been considered, as it should have been if the humanistic approach were really being followed.

However this argument cuts both ways, and the same charge of pre-judging student preferences can be applied to a humanistic argument for TILT. As with any other recommended strategy for humanistic learning, it must always remain provisional and subject to the veto of students. If there is a lesson to be learnt from the failures of 20th century language teaching and its succession of beliefs, it should be that no single approach should be presented as being attractive to all students of all types, in all places, for all time—and TILT should be no exception. There are, nevertheless, good reasons to suppose that TILT might be more conducive to student satisfaction than has commonly been imagined. In Chapter 3 we surveyed studies which found that when the views of students from a variety of settings, ages, and stages were actually canvassed rather than being simply assumed, Direct Method was often perceived as unsatisfactory and disempowering. Many students, in other words, look more favourably upon bilingual instruction—and therefore potentially upon translation—than has previously been assumed. That this preference is widespread is also suggested by the dominance of bilingual materials for self instruction (discussed in Chapter 1) and by the continued prevalence of TILT in many settings, despite the onslaught it has sustained from theorists. There is also the strong possibility, though research is needed to verify the claim, that for many students the conundrums of translation provide a satisfying intellectual challenge (along the lines of popular pastimes such as Sudoku, crosswords, or chess) and aesthetic satisfaction, in that it involves the crafting of a complex artefact.

TILT as academic education

Making a case for TILT as fulfilling an academic educational purpose presents something of a paradox. In some quarters it might be conceived as being an argument against it. It is the perception that TILT is *too* academic which contributed to its downfall in the late 19th century and has fuelled its continuing exclusion ever since. It is seen as divorced from real-world activities and needs, and preoccupied with declarative rather than procedural knowledge. It is also associated with deductive rather than inductive teaching, accuracy rather than fluency, writing rather than speech, and invented rather than actual language use. Yet while these are the characteristics of Grammar Translation, they are by no means necessarily features of TILT as a whole, which may be as focused on the real-world processes of communication as on the teaching of any other common social use of language.

It is true, nevertheless, that instruction in translation and discussion of translation problems is likely to involve an academic element, in that it necessarily involves explicit declarative knowledge about language and languages, and a metalanguage for their formal description, as argued in Chapter 4. In discussing, for example, the tensions between literal and free translation, TILT will need, in some shape or form, to make use of the distinction between linguistic forms and functions, and semantic and pragmatic meaning. So for such purposes, rather than trying to come up with some new terminology *ad hoc*, it would seem only sensible to draw upon established theories and descriptive apparatuses already developed in the formal academic study of language, and that is what most TILT does, whether it makes use of traditional grammar and literary critical terminology, or a more rigorous descriptive system from linguistics. Thus TILT provides students, as a kind of by-product of their studies, both with an academic metalanguage for the analysis of any language, and a deeper understanding of the nature of language and language use in general. It is, in short, a way into the most academic study of language of all—linguistics. When it is combined with literary study, as it often is, this too adds to its academic feel.

TILT does then involve an academic dimension and draws upon a tradition of existing scholarship. But is this of itself necessarily detrimental to good language learning, as has been implied by many 'communicative' critiques? Here, as so often in discussions of language teaching, there are underlying assumptions which need teasing out, and which, when they have been teased out, emerge as highly questionable. A first assumption seems to be that an academic approach is somehow incompatible with a practical focus, in which the aim is to be able to use language for communication. Developing academic knowledge is seen as having no relation to practical skills, and as taking up valuable time which might have been better spent on more useful activities. Made explicit in this way, this assumption is rather strange. Applied to other fields of learning, the notion that there is no relation between declarative and procedural knowledge, that knowing about something is a hindrance to knowing how, seems quite bizarre. Medical students' study of anatomy, homeostasis, and biology, for example, is generally considered a help rather than a hindrance in the diagnosis and treatment of illness, even if it is not enough in itself to make a good doctor. In musical academies, musical theory is studied as potentially helpful to an ability to perform or compose, even though no one would claim it to be sufficient, and so forth. In a similar way, there is no reason to suppose that knowledge about a language should impede someone's ability to use it. Indeed it is hard to see how one could prevent language students from hypothesizing about the structure and relation of the two languages in the light of the evidence provided by their study or, to put it another way, how one could stop them taking an 'academic' perspective (Widdowson 2003: 1–19). Theorizing in the light of evidence is after all both a natural human way of dealing with new knowledge and the essence of academic study—unless one takes the extreme and demonstrably false view that no academic knowledge and enquiry has any relation to the 'real world'. This is not to say that all academic study is to be judged by its practical applications, nor to deny that there are instances of intellectual enquiry which are abstruse and sterile. It is, however, to assert the value and inevitability of academic enquiry, the right of students to benefit from it in their studies and also, for they are not just passive imbibers of academic wisdom, to acknowledge the active contribution which they themselves can make to the overall understanding of language and translation.

In defence of the academic nature of TILT, and against those who see it as detrimental to language learning, there is a weak and a strong argument. The weak argument sees this academic dimension as no threat to the development of language use, and not detrimental to the other purposes of education described in this chapter (to provide needed skills, promote positive values, and enable personal fulfilment). The strong argument sees it as a positive force, both of value in its own right, and as strengthening the acquisition of practical proficiency. In this latter mode it might be argued, as of academic enquiry in general, that a detached and systematic analysis of the object of study can promote critical thinking and serve as a bulwark against manipulation and deception. In a world where casual or uninformed translation can cause so many problems, academic understanding of the processes involved has a great deal to contribute, not only to the academic world itself but to the real world as well—suggesting, in fact, that this artificial opposition of real and academic worlds is yet another damaging language-teaching myth.

The argument of this chapter has been that, whatever the underlying educational philosophy on which teaching practice is based, TILT has a role to play in promoting it, and that it can satisfy a range of criteria, rather than appealing to only one or two. The best educational rationales are always those which acknowledge and respect the multiple motives and effects of educational programming, and which take into account the variety of interested parties. Students, teachers, parents, governments, academics and society at large (and the majority and minority groups within each category) all have a legitimate stake in what happens. Educational programmes which focus too closely on any one rationale or interest group tend to be weak, and to contain the seeds of their own destruction. All elements have a role to play, and inevitably intertwine. TILT has the potential to reconcile competing interests and competing criteria.

The details of moving from principles to practice are always problematic however, and it is to a consideration of practice that we move in the next chapter.

Notes

1 In this they draw heavily on Skilbeck (1982).

2 Clark (1987), whose taxonomy is also influential, uses the terms 'classical humanist' (broadly equivalent to Allen's 'academic'), 'reconstructionist' (broadly equivalent to Allen's 'social reformist') and 'progressivist' (broadly equivalent to Allen's 'humanistic'). Clark has no separate category for Allen's 'technological'.

3 In norm-referenced assessment, each student is assessed relative to the others. To succeed means to do better than the other students; to fail means to do worse than the others; to be average means to be half-way down the scale. In criterion-referenced assessment, by contrast, students are judged by whether they have achieved the objective rather than in comparison with each other, and it is therefore possible for all students to succeed or for all students to fail.

4 Also known as EMILE: *Enseignement d'une Matière par l'Intégration d'une Langue Etrangère.*

5 http://curriculum.qca.org.uk/key-stages-1-and-2/Values-aims-and-purposes/index.aspx (accessed 10 May 2009).

6 Chinese Communist Party Central Committee and the State Council China Reform and Development Program, February 13, 1993 http://news.rednet.cn/c/2008/06/19/1533296.htm (accessed 15 May 2009, translation by Guozhi Cai).

7 Translated for the author from the original Chinese by Guozhi Cai.

8 Translated for the author from the original Portuguese by Denise Santos.

9 For critiques of this idea, see Widdowson 1983, 1984: 189–200.

10 http://europa.eu/languages/en/chapter/15 (accessed 17 May 2009).

11 http://ec.europa.eu/dgs/translation/index_en.htm (accessed 17 May 2009).

12 This translation is from Morgan 1959: 276. The name of the translator is not given.

13 http://www.clilconsortium.jyu.fi/index.php?option=com_content&task=view&id=5&Itemid=6

14 CLILConsortiumhttp://www.clilconsortium.jyu.fi/index.php?option=com_content&task=view&id=21&Itemid=39

15 http://sarolta.wordpress.com/category/efl/clil/

16 http://www.koreatimes.co.kr/www/news/nation/2008/03/117_21054.html

17 Contrary to the accepted wisdom of modern linguistics that all languages are equally complex, N. Ellis and Larsen-Freeman (2006: 573) interestingly suggest that some languages are easier to learn, and that this 'easiness' may be related to the amount of contact the language has had with outsiders, including those people learning it. Ironically, if true, this claim would mean that it is the world's least powerful languages which become the most complex, as these are those least likely to have had most learners.

18 A widely cited source is Lewis 2009.

19 Also known as Mandarin Chinese.

20 Often considered by linguists to be different version of one language. They are mutually intelligible, but use different writing systems. (Dil 1992).

21 Again estimates vary: some sources (e.g. Lewis 2009) put the number of Ingush speakers much higher.

22 The Welsh Language Act 1993 and the Government of Wales Act 1998.

23 I am aware of a danger in this discussion of confounding language with culture and ideology. The idea that a set of ideas is shared by all speakers of a language is of course a gross simplification—not all Russian speakers were pro-Soviet during the days of the Soviet Union, nor all native British English speakers imperialist during time of the British Empire, any more than all Arabic speakers are Islamist fundamentalists today. However, such over-generalizations do fuel policy and attitudes in foreign language learning.

24 With some exceptions. See the discussion of Suggestopaedia and Community Language Learning in Chapter 2.

7

Pedagogical arguments

Grasping the nettles

There is no point in any recommendation about how to teach or learn languages, however much linguistic and psychological evidence there may be in its favour, unless it is going to work pedagogically. If there is no case for TILT on this score, then there is little point in pursuing the earlier arguments in this book, other than as an academic exercise. We need to leave behind generalizations, and to be more specific about what kinds of translation can be used, in which circumstances, by which teachers, and with which students.

As we have already seen, many arguments have been advanced against TILT. It has been claimed—or insinuated—that it is unhelpful to learning, unusable, dull, authoritarian, unpopular, artificial, and slows students down. This is a long catalogue of crimes. The task of this chapter is to show how it need be none of these things. A few nettles need to be grasped.

The book so far has been largely theoretical. We have examined the history and causes of TILT's rejection (Chapters 1–3), evidence-based and educational arguments (Chapters 5–6), and in between, the nature of translation itself (Chapter 4). This is in line with the purpose expressed in the Introduction. Neither the book as a whole, nor this chapter, are intended as a practical teaching manual, or a comprehensive catalogue of ways in which translation might be used. (For more extensive coverage of this kind the reader is referred to the books frequently cited in this chapter, such as Duff 1989; Deller and Rinvolucri 2002; González Davies 2004; Butzkamm and Caldwell 2009.) Nevertheless, theoretical discussion inevitably raises questions about how ideas should be implemented. This chapter directly addresses some of these practical issues.

Questions of what, when, what for, by whom, and with whom cannot be kept neatly separate from each other; it is necessary to move backwards and forwards between them. There are connections, for example, between viable activity types, teacher competences, and class composition. To keep things clear, it will be helpful to set out a list of questions which the chapter seeks to answer, and use these as section headings.

- Which teachers will TILT work for?
- Which students will TILT work for? How should its use vary with the ages and stages of learners, or with other learner characteristics?
- What types of TILT activity can be used? Can TILT be used with mixed language classes? Can TILT be used by teachers who do not know their students' own language?

Which teachers?

One nettle that needs to be grasped is this: a case for rehabilitating translation in language teaching immediately runs into two obvious objections. One concerns classes where the students share a single language but the teacher does not speak it. The other concerns the use of translation in mixed-language classes. This section will deal with the first of these. The second will be dealt with in a later section on types of activity.

Teachers who do not speak their students' language(s)

Any radical change in teaching has implications for teacher education and for the status and self-perception of teachers already in the profession. The spread of Direct Method has had just such an effect. It brought to an end the notion that a language teacher should know their students' own language, and opened up an employment market for native-speaker teachers whose native-speaker proficiency and the ability to teach monolingually were regarded as sufficient expertise. They had the first of these by definition, and could acquire the second through training. Non-native speakers on the other hand, however expert they might be in the language they were teaching and however well they might teach it, could never—also by definition—become native speakers. This elevation of the native-speaker teacher had a profoundly detrimental impact on the status of non-native bilingual teachers (Medgyes 1994; Braine 1999; Seidlhofer 1999; TESOL 2006; Clark and Paran 2007) and the assumption that native speakers make better teachers than bilingual non-natives is widespread to this day. One typical online Internet language-teaching site[1] advertising 'Real English Lessons with Real English Teachers' at the time of writing boasts that its teachers:

- are all native speakers of English—from England
- are fully qualified and experienced in teaching English as a second language—ESL
- are really nice people—friendly, outgoing and focused on your individual learning needs.

Another[2] proudly claims that:

All our teachers are native speakers of the language being taught. We are unable to make any exceptions. If you are a native speaker of a language we don't yet offer, please contact us to discuss future opportunities.

Such attitudes can be taken to extremes, as illustrated by the following report from the *EL Gazette*, March 2000:

> A Japanese court has rejected the unfair dismissal claim of a native-speaker English teacher who was dismissed for being too Japanese. Teacher Gwendolen Gallagher, 44, was dismissed by the private sector Asahikawa University, having worked there for 12 years. On February 1st Asahikawa District Court chief judge Saiki Norio found that the university was justified in dismissing Gallagher, having heard evidence from the university that she was over Japanized as a result of spending a long time in Japan and the fact that her husband is Japanese. The university claimed that this reduced her effectiveness as a teacher of foreign culture, and that it needed to employ fresh foreigners.

Curiously—and perhaps cunningly—the teacher in this case is defensively described by her employer as 'a teacher of foreign culture' rather than 'a teacher of foreign language', suggesting that the native-speaker teacher's role was seen in this university context as auxiliary to the serious business of *language* teaching, which was probably carried out by Japanese teachers of English. This raises issues about the potentially complementary roles of native-speaker monolingual teachers and non-native speaker bilingual teachers to which we shall return later. Yet culture and language are not, as we have seen, so easily separated. In addition, the inevitably complex identity of individuals who live between two cultures and languages, and the hybrid forms that emerge from this—including the linguistic phenomenon of 'expat syndrome' where resident teachers begin to make the same interference errors as their students—should not necessarily be treated as undesirable. To do so has an element of the purism which seeks to keep nations and languages clearly distinct (discussed in Chapter 3). In short, the discrimination seems more than unfair, given that bilingualism and biculturalism can be validly conceived as positive forces rather than disadvantages.

The question arises as to whether a return to bilingual teaching and translation in those contexts where it has been outlawed might have a similarly negative effect on native-speaker monolingual teachers as Direct Method had on non-native bilingual teachers. It is not likely, however, that such native-speaker teachers will be left out in the cold. Given the number of monolingual teachers who do not know their students' languages and the number of mixed language classes (especially in private language schools and in classes for immigrants), a mass return to exclusively bilingual education is highly improbable. This is not just a practical matter, however. The extremism of the Direct Method should not be repeated in reverse. An advocacy of translation should be more sensitive to the position of monolingual teachers than the Direct Method revolution was to that of non-native speaker teachers, whom it relegated to a second-class status, and who still suffer discrimination by many employers. It would be wrong if arguments for translation were seen as undervaluing in a similar way the work of those who teach monolingually.

What is needed is an accommodation between intra-lingual and cross-lingual teaching in which each recognizes the complementary strengths of the other, supplemented by an inventory of ways in which translation can be used in mixed language classes and by monolingual teachers. Contrary to Butzkamm and Caldwell (2009: 25), in whose view *all* teachers should be bilingual, I believe there is still a role for the monolingual teachers, especially in mixed language classes, or working in tandem with a bilingual teacher. The section on activity types below discusses ways in which translation can be used even in mixed language classes or by monolingual teachers.

The issue of who can teach through translation does not entail a simple distinction between native and non-native speaker teachers, however. There are certainly native-speaker teachers of single-language classes who are also adept speakers of their students' language and can therefore make the same connections between the two as their non-native colleagues. In the words of one former learner of English in Brazil:

> My best English teachers had something in common—both knew *a lot* about English *and* Portuguese. One was a Brit, the other a Brazilian.

Indeed the question of whether a teacher is monolingual is, in a sense, separate from (though obviously related to) whether they are teaching using a monolingual approach. Absolutist Direct Method has led to situations where bilingual teachers have been obliged, or have decided, to hide their knowledge of their students' own language. In addition, language knowledge is not immutable— obviously so, as otherwise there would be no point in teaching or learning—and teachers who do not know their students' own language, or do not know it very well, can set about learning it or improving their proficiency in it.

There is nevertheless, especially among native-speaker teachers of English, a significant itinerant population who, while they may have some knowledge of the local language, do not have the level necessary for extensive translation use in class. In their defence, there are many extenuating circumstances. Career patterns and employment pressures make many native-speaker teachers move from place to place, with the result that they know something of several languages but none of them in depth. In addition, there is often little need or motivation for English speakers to learn other languages, because in many countries they can function without knowing the language. This is true not only at the mundane level of survival (finding the way, shopping, and so forth) but even in the establishment of relationships and social networks, especially for teachers whose local colleagues are teachers of English and therefore not only speak the language very well, but have a professional interest in using it. Moreover, the tendency for the economically and politically more powerful language to dominate in cross-linguistic communication between individuals (Baker and Prys Jones 1998: 30) adds to the likelihood that communication between English native speakers and speakers of other languages will take place predominantly in English—and this can hardly be laid at the door of individuals. All this means that it would be unrealistic to expect large numbers of teachers to 'retrain' quickly, acquiring another language to a level at which they can use it for teaching through translation, even if there were resources for this, and even if they wanted to.

More practical, more likely, and more desirable than any such wholesale change would be an accommodation between the two approaches, with gradual shifts of emphasis and value. There could be a widespread recognition that bilingual teachers are able to engage in valuable cross-lingual activities which monolingual teachers cannot do as extensively. Monolingual teachers, for their part, could recognize the benefits of learning or at least starting to learn their students' language(s). Apart from the possibilities this opens up for more varied classroom activities, it can also serve to motivate students and strengthen relationships, since students will see their teacher struggling with the same kinds of problems as they have. Just as the bilingual teacher is a model of successful language learning, so the monolingual teacher could seek to become one too.

Which learners?

A second nettle to be grasped is the degree to which TILT is appropriate for all types of learners. So far, this book has largely treated TILT generically without making distinctions, and this is justified to an extent, as many of the arguments apply to all types of learners in all types of contexts. Nevertheless, the type, quantity, and function of translation activity must vary with the stage which learners have reached, with their ages, and with their own preferences, learning styles, and experience.

Beginners

The function of TILT with beginners will be very different from its function with advanced learners. Beginners, by definition, do not know the new language, and for this very reason their own language is particularly needed at the outset of their studies for communication of anything other than the very simple and highly artificial messages which can be constructed using the language encountered in the first few lessons. While teachers and students may want to enter into a pact to use only the new language for some parts of the lesson or for certain types of activity, and to specify clearly which these are, this is very different from extending such a monolingual strategy to every part of every lesson. As before, I am treating translation as both an inevitable feature of any bilingual teaching, and as a specific activity in itself. Translation can be part of a general use of the students' own language, called upon when necessary to augment explanation and resolve difficulties; it can also be the main focus of attention at other times. Given the perennial problems of time management for language teachers, it will be very important that adequate and clearly demarcated sections of each lesson are allocated for this latter purpose.

Without any use of the students' own language, or clarity as to when and for what purposes it can be used, lessons can be both confusing and demoralizing. Brooks-Lewis' study of student attitudes to Direct Method is prefaced by an account of her own language-learning experience which is worth quoting at length, as it eloquently sets out what may well be a very widespread experience:

> The research evolved from the personal experience of my return to the foreign language classroom as an adult. My first language is English, and I wished to learn Spanish. I attended Spanish as a foreign language classes at two universities in Texas, and although I made excellent grades, it was a disappointing, discouraging experience. While I may have learned some grammar rules, I learned no usable Spanish, and worse yet, I came to doubt my ability to learn at all. This began the very first day of class when the teacher spoke only Spanish. I felt I had walked into the second act of a three act play, or that I had gotten into the wrong classroom. I had enrolled in a beginning class because I wanted to learn the language, so of course I could not understand anything the teacher was saying, and wondering why she acted as if I should was worrisome, making an already stressful situation even more so. ...As I became ever more uncomfortable with subjecting the people I was working with to experiences I had found disquieting and disillusioning I began to analyze my own learning experiences and those from teaching. Two factors stood out that were common to both of these experiences: the learner was ignored and there was no *beginning*, no 'first act' in the teaching of foreign language when working with adults.
> (Brooks-Lewis 2009)

Ironically, the highly artificial strategy of such total monolingualism needs explaining to the students in their own language, if they are not to experience in the first lesson the kind of confusion and disorientation described by Brooks-Lewis. Such own-language explanation is exactly what happens in statements and prefaces to Direct Method courses. The Rosetta Stone 'unique language learning software program', for example, 'built around a concept called Dynamic Immersion' which 'never ask[s] you to translate back into your native language or memorize vocabulary lists'[3] has nevertheless—as these quotations illustrate—to explain to students in their own language that they will not be using their own language! Such statements undermine themselves, and in so doing illustrate perfectly why, with beginners, not everything can be done in the new language.

So even the most extreme monolingual teaching is, of necessity, framed by bilingual explanation. Allowing alternation between languages, including frequent translation, seems eminently more sensible for beginners. This does not mean that the teacher will not sometimes oblige students to use the new language when they are tempted to take the easier option of resorting to their own language. But a flexible approach will allow the student to ask for clarification and the teacher to give it when necessary. In this way the teacher is able to monitor students' understanding, to ensure that they do not feel lost, and allow them to express their own thoughts, needs, and worries. For these reasons, own-language use including translation, is likely to be far more empowering and student-centred than monolingual teaching, which is a sure way of concentrating power and control in the hands of the teacher alone.

Yet there are many signs of change, and suggestions for constructive ways of relinquishing some of this demotivating use of power by allowing movement between new and own language. The International Teacher Training Organization now recommends to its trainees that:

> Finally, a great tool to use in the TEFL classroom is a L1 problem session. This is a period of time that is regularly scheduled for students to discuss, in their own language, any questions they have about lessons and vocabulary. It can be 10 minutes at the end of class or set on a weekly or monthly basis as needed. Since your students will know in advance, they will really have time to think about any problem areas they may be having. Motivation increases as well. When your students know that they will have the chance to discuss something in L1 in the future, it is easier for them to actually try during activities in English. Most students will be relieved and have a better attitude if you will allow a time and place for L1, rather than saying that there is no place for their mother tongue in the classroom.
> (ITTO 2009)

Advanced learners

Let us jump now to the other end of the stages continuum—advanced learners. From there, we shall move back to intermediate learners in the following section.

Generally, advanced learners are able to use the new language to communicate what they want to say, voicing their views, needs, and questions to the teacher. (Indeed the terms 'new language' and 'learners' do not seem so appropriate for them since they are already established users whose expertise should be treated with respect.) The arguments for TILT as an answer to a real communicative need do not therefore apply to advanced learners in the same way as they do to beginners, and discussion and activity in the new language can generally proceed without translation. Nevertheless there will be occasions, as with beginners and intermediate students, when a communicative problem may be swiftly overcome by translation. There is nothing necessarily 'learnerish' about this however. It is a possible and frequent communicative strategy for anyone who knows more than one language. Translation is often used by bilinguals to clarify something in either of their languages, and even by native speakers to remedy a gap in their own language vocabulary by reference to another. (This is most often the case with technical vocabulary. A native

Russian speaker who learnt to drive in England for example tells me that she learnt the Russian word *stsepleniie* (сцепление) by looking up 'clutch' in the English–Russian section of a bilingual dictionary.) All this should remind us that at the advanced level categories are fuzzy and complex. It is hard to say when someone ceases to be a 'learner' and becomes an 'expert speaker' or 'bilingual'. Nor is there any reason why a native speaker or bilingual should always know more than the 'learner'. Where the level of knowledge is so close, it will lead to discussion rather than telling by the teacher. It may be that in advanced classes the role of the teacher is as much to provide explanation of cultural background or commentary on problematic language forms used (idioms, or examples of language variation and change that may deviate from the 'rules' the student has learnt previously) than to focus on developing accuracy and fluency with the basic forms of the language.

Such discussion is however only one function of TILT in the advanced class. Two others are of particular and perhaps greater importance. One is to develop translation as a needed skill in itself. The other is to deepen, through discussion of translation problems, explicit knowledge of the two languages and the relation between them. Both will be discussed in the sections on activity types below.

Intermediate learners

Intermediate learners are, by definition, midway on a continuum between beginners and advanced learners. Not surprisingly, therefore, TILT for intermediate students can share elements of its use with both beginners and advanced learners, but with some adjustments. Specifically, with intermediate students the amount of TILT for explanation may decrease, while the amount of TILT for developing translation skills and explicit knowledge may increase. As with beginners, there can be *ad hoc* translation and movement back and forwards between languages to aid explanation, as well as clearly designated times—the 'pacts' referred to above—when only the new language can be used. There can also be lessons, or sections of lessons, in which students are explicitly taught to translate. These strategies, in addition to developing translation skills *per se* will also help diagnose and tackle difficulties and, as with advanced learners, develop declarative knowledge of the two languages. Intermediate students can study new vocabulary as translation equivalents; they can discuss in their own language difficulties which arise concerning particular translation problems, such as the lack of exact equivalence between a particular word and its conventional translation; they can be encouraged to use bilingual translation resources, such as bilingual dictionaries and vocabulary lists, and watching subtitled films, in ways which will become increasingly important if they move on to an advanced level. By relating new to existing knowledge, such activities will also give intermediate students a sense of confidence in what they know and of order in what they are learning. This is all too often lacking in monolingual teaching, where the teacher may know what is happening but the students do not, and suffer as a result from a disconcerting sense of disorientation and loss of control, as their main means of understanding the world—their own language—is artificially and autocratically pulled out from under them. In the transition from intermediate to advanced proficiency, TILT can be play a key role in avoiding this problem.

Young learners

The issue of how the use of TILT should vary with student ages, and how ages relate to stages, is complex. Though there is no necessary relation between stage and age (and beginners can certainly be of any age), advanced students tend to be older, while young children are most usually beginners. So with an eye to exceptions, this section considers the difference between young learners who are beginners or lower-intermediate learners, and teenage and adult learners of all stages. What has been said so far in this chapter applied mostly to older learners. We need now to consider in what way younger learners might be different. (For reasons explained below, the terms 'young learner' and 'child(ren)' refer to learners before puberty.)

Views on how best to teach languages to young learners suffer from a popular misconception about children's language learning abilities, and confusion between language learning in family and school contexts. It is well known and well documented that if life circumstances lead to a child moving from one language environment to another before puberty, they are able to acquire native-speaker competence in the new language without formal instruction (Lenneberg 1967). Thus, for example, a Somali-speaking child adopted by a German-speaking family, brought up in Germany and sent to a German-medium school, will become a native speaker of German and—in the absence of any maintenance—lose their Somali. In addition, children who use one language at home but another outside, may become bilingual, having native competence in both languages. Thus, for example, the children of a Japanese-speaking family brought up in Spain and educated in Spanish schools who continue to use Japanese at home, are likely to have native-like ability in both Spanish and Japanese. (The balance between the two in later life will depend on many different factors.) The fact that all this can take place without instruction has led to a popular misconception that children can acquire a language on the school curriculum in the same way, leading to great enthusiasm for 'early start' programmes in primary schools. Research and experience, however, show this to be wishful thinking (Poole 1999). Limited classroom exposure to a few lessons a week with no genuine communicative need to use the language is very different from the all-day every-day exposure to a new language of a child who has moved from one language community to another, and who needs this new language in order to function as a social being.

This is not to deny, however, that the ways young children relate to a new language are significantly different from those of older students. The differences, however, cut both ways, and being a young learner brings both advantages and disadvantages. On the one hand, children may have fewer barriers to certain kinds of new knowledge. They may have, for example, a great ability to imitate sounds and intonation patterns successfully. They are less inhibited by stress, self-consciousness, and worry about final outcomes. On the other hand, these same qualities of openness, spontaneity, and intuition may hinder them in other ways. They are less likely to work hard outside lessons. They have less ability to think metalinguistically, or to organize understanding and categorize new knowledge in the ways which help older learners. This means that the rationale for TILT as a means of developing declarative knowledge of the relationship between the two languages is of less relevance to young learners. Form-focused activities such as corrected close translation (to be discussed below) are perhaps best avoided. In short, with young learners there is a case for a more or less exclusively 'communicative' focus—learning language by using it. This need not mean, however, that translation or explanation is of no use. There are plenty of communicative ways to use translation as we shall see shortly. If one of the virtues of young children is to be more relaxed and spontaneous about learning, then a flexible and adaptable approach in which translation is used as and when required would seem to be best for them.

Learner styles, experience, and preferences

In addition to the factors already discussed, such as teacher bilingualism (or lack of it), and learner stages and learner ages, there are a host of other factors which may affect the degree and type of TILT which is used. Perhaps the single worst feature of the Direct Method era is its dogmatic insistence that the teaching approach or method of the moment is a universal truth applicable to all students everywhere. I referred to this in Chapter 1 as the fourth pillar of the Direct Method: absolutism. It would not be in the spirit of the argument against this dogmatism simply to repeat it in reverse, insisting that the use of translation is an absolute good in all circumstances. Different students in different contexts may need, like, or benefit from TILT to a greater or lesser degree, depending upon their learning purposes, their previous experience of education, and their styles of learning. Early Direct Method and communicative language teaching often rode roughshod over the wishes and experiences of students and teachers whose frame of reference had developed in earlier times or in different traditions. Now, however, after a century of Direct Method and forty years of CLT, both have become deeply embedded in the beliefs of many teachers and students. For them, TILT can seem as inimical and contrary to cherished beliefs as Direct Method and CLT did to previous generations. Nothing is to be gained by imposing any teaching approach upon people who are deeply opposed to it. So it is to be hoped that

TILT, where espoused, will be applied with a greater sensitivity to differences than the approaches which it seeks to replace.

In addition to learner needs, styles, attitudes, and beliefs, the realization of TILT will also vary, like any other pedagogic programme, with practical factors such as class size, time available, and resources. In particular, as already discussed, it will also of necessity vary with class composition and teacher ability, as it cannot be used as extensively in mixed language classes, or in single language classes taught by monolingual teachers. The issue of teacher knowledge has been discussed above. How TILT might be used in mixed language classes will be returned to later in the chapter.

What types of activity?

TILT, as we have seen in earlier chapters, has been relentlessly associated with the 'traditional' half of a number of dichotomies, concerned with:

FORM	rather than	MEANING
ACCURACY	rather than	FLUENCY
ARTIFICIALITY	rather than	AUTHENTICITY
DECLARATIVE KNOWLEDGE	rather than	PROCEDURAL KNOWLEDGE
AUTHORITARIAN TEACHING	rather than	COLLABORATIVE LEARNING

I shall refer to the focuses in the left-hand column of this table as 'traditional' and those in the right-hand column as 'communicative'. As the scare quotes indicate, however, neither term is satisfactory. 'Traditional' teaching often involves communicative elements, while activities described as 'communicative' are often, in the words of David Nunan (1987: 144), 'not…very communicative at all'. The legitimacy of all the component dichotomies can be questioned too. Taking each in turn, possible objections include the following:

- Form and meaning are not alternatives but aspects of the same phenomenon, and all instances of language inevitably have both (Widdowson 1990b; G. Cook 2000: 48–52, 163–167).
- Accuracy and fluency are complementary, and both are needed for effective communication (Brumfit 1984).
- Artificiality and authenticity are aspects of how something is used rather than fixed qualities, so the same text or activity may be either, depending on how teacher and student relate to it (van Lier 1996: 127–8; Widdowson 1978:80).
- Declarative knowledge feeds into procedural knowledge and *vice versa* (Johnson 1996).
- There is a difference between authoritarianism and authority, and to impose collaborative learning or deny teachers the right to intervene authoritatively when needed can be highly authoritarian in itself.

However, given the currency of these dichotomies in language teaching theory, I shall make use of them in this section. Ultimately however, I hope to show that 'traditional' and 'communicative' focuses are complementary rather than alternatives, and that TILT excels in promoting attention to both, creating what Butzkamm and Caldwell (2009: 44–46) refer to as a 'dual focus'.

I start with a defence of some 'traditional' focuses, and in the latter part of the chapter move on to more 'communicative' ones, including activities which can be used by teachers who do not know their students' language, or who teach mixed-language classes.

Types of activity 1: corrected close translation

Translation can, as we have seen, be interpreted in a very loose sense to mean all types of mediation between different languages. Applied to language teaching, this loose definition can encompass own-language explanations of encountered difficulties, teacher glosses of unknown words and expressions, reference to a bilingual dictionary, or discussion of different cultural norms. Alternatively (as discussed in Chapters 4 and 6) translation can be defined more strictly as: 'the replacement of textual material in one language by equivalent textual material in another language' (Catford 1965: 20). Even within this sense though, there is room for a loose interpretation and a tight one. We might ask students to produce a 'free' translation or a 'literal' one. Here, however, I want to take the tightest of tight definitions, and consider the usefulness of asking students to produce translations in which they are to keep as close as possible to the original (taking into account the limits to 'closeness' discussed in Chapter 4). Such form-focused close translation is the most controversial and the most vilified manifestation of TILT. But does it deserve its bad reputation?

It certainly, by definition, curtails student freedom and room for manoeuvre, and is therefore out of tune with the ethos of most current approaches to language teaching, which prefer to give students options. Yet this restriction has many advantages. It prevents students from simply bypassing difficulties and gaps in their knowledge. Imagine, for example, an English speaking student of Spanish who has problems using the subjunctive, and does not know the Spanish for 'humble', asked to translate as closely as possible the sentence:

I hope the next President will be more humble.

The answer should be:

Espero que el próximo presidente sea mas humilde.
(*Sea* is the present subjunctive of *ser*.)

If they wanted to express a similar meaning in a monolingual class, however, they might easily avoid both this structure and this word, by saying:

Según mi parecer un presidente menos arrogante será una cosa buena.
[In my opinion, a less arrogant president would be a good thing.]

While the ability to innovate and paraphrase in this way has its place, there are also times when students need to confront the difficulties it can help them avoid. The demand for a close translation makes this avoidance strategy impossible. It draws both the student's and the teacher's attention to the problem, and is thus the first stage towards its solution—though the teacher of course needs to deliver corrective feedback in ways which the student will take on board (Bitchener and Knoch forthcoming; Truscott 1996).

Against this, advocates of TBLT might point to the existence of so-called structure-trapping tasks (discussed in Chapter 5), designed to elicit use of a particular structure. But these are not failsafe. There is always the 'danger' that students will successfully complete the task without the targeted structure, and if they do, it is hard to see how they can be 'corrected' without abandoning the TBLT principle of maintaining a primary focus on meaning and task completion. Form-focused translation does not have this problem. It achieves its aim by reducing options for avoidance—but this is not necessarily restrictive in a negative sense. Indeed, by making more structures and more lexis available, it opens up more possibilities for the future.

The sentence in Spanish I have just used to put forward this argument may appear to be one which I have invented simply to illustrate a grammatical point and, as such, to have no context. If so, it is open to the usual charges made against the use of isolated, invented sentences. But these arguments, whatever their merits, are not relevant to the point I am making here. Close translation can equally well make use of examples which have or have not actually occurred. Gaps in student knowledge will be revealed by either kind of example. Indeed, nobody can know for sure, unless they are told, whether a given sentence has been invented to illustrate a language point or retrieved from an actual act of communication. Thus the reader here has no way of knowing whether the sentence about the humble president was invented by me or did actually occur. Nor does it matter! The fact that it could be either attested or invented merely illustrates the irrelevance of the distinction for these purposes (G. Cook 2001a). The most artificial sounding utterances can actually occur. 'The cat sat on the mat' is famous for being one of the most obviously artificial sentences imaginable. Yet when my daughter was very young, she came very close to producing it quite 'naturally'. Seeing a cat in front of our house, she said to me quite spontaneously, 'Look Dad! The cat is sitting on the mat.'

In addition to the gaps in student knowledge of which they are already aware, there are also instances where students may think they know something, but be mistaken. At the lexical level, the classic example is the *faux ami* (false friend)—the word which seems to be the same in the new language, but is not. (In Italian for example *un preservativo* is a condom, not a preservative.) Strangely, as already discussed in Chapter 5, one of the main charges against translation has been that it promotes a sense of false equivalence. That may be so, but only if false equivalence goes uncorrected. In the mono-lingual classroom, on the other hand, confusion of *faux amis* is likely to pass undetected. The student who does not realize that in French *la librairie* is 'the bookshop' and *la bibliothèque* is 'the library', and who means to say that they spent an hour in the library, will say:

J'ai passé une heure dans la librairie.
[I spent an hour in the bookshop.]

But as this is a grammatical and meaningful utterance, the teacher may not realize anything is wrong. As the right and wrong meanings of *faux amis* are often connected, the correction of translation is a particularly effective way of making sure that such misunderstandings emerge. And this applies not only at the lexical level but at the grammatical and pragmatic levels too. French *passé composé* for example is syntactically equivalent to the English present perfect but its use and meaning are sometimes different; Russian and English imperatives may be grammatically equivalent but have different interper-sonal force.

Close translation not only reveals problems, however, it can also be used proactively, in order to deliberately draw students' attention to difficult aspects of the new language. For the bilingual teacher or materials writer who already knows their students' language and the problems which are likely to emerge for them in the new language, it is possible to design close trans-lation activities which will concentrate attention on these problem areas. (This is also, incidentally, an argument for invention—or at least very careful selection—of single sentences.) This is, of course, a technique which goes back to Grammar Translation, and which also subscribes to the contrastive analysis hypothesis, but as argued in Chapters 2 and 5, there is no evidence to discount it for these reasons.

Types of activity 2: word-for-word translation

Close translation is not often the same as word-for-word translation. Strict maintenance of word order often produces grammatical inaccuracies. Word-for-word translation of the expression *in-shâ'-llâh* (إن شاء الله) would be 'if wishes God', which is not grammatically correct in English. Some adjust-ment is needed to conform to the target language grammar ('If God wishes'). This does not mean however that producing such word-for-word equivalents has no role as a teaching and learning exercise. There is a valid distinction to be drawn between translation for consumption in the world outside the classroom and translation as a useful exercise for language learners. Though approaches such as TBLT insist that classroom activities should imitate real-world ones immediately, artifice can play a role in the development of skills. The accomplished professional translator who avoids the clumsiness of excessive literalism does so from choice rather than necessity, rather as an artist who is capable of accurate mimetic drawing might nevertheless choose to produce an abstract painting. At an earlier stage, both may have performed useful imitative technical exercises. Word-for-word translation can be just such an exercise, drawing students' attention to each component so that they may better understand the mechanics of the whole.

For learners, the choice between literal and free translation can only be made once basic skills have been acquired. Before that stage is reached, pragmatic translation may be their only option. They may be unable to break down the original into components, and may even be using pragmatic equivalence as a strategy for avoiding gaps in their own knowledge. Thus someone who knows that in Arabic *in-shâ'-llâh* (إِن شَاء الله) sometimes performs the same pragmatic function as *perhaps* without knowing its literal meaning ('if God wills') has no option of using this more literal translation where appropriate. Nor can they use it to generate analogous sentences such as *in-shâa al modarris* (إن شاء المدرس)—'if the teacher wants'[4]. Butzkamm (2001)[5] gives the example of French *S'il vous plaît*: understood word for word (*If it you pleases/If it pleases you*), rather than just as the pragmatic equivalent of *Please*, it can generate new utterances such as *Si le jardin vous plaît* (= If you like the garden).

Conversely, the inability to reduce units to their components, which can be a consequence of pragmatic translation not only prevents such generation of new utterances, but can also produce errors such as:

*Comment t'appelles-tu la fille?
(Example in Myles et al. 1999)

This attested error is caused by the pupil's perception of *Comment t'appelles-tu* as a single unit without being aware of the meaning of each component (*How yourself call you?*) making them unable to produce by analogy the correct French for 'What's the girl's name?', namely *Comment s'appelle la fille*. Such errors echo the well documented and often amusing segmentation errors of children acquiring a first language, such as:

Adult: Behave!
Child: I am have. (pronounced /heɪv/ as though it rhymes with 'rave')
(Peters 1983: 43)

in which the child has interpreted 'Behave!' as analogous with 'Be good!' or 'Be quiet!', to which the answer might be 'I am good' or 'I am quiet. Or:

Mother: Don't argue.
Child: I don't arg me.
(Crystal 1986: 108, quoted in Butzkamm 2001)

Such mis-segmentations are particularly common in children's hearing of prayers and songs:

'Life is butter cream' for 'Life is but a dream'.
(Peters 1983: 64)

'Gladly, the cross-eyed bear' for 'Gladly the cross I'd bear.'

Drawing explicit parallels with the ways parents may disentangle the segmentation errors of their children, Butzkamm (2001) advocates the pedagogic use of word-for-word translation, which he refers to as 'mirroring', on the grounds that:

> Practising communication is an important classroom activity, but communication is not everything. Learners must also learn to divide messages into their component parts, otherwise each new message would have to be taken over from others and memorized, in which case there would never be any really new messages. Language only comes into its own when the learner discovers its sequential combinatorial system ... Anyone who has tried to learn an unfamiliar language will be easily convinced of the great advantage of mirroring structure in the native language.
> (Butzkamm 2001: 149)

As Green succinctly illustrates the point:

> 'Literal translation ... is sometimes a striking way of highlighting structural features such as word order. As an example ... an Englishman beginning Hindi may find it helpful to remember that in Hindi *I like it* is often rendered as *to me pleasing is*.'
> (Green 1970)[6]

Types of activity 3: teaching vocabulary

One traditional but effective use of translation is to introduce new vocabulary. Indeed for all but material objects which happen to be present in the classroom, or objects or actions which can be unambiguously illustrated or mimed—which is not very many—it is essential. This has long been recognized by theorists whose ideas are anchored in classroom reality. Swan nicely illustrates the foolishness of monolingual vocabulary teaching, and the inevitability of students translating anyway:

> teachers would go through contortions to explain and demonstrate the meaning of words without translating. What often happened, of course, was that after the teacher had spent a few minutes miming, say, *curtain* to a class of baffled French students, one of them would break into a relieved smile and say 'Ah *rideau*'.
> (Swan 1997)

As with *faux amis*, the argument that learning induces a sense of false equivalence could not be further from the truth. If a word in one language is given as unproblematically equivalent to a word in another, then there are indeed likely to be problems. But if there is explicit discussion of the degree of equivalence in different translations, then learning translation equivalents is likely to be helpful. This is evident from the kind of discussion which occurs frequently on language-learning blogs. Take, for example, the polysemantic and polyfunctional Italian word *prego*, which has no single straightforward equivalent in English. Here are two exchanges concerning this word. Significantly, the first starts from student frustration with a Direct Method course, which does not use translation, while the second revolves around the connection between the multiplicity of *prego*'s contemporary functions and its literal meaning of 'I pray'.

Blog extract one
http://able2know.org/topic/20164-1

Note: All texts below are exactly as written by the bloggers.

KICKYCAN: I am trying this online Italian course, and they use the word prego to mean different things, and it's kind of confusing me. In one example, there is a waiter asking 'Prego?', meaning 'What would you like?'. In another, a woman asks if she may sit down at a spot at a bar, and a man says 'prego' meaning, 'of course'. And it's used to mean 'your welcome' after someone says 'grazie'. I get how it could mean 'of course' or 'your welcome', but the most confusing useage for me is the waiter using it to ask 'What would you like?'

LITTLEK: Does anyone know the exact translation of the word in english? Are there also other meanings for the word? And is this the common way to ask someone what they would like, or is it specific to the situation?

OSSOBUCO: let's see... my dictionary says it means all those things you say it means, except not in the waiter context. I dunno why waiter's say it, just a usaeage. Maybe it's one of those things you must accept without understanding, grasshoppah.

IDURU: So what I gather from my mother is... When you walk into the restaurant they would say something to the effect of 'si prego' or 'si accomodi' which both essentially mean 'yes, how can I accomodate you' or 'what can I do for you' She says that nothing is very literal in the italian language and that there are many different meanings and ways to express most words. hope this helps.

Blog extract two
http://slowtalk.com/groupee/forums/a/tpc/f/534601885/m/3311098261

SPINNAKER: I know 'prego' is used for 'you're welcome' after a thank you correct? But I thought I have heard it used elsewhere. Am I mistaken or can it also be used for 'please'? If so in what situations? Why not use 'per favore'? What other situations is 'prego' used?

JUIDTH IN UMBRIA: It literally means 'I pray' so think antique English, as in when someone says, I pray you will… It is quite strong as a query, 'I beg you will or will not do this.'

KIMC: You might also hear it used as 'please' in a form like 'please accomodate yourself.' As decobabe says, it's more the 'I pray you will' form. So in a restaurant, someone might say 'Prego' as they show you your table, meaning, 'please sit here' or 'please make yourself comfortable.' As a traveler, that's probably the most common usage you'll hear apart from the standard 'you're welcome.'

BARBARA (AND ART): When someone comes to the house they say 'permesso?', asking permission to enter, and we say 'prego' meaning 'please come in'.

SPINNAKER: I think it is really funny to learn that 'Prego' means 'I pray'. We have a jarred spaghetti sauce in the States called Prego. Could it mean 'I pray that it is good' ☺ Actually it is very good for a jarred sauce.

G-JAH: I never realized that Prego meant I pray, it seems like the all-purpose word meaning 'how can I help you?' 'after you,' 'you're welcome.' My guess was that it meant something like 'be my guest.' Thanks for the insight!

In both cases, discussion of translation occurs spontaneously and enthusiastically. It is the lack of exact fit between the Italian word and any English translation which seems to interest the students.

Types of activity 4: discussion of translation problems

One common way of characterizing the difference between 'traditional' and 'communicative' approaches is the claim that the former promote knowing about a language while the latter promote using it. Among traditional ways of learning about the language, metalinguistic activities such as parsing, or the study of rules and paradigms, have been especially vilified as being associated with the driest, dullest, and most authoritarian traditional teaching. Such activities have their place however, and are not as unpopular with students as supposed. It is in any case not necessarily the case that thinking about language and talking metalinguistically entail a 'traditional' focus, nor that they put students in a position of particular passivity. There are many other activities which involve thinking or talking about language in engaging and active ways, and which feed directly into improved language use. (There is some irony, moreover, in the fact that the people who claim that talking about language is demotivating and dull obviously do not find it so themselves. As applied linguists they have devoted their lives to such reflection and paradoxically the claim that metalinguistic discussion is demotivating is itself a metalinguistic observation!)

Discussion of translation is a particularly fruitful way to get students to think explicitly about the language they are learning. Thus González Davies (2004), for example, is full of stimulating and entertaining activities which focus upon knowledge about language without abandoning her principle that learning should involve students in their own learning in as humanistic a way as possible. Suggestions include:[7]

- discussion of mistranslations ('plate of the house' for *plato de la casa*)
- critical assessment of film subtitling (Cop: 'I must chase you, as you run away.' Crook: 'I must run away from you, as you are after me.'[8])
- critical assessment of title translations (Is the Swedish *Garp och Hans Värld* ('Garp and His World') an adequate translation of *The World According to Garp*?)
- comparison of different translations of the same text
- reflection on translation dilemmas (such as whether sexist or racist language should be maintained in a translation)
- how to deal with the untranslatable (for example, puns in ads).

All of these activities can be entertaining, while at the same time highlighting and making memorable specific points about the language being learnt. Examples can be short and interesting, making use of texts which students know and care about—such as extracts from favourite songs or film scripts. They can also be playful, memorable, or just downright funny. Mistranslations for example, like children's segmentation errors, are the stuff of endless travellers' anecdotes, which are not only intrinsically amusing and memorable, but fix a language point in the mind. Think back to the apparently rather abstruse point about Russian verbs of motion in Chapter 4. The student of Russian who has been laughed at, as I have, for saying that they have just walked to Moscow from London, or taken a bus from the kitchen to the sitting room, becomes more aware of this distinction between those verbs which mean 'to go by transport' and those which mean 'to go on foot'. Examples abound in the experience of anyone who has been involved in language teaching. I was once asked by an Italian student making an inviting gesture towards a bowl of peanuts on a table, *Come si dice in inglese?* (How is this said in English?'), to which I answered 'peanuts'. A few days later this same student opened the door for a teacher in the school where I was working, and motioning her to go through before him, said with courteous aplomb, but to everybody's great amusement, 'Peanuts!' What he had asked me for originally was the English for the Italian word discussed above: *Prego*!

Types of activity 5: 'traditional' focuses in a 'communicative' frame

The constant bad press of recent decades for everything 'traditional' and the accompanying lauding of everything 'communicative' has meant that those few activity designers who have promoted translation have often been keen to reject the former and ally themselves with the latter. Alan Duff's 1989 resource book for teachers *Translation* provides a good example. Published in the heyday of the communicative approach, its introduction is at pains to distance the book from the image of TILT as:

> a pointless routine exercise, a chore, a punishment... a lone, pointless struggle between student and text

and to present itself instead, using watchwords of the communicative movement, as:

> natural and necessary... two-way not one-way... authentic not 'made up'... useful

assuring us that:

> translation does not mean setting written assignments to be returned to students with errors marked in red. It means rather giving the students regular opportunities to compare and discuss their work, and to respond to suggestions
> (Duff 1989: 5–8)

To live up to these ideas, activities are to have warm-up routines, pair work, group work, authentic texts, and collaborative student self assessment.

Ironically however, when we come to the body of the book, which is a series of activities grouped under five headings, we do not always find these orthodox 'communicative' principles put into practice. Instead, many activities are quite 'traditional'. They focus on forms, use decontextualized examples, and demand solitary written translation for correction by the teacher. In a section with the heading[9] 'Time: tense, mood and aspect', for example, we find instructions to the teachers such as:

> Select passages containing *-ing* forms, and participles with *-ed* or *-en* endings.
> (op. cit. 74)

and instructions to students:

> Translate the passage below from the beginning of line 7. Concentrate in particular on ways of rendering the expressions with not, such as *not drinking, not spitting, not speaking your mind*, etc.
> (op. cit. 77)
> Out of class, translate in writing the passage below.
> (op. cit. 80)

Though preceded with warm up exercises and followed up by sociable collaboration with other students, it is hard to see how such activities do not in part maintain the old outlawed 'traditional' emphases (focus on forms, accuracy, solitary study, and teacher correction).

A similar phenomenon pertains in González Davies' *Multiple Voices in the Translation Classroom: Activities, Tasks and Projects* (2004), a book primarily 'addressed to translation trainers and students' but also 'to foreign language teachers who wish to include translation activities in a communicative and interactive way in their classrooms' (op. cit. 6). In an effort to 'bring translation teaching up to date' it 'draws mainly from humanistic teaching principles, the communicative approach, cooperative learning and social constructivism' (op. cit. 12) and:

> the students are actively involved in their learning process by
> making decisions and interacting with each other in a classroom
> setting that is a discussion forum and hands-on workshop
> (op. cit. sleeve notes).

In keeping with these principles, the activities—which form the bulk of the book—concentrate very much upon speed and collaboration. (See the example in Figure 4 on page 146.)

However, while such activities are wrapped around with elements trying to lighten the load of language learning, the core remains hard work of a more 'traditional' kind. Thus it may be fun to warm up or warm down, whisper and jot things down, sit side by side and so forth, but in practice the main part of these 'communicative' activities inevitably remains the difficult task of translation. Students still need, as in more 'traditional' activities, to reach inside their own minds and pay careful attention to the text. The teacher is needed to offer guidance in the form of prompts, corrections, and explanations, of a kind and quality which other students probably can not.

This union of 'traditional' and 'communicative' is evident in another book making frequent use of translation exercises, Deller and Rinvolucri's *Using the Mother Tongue* (2002). The emphasis is very much upon fun, interaction, and embodied experience, but the same inevitable focus on form and the use of teacher correction seems to be entailed. Take, for example, the activity called Bilingual Sentence Building, in a section whose overall aim is to make grammar 'less frightening'. (See Figure 5 on page 147.)

Although the *description* of this activity focuses upon its spontaneous physical interactive side, its *execution* is likely to be quite different. If students are not to finish it with wrong ideas about differences between the structure of French and English, then either during or after, they will need specific information and correction about such matters as the order and agreement of adjectives and nouns in the two languages and so forth. The description of the activity in other words deals with the framework, which is 'communicative', but the heart—what most of it will involve—is likely to remain quite 'traditional'.

Activity 59. Film shadowing and translating

Aims

– To practise pre-interpreting skills
– To reflect on the transfer skills needed to translate orally
– To practise speed translation
– To discuss the process of translation

Level

Intermediate or advanced

Grouping

Individual or pairs

Steps

a. A video film or documentary chunked into workable sections (between 5 and 10 minutes the first time this activity is carried out).

b. The students sit looking at the screen. They follow the dialogue silently by moving their lips and repeating *exactly* what is being said in the film (shadowing).

c. Once they have completed step one satisfactorily, they proceed to translate as they watch. This they should also carry out mentally, in silence.

d. The teacher turns up the sound and the students try to translate the dialogue orally but silently, only by moving their lips at the same time as the scene is played. In classes with few students this can be done aloud in pairs.

e. A discussion on what was going on in their minds, the problems they had and on the results of using pre-interpreting skills may follow.

N.B. This is the kind of activity that the students can carry out to develop their competence at home, without the help of the teacher.

Figure 4 A communicative translation activity focusing on fluency: Film shadowing and translating (M. González Davies 2004: 178)

All these writers are right to insist that there is nothing inherently uncommunicative or heartlessly formal in TILT. They show how translation is indeed an authentic, meaning-focused, real-world activity, and as such fits well into communicative paradigms, lending itself as easily to warm-up activities, communicative tasks, and to collaborative feedback, as it does to formal exercises concentrating on accuracy. Yet although fluent, meaningful, authentic language use is the goal of language learning, it is not the only means. Translation can also foster the more 'traditional' perspective that 'communicative' approaches tended to dismiss.

The tension between the 'traditional' and the 'communicative' in these three books and the inclinations of the authors to nail their colours to one mast only, coupled with the fact that they do not entirely practise what they preach, suggests a weakness in the view that old TILT practices

Bilingual Sentence Building

Teacher	working knowledge of students' MT
Class	monolingual
Level	elementary to advanced
Purpose	to make students quickly aware of contrastive grammar

1. Tell the students to stand in a circle. If you have a large class, have two or three circles.
2. Tell them that they will be 'handling' words and phrases round the circle. They pretend the word or phrase they 'pass' to the next person is an object (giving a sense of its weight and temperature, for example). They also say the word loudly and clearly.

If the class MT is French, this is the way the activity might go:

- Student A hands and says a word of their choice to student B: **lapin**
- Student B receives the word and then hands it to student C, translating it: **rabbit**
- Student C receives the word and adds another word: **grey rabbit**
- Student D translates the phrase into MT: **lapin gris**
- Student E adds a word: **viens, lapin gris**
- Student F translates the phrase into English: **come, grey rabbit**
- Student G adds a word: **come here, grey rabbit**
- Student H translates the phrase into French: **viens ici, lapin gris**

3. Get the words and phrases flowing bilingually round the circles. Stop the students before the sentences get too unwieldy, around ten to twelve words long.
4. Put the students into pairs and ask them to reconstruct the bilingual sequence in their notebooks.

NOTE: This is a linguistic spontaneity activity, so you can't pre-plan the sequences

Figure 5 A collaborative translation activity focusing on grammar (Deller and Rinvolucri 2002: 29)

should be entirely 'communicative'. A stronger case might be to see these communicative frames as an addition rather than a replacement. The great strength of TILT is that *unlike* hard-line 'communicative' teaching which struggles to develop declarative knowledge and formal accuracy without abandoning its own principles, the focus of TILT can easily be *both* 'traditional' and 'communicative'. The act of translation can sometimes be used (as, for example, in González Davies' film-shadowing task) to keep students locked into the pressing and immediate flow of communication, but it can also at other times allow a pedagogically complementary detachment, as in Duff's more traditional form-focused activities, in which there is room for more measured reflection, developing declarative knowledge of the relationship between the two languages, of the kind investigated in Chapter 4. While 'communicative' critics of 'traditional' teaching undoubtedly have a point when they say that declarative knowledge is insufficient for fluent communicative competence, this does not mean that teaching should exclude the opportunity to strengthen and deepen such knowledge, and the sense of confidence, order, and satisfaction which its development can give to both students and teachers. The strength of TILT is that it lends itself perfectly to a marriage of the 'traditional' and 'communicative' which has been missing from language teaching for so long and is the cause of so many unproductive swings of fashions. Writers like Duff, González Davies, and Deller and Rinvolucri all demonstrate this union effectively, even when they may be unaware of it. The problem is not the activities themselves—which are all innovative, stimulating, useful, and carefully designed—but the perceived need to disguise their 'traditional' aspects in order to make a case for TILT within the dominant 'communicative' orthodoxy.

Despite this internal theoretical contradiction, all of these books do undoubtedly contain genuinely innovative and stimulating ways to use TILT. Yet more convincing perhaps, and certainly more influential in English language teaching worldwide, have been widely distributed mainstream course materials by major publishers which, without feeling the need to tip their hats at conventional language-teaching orthodoxies, have since the 1990s also begun to integrate translation into activities (Soars and Soars 1986 onwards; Swan and Walter 1990 onwards; Littlejohn and Hicks 1996 onwards). There is always a tension for publishers between the desire for worldwide distribution, which pushes materials away from reference to specific languages, and the necessarily language-specific focus of TILT, which leads towards more localized focus. The need for this latter direction is now acknowledged by institutions with a worldwide, and some might say hegemonic, perspective. Thus the British Council and World Bank have also been working with local teachers in several countries on large-scale textbook projects to produce localized EFL teaching materials (Bolitho 2003). Yet these two apparently opposed directions need no longer be in conflict. Just as this commercial imperative towards homogeneity worked in favour of Direct Method in the days of laborious manual typesetting and industrial printing presses, so the revolution introduced into publishing by computers allows swifter adjustment of electronically stored text and therefore permits greater diversity of materials without affecting profit margins. Thus the means of production continues to influence the ideology of language teaching just as much as it did in the late 19th century.

Types of activity 6: communicative translation

'Traditional' activities have an important role to play as a diagnostic and remedy for gaps in student knowledge and as a way of developing declarative knowledge of the two languages and their relationship. Yet there is much more to translation, and many more ways in which it can be used in the classroom. Translation can also be truly communicative—oriented towards meaning, focusing upon fluency, and honing procedural knowledge in activities in which teacher intervention is minimized and success is measured in terms of achieving a communicative goal, rather than formal accuracy for its own sake.

Suppose, for example, that students are divided into groups, and some members of the group are given a text, or played a recording which they then have to translate for the others, and that this translation is needed for the completion of a communicative task. Success might be measured by completion of the task, and—to make it more enjoyable—by competition between groups to complete the task first. A translation element or stage of this kind could be incorporated into virtually any of the many different task types which have been developed in TBLT. This use of translation involves extensive interaction and negotiation, as the translators in the group will discuss problems together, and the recipients of the translation will ask questions, demand repetitions, and discuss their understanding (or lack of it) together. Once initiated, the teacher need not intervene unless absolutely necessary, though there may be feedback afterwards.

In short, such a use of translation has all the strengths and characteristics of the best communicative meaning-focused tasks, but with an extra dimension. And in the spirit of task-based teaching, it mimics real-world situations. For example, a company entering negotiations with a foreign partner may receive documents and communications which first need translating by its bilingual staff before they can be discussed and actions decided upon by its monolingual staff. Or, on the level of social interaction, a group of diners in a restaurant may first need to have the menu translated for them before they can embark on the task of choosing their food. In court, evidence may need translating before a judgment can be made. All such tasks (business decision-making, social choices, evaluation of evidence) are well established in monolingual teaching, but all can have a translation element introduced.

Types of activity 7: 'sandwiching' as an aid to fluency

One of the many criticisms of TILT is that, by slowing everything down, it is at odds with one of the goals of communicative teaching: fluency. However, although this seems to have logic on its side—translation, after all, roughly doubles the amount of what is said—it can have the opposite effect. By swiftly indicating the meaning of an unknown word or phrase, translation may be used by the teacher to keep things moving and maintain the speed of communication. Butzkamm and Caldwell (2009: 33–35) illustrate this potential through their description of a technique they call 'sandwiching', in which an unknown expression is quickly glossed by the teacher and then repeated, enabling the new expression to be used communicatively, and perhaps even learnt, even though it was not known before:

> German teacher of English: "You've skipped a line. Du hast eine Zeile übersprungen. You've skipped a line...."
> This technique of sandwiching the translation of an unknown expression can be carried out very discreetly in the tone of an aside, as a kind of whispered interpreting. It should be a central technique of any foreign language teacher.
> (Butzkamm and Caldwell 2009: 33)

Their advocacy of sandwiching is part of their more general argument that a structured and principled deployment of the student's own language—as opposed to the chaotic way it tends to appear, despite restrictions, in mono-lingual teaching—can increase rather than decrease the use of the new language for communication.

> paradoxically a targeted yet discreet use of L1 makes it easier to achieve a foreign language atmosphere in the classroom.
> (ibid.)

A similar view is a expressed by Prodromou (2002: 5) in his argument that tolerance of the students' own language(s) actually aids the communicative use of the new one (see also Chapter 3):

> Our strategic objective will continue to be maximum interaction in the target language and the role of the mother tongue will be to enrich the quality and the quantity of that interaction in the classroom, not to restrict or impoverish it.
> (Prodromou 2002: 5).

It is worth noting again (see Chapter 1) that Michel Thomas's highly commer-cially successful language courses also shadow utterance in the new language with translation and explanation in the old.

Sandwiching is, however, in Butzkamm and Caldwell's view, distinct from concurrent translation of everything—a practice which in their view encour-ages an undesirable reliance on the students' own language(s). This is indeed a real danger. Given information in two languages at once, receivers tend to rely automatically upon the language they know better. Own-language subtitles may make someone cease to pay attention to the soundtrack of a film. Parallel texts, in which each page of the original has a translation on the opposite page, tend to be self-defeating, for if the readers become involved in the story, they are likely to end up reading the version in their own language.

Sandwiching is not dissimilar from a number of other bilingual techniques which allow macaronic speech. Students can be allowed for example, as suggested by participants in one ELT teachers' blog[10], to demonstrate their understanding of what the teacher has said by responding in their first language, or speak in their own language to have their words reformulated by the teacher. In one particularly radical proposal (Giauque and Ely 1990, discussed in V. Cook 2001a), beginner students are allowed to mix words from their first language into utterances in the language they are learning, producing such hybrid creations as:

Je am having difficulté with this learning activité.

The idea is that the proportion of their own language will decrease as knowledge of the new language increases. A similar suggestion is made by Celik (2003) with regard to the teaching of vocabulary through code-mixing. Students are first told a story in the new language (English) in which targeted words are inserted in their own language (Turkish). There is, as Celik remarks, nothing artificial or inauthentic about this; it is after all 'a common occurrence in bilingual or immigrant communities'. Thus the story used in his study contains lines such as the following:

> However, there is another problem. It is to do with police officers. You see, they are very *müsamahakar* towards drivers. They tend to let them go when they break traffic rules.

Students were then guided towards replacing these with the correct English words in subsequent discussion and writing.

Types of activity 8: TILT in mixed-language classes

We come now to the question of whether TILT can be used at all in mixed-language classes, and if so how. At first glance it might seem that it cannot and that this is therefore a major limitation to TILT.

The problems are not, however, as fatal to an advocacy of TILT as might appear—for two reasons. Firstly, although they are undoubtedly an issue within the English-speaking countries, where mixed-language classes are common, they are by no means the default situation. Worldwide, the majority of language teaching still takes places in single-language classes conducted by bilingual teachers who are themselves native speakers of the students' language and former learners of the language they are teaching. Secondly, it is not the case that TILT has no place at all in mixed-language classes. Though it cannot be used in all the ways possible in a single-language class—as a teaching, diagnostic, or corrective tool—it is possible nevertheless.

- Pair or group work involving translation may be possible in a class where each language has more than one representative. Students who share the same language can be encouraged to translate to and for each other.
- Students can be encouraged to reflect upon and explain translation problems they encounter (even though the teacher may not be able to verify them).

- Students may be asked to bring in short significant texts or recordings (appropriate to their level) from their own language and translate them for the class—a truly communicative task which will also help to establish a link between their own and their new language identities.
- Students can be encouraged to make use of bilingual resources both inside and outside the classroom, such as bilingual dictionaries and subtitled films. They can also take advantage of online resources, for example, joining a blog in which speakers of their own language share experiences and insights into the new language, including discussion of translation (as we saw in the blog discussion cited earlier).

All these activities will have limitations and cannot form a staple part of procedures, as TILT does for the bilingual teacher in the single-language class. Nevertheless they help to establish the presence and relevance of the own language, and the importance of translation in real-world bilingual language use.

Types of activity 9: TILT for teachers who do not speak their students' language(s)

Similar practical problems arise in the use of TILT for the teacher in a single-language classroom who does not share their students' own language. A key difference however, is that such teachers are often working in institutions where there are also bilingual teachers who *can* use TILT. (An exception to this is those private language schools with single-language classes which recruit only native-speaker teachers and have a largely itinerant staff.) Sadly however, in contexts where there are both types of teacher, they often work separately. The Direct Method myth of the superiority of the native-speaker teacher has created a deep tension and mistrust, and an unwillingness on both sides to collaborate. Monolingual native speakers often feel excluded from the lessons where translation is being used; bilingual local teachers feel reluctant to venture into the native-speaker's lessons in case their own proficiency is called into question. (As pointed out before there are of course many exceptions to both these categories: native-speaker teachers who are also bilingual in their students' language, non-native-speakers with an expert command of the language they teach.) Perceived differences very often lead to a tacit division of labour. Native-speaker teachers tend to deal with fluency, conversation, idioms, and cultural context; non-native teachers with the 'nuts and bolts' of grammar, reading, and writing. Some breaking down of this rigidity, acknowledgement of difference rather than a quest for superiority, and recognition that both bilingual and monolingual teaching have a role to play in a rounded language course, might enable this mutual suspicion to be replaced by a dynamic collaboration between two styles of teaching—the one using code-switching and translation, the other conducting the lesson monolingually, so that those aspects of language teaching which are best dealt with by translation are handled in one type of lesson, and those best dealt with by Direct Method in the other. Yet this need not mean that the monolingual teacher cannot consult the expertise of the bilingual where necessary, or that the non-native speaker should somehow steer clear of working on the less mechanical aspects of language learning. Native monolingual and non-native bilingual working in the same institutions could treat each others' expertise as an invaluable resource to be called upon as much as possible. They might even teach together, if circumstances permit.

Meanwhile those teachers who have transcended these categories (the native speakers who are fluent in their students' language(s) and the non-native-speakers who have acquired such expertise in the language they teach that it calls into question the very definition of 'nativeness' and the assumption that natives always know the language best) would have a particular and highly deserved authority—an authority which has been consistently undervalued in monolingualist regimes where bilingualism is simply not considered an asset.

Notes

1 Doyouspeak.com (accessed August 2009).
2 http://www.avatarlanguages.com/requirements.php (accessed August 2009).
3 http://www.rosettastone.co.uk/personal/how-it-works (accessed August 2009).
4 Arabic *in-shâa* is in fact the past tense, though it may refer to the present. (Khalid Al-Balushi, personal communication)
5 See also Butzkamm and Caldwell 2009: 52.
6 This edited version of the quotation is from Thomas 1976.
7 Apart from the first one, the examples are my own, not from González Davies.
8 Subtitle sequence from Sau Leung Ko's *Curry and Pepper* (1990), quoted in David Parkinson 'Ask Parky: Lost in translation' *Guardian* Wednesday, 19 November 2008.
9 Although 'time', it could be claimed, is a notion rather than a form.
10 IATEFL Literature, Media and Cultural Studies Special Interest Group http://groups.yahoo.com/group/LMCSSig/

Conclusion

The purpose of this book has been twofold. One aim has been to show the weakness of exclusively monolingual language teaching—that the reasons behind it are more commercial and political than scientific, that it is supported only by selective evidence and shaky reasoning, and that it disregards learner and teacher needs. A second aim has been to show that translation has an important role to play in language learning—that it develops both language awareness and use, that it is pedagogically effective and educationally desirable, and that it answers student needs in the contemporary globalized and multicultural world.

There are times in history when a reigning power which seemed to be both secure and permanent proves suddenly to be both insecure and ephemeral. In the 20th century, for example, the power of the Soviet Union was of this kind. Almost until its collapse, it seemed an unshakeable feature of the political landscape. Yet as things turned out, it did not even outlast the century in which it began. Now, in retrospect and from the standpoint of the 21st century, it increasingly appears no more than a brief and curious historical interlude.

Academic and educational history displays similar phenomena. The idea that a language should be taught monolingually and without recourse to translation may prove to be of this kind—a power which reigned unquestioned in the 20th century, but will seem increasingly curious as we move into the future. When time has elapsed, this may not seem surprising. Like short-lived political movements, monolingual language teaching attempted to ignore and override the inclinations and wishes of the very people it was supposed to benefit. It was grounded in theory but not reality, and it ran counter to stronger imperatives than its own. Humans teach and learn by moving from the familiar to the unfamiliar, by building new knowledge onto existing knowledge. Language learning and teaching are no exception to this general rule. Translation is just such a bridge between the familiar and the unfamiliar, the known and the unknown. To burn that bridge or to pretend that it does not exist, hinders rather than helps the difficult transition which is the aim of language teaching and learning. Learners moreover need that bridge to maintain the links between their languages and identities. They should never be forced to leave everything behind them, simply because they are speaking another language.

These are powerful forces in favour of translation, and have made monolingualism insecure from the outset. A relentless propaganda campaign has been needed to make teachers and learners keep away from translation, but the results of that campaign have not been entirely successful. There has been a dislocation between theory and practice, or (to put it in more human terms) between theorists and practitioners. Some teachers and learners have been seriously disturbed and disoriented by the theorists' diktat never to translate. For others there has been a kind of schizophrenic accommodation between the party line and reality. They have continued to translate while simultaneously denying that they do, and arguing that it is wrong. Some teachers have talked of any use of the students' own language as a kind of professional misconduct (Mitchell 1988: 28). Yet as the weaknesses of monolingualism and the absence of any convincing reason not to use translation become apparent, teachers' allegiance to monolingualism often evaporates too. A reinstatement of TILT in theory as well as practice has the potential to bring the voices of applied linguistic theorists and language teachers closer together and to encourage each to listen more to the other. It could help to end the rather authoritarian tone of much applied linguistics theorizing in the monolinguistic mould. It could usher in a more reasoned and historically contextualized approach to translation which would do a great deal to restore the authority—as opposed to the authoritarianism—of theory.

In contrast to the exclusive dismissal of TILT by Direct Method theorists in the past, the view in this book has been that both bilingual explanation and translation, and periods of monolingual practice have a role to play. What is needed is not another lurch of fashion from one extreme to another, but a symbiosis in which students can benefit from varying and complementary strategies. Only this would bring to an end the unproductive sense of division, and heal the self-inflicted wound of Direct Method dogmatism.

This book has set out an argument for change, but a great deal remains to be done before TILT can be rehabilitated and developed in the way that it deserves. The insidious association of TILT with dull and authoritarian Grammar Translation, combined with the insinuation that Grammar Translation had nothing good in it at all, has lodged itself so deeply in the collective consciousness of the language-teaching profession, that it is difficult to prise it out at all, and it has hardly moved for a hundred years. The result has been an arid period in the use and development of TILT, and serious detriment to language teaching as a whole. If the benefits of TILT were to be recognized in theory as well as practice by those in positions of power and influence as well as by rank-and-file teachers, it would have positive repercussions, and would initiate activity and innovation in many areas beyond classroom practice itself. New materials would need to be written, new tests designed, and new elements introduced into teacher education. New applied linguistic research would be needed too, on the theory, practice, and effect of TILT—areas of enquiry so spectacularly lacking in recent decades.

Bibliography

Adendorff, R. D. 1996. 'The functions of code switching among high school teachers and students in KwaZulu and implications for teacher education' in K. M. Bailey and D. Nunan (eds.): *Voices from the Classroom. Qualitative research in second language learning.* Cambridge: Cambridge University Press.

Al-Balushi, K. 2007. *Teaching English language through literary translation in Oman.* Unpublished PhD thesis: University of Nottingham.

Allen J. P. B. 1983. 'General purpose language teaching: a variable focus approach' in C. J. Brumfit (ed.): *General English Syllabus Design. ELT Documents No. 118.* London: Pergamon Press and The British Council.

Althusser, L. 1971. *Lenin and Philosophy and Other Essays* (trans. B. Brewster). London: New Left Books.

Angiolillo, P. F. 1947. *Armed Forces' Foreign Language Teaching. Critical Evaluation and Implications.* New York: Vanni.

Anthony, E. 1963. 'Approach, method and technique.' *English Language Teaching Journal* 17 (2): 63–67.

Arthur, J. A. 1996. 'Code switching and collusion: classroom interaction in Botswana primary school.' *Linguistics and Education* 8 (1): 17–33.

Asher, J. 1977. *Learning Another Language Through Actions: The Complete Teacher's Guidebook.* Los Gatos, CA: Sky Oaks.

Atkinson, D. 1987. 'The mother tongue in the classroom: a neglected discourse.' *English Language Teaching Journal* 41 (4): 241–247.

Auerbach, E. 1993. 'Reexamining English Only in the classroom.' *TESOL Quarterly* 27 (1): 9–32.

Austin, J. L. 1962. *How to Do Things with Words.* Oxford: Clarendon Press.

Baker, A. 2008. 'Special report: the bigger picture.' *Language Travel Magazine* November 2008.

Baker, C. and **S. Prys Jones.** 1998. 'Types of bilingual family' in C.E. Snow, C. Baker, and S. Prys Jones (eds.): *Encyclopaedia of Bilingualism and Bilingual Education* 28–36. Clevedon: Multilingual Matters.

Baker, M. 1992. *In Other Words.* London: Routledge.

—— 2007. 'Reframing conflict in translation.' *Social Semiotics* 17 (2): 151–169.

—— and **L. Pérez-González** (forthcoming). 'Translation and interpretation' in J. Simpson (ed.): *The Routledge Handbook of Applied Linguistics.* London: Routledge.

Baker, P. and **J. Eversley** (eds.). 2000. *Multilingual Capital: The Languages of London's Schoolchildren.* London: Corporation of London.

—— and **Y. Mohieldeen.** 2000. 'The languages of London's schoolchildren' in P. Baker and J. Eversley (eds.): *Multilingual Capital: The Languages of London's Schoolchildren* 5–60. London: Corporation of London.

Ball, A. F. and **S. Warshauer Freedman** (eds.). 2004. *Bakhtinian Perspectives on Language, Literacy, and Learning.* Cambridge: Cambridge University Press.

Barnard, T. C. 1975. *Cromwellian Ireland.* Oxford: Oxford University Press.

Bassnett, S. 1980 (revised edn. 1991). *Translation Studies.* London: Routledge.

Bates, E., W. Kintsch, C. R. Fletcher, and **V. Giulani.** 1980. 'The role of pronominalisation and ellipsis in texts: some memorisation experiments.' *Journal of Experimental Psychology: Human Learning and Memory* 6: 676–691.

Baynham, M. 1983. 'Mother tongue materials and second language literacy.' *English Language Teaching Journal* 37 (4): 312–318.

Bell, R. 1991. *Translation and Translating: Theory and Practice*. London: Longman.

Benson, M. J. 2000. 'The secret life of grammar-translation' in H. Trappes-Lomax (ed.): *Change and Continuity in Applied Linguistics*: 35–51. Clevedon: Multilingual Matters.

Benwell, B. and E. Stokoe. 2006. *Discourse and Identity*. Edinburgh: Edinburgh University Press.

Bhatia, T. 1992. 'Discourse functions and pragmatics of mixing: advertising across cultures.' *World Englishes* 11 (2): 195–215.

Bialystok E., F. Craik, C. Grady, W. Chau, R. Ishii, and A. Gunji. 2005. 'Effect of bilingualism on cognitive control in the Simon task: evidence from MEG.' *NeuroImage* 24: 40–49.

——, F. Craik, and M. Freedman. 2007. 'Bilingualism as a protection against the onset of symptoms of dementia.' *Neuropsychologia* 45: 459–64.

—— and X. Feng. 2009. 'Language proficiency and executive control in proactive interference: evidence from monolingual and bilingual children and adults.' *Brain and Language*. 109 (2–3): 93–100.

Bitchener, J. and U. Knoch (forthcoming). 'The contribution of written corrective feedback to language development: a ten month investigation.' *Applied Linguistics*.

Block, D. 2003a. *The Social Turn in Second Language Acquisition*. Edinburgh: Edinburgh University Press.

—— 2003b. 'Review of Michel Thomas's language courses.' *Language Learning Journal* 27: 74–8.

—— 2006. *Multilingual Identities in a Global City: London Stories*. Basingstoke and New York: Palgrave Macmillan.

—— 2007. *Second Language Identities*. London: Continuum.

—— 2008. 'On the appropriateness of the metaphor of LOSS' in R. Rubdy and P. Tan (eds.): *Language as Commodity: Global Structures, Local Marketplaces* 187–203. London: Continuum.

—— and D. Cameron. 2002a. 'Introduction' in D. Block and D. Cameron (eds.): 1–11.

—— and D. Cameron (eds.). 2002b. *Globalization and Language Teaching*. London: Routledge.

Bloomfield, L. 1935. *Language*. London: George, Allen and Unwin.

Blunkett, D. 2002. 'What does citizenship mean today?' *The Observer* September 15, 2002.

Bolitho, R. 2003. 'Designing textbooks for modern languages: the EFL experience.' *Center for Languages, Linguistics and Area Studies* available at http://www.llas.ac.uk/resources/gpg/1470.

Bourdieu, P. 1977. *Outline of a Theory of Practice* (trans. R. Nice). Cambridge: Cambridge University Press.

—— 1991. *Language and Symbolic Power* (trans. G. Raymond and M. Adamson). Cambridge, MA: Harvard University Press.

Braine, G. (ed.). 1999. *Non-Native Educators in English Language Teaching*. London: Lawrence Erlbaum.

Breen, M. P. 1984. 'Process syllabuses for the language classroom' in C. J. Brumfit (ed.): *General English Syllabus Design. ELT Documents No. 118*: 47–60. London: Pergamon Press and The British Council.

—— 1987. 'Learner contributions to task design' in C. Candlin and D. Murphy (eds.): *Language Learning Tasks* 23–46. Eaglewood Cliffs NJ: Prentice Hall.

Brooks-Lewis, K. A. 2007. *The significance of culture in language learning: working with adult EFL learners in Mexico*. Unpublished PhD thesis: University of Kent at Canterbury.

—— 2009. 'Adult learners' perceptions of the incorporation of their L1 in foreign language teaching and learning.' *Applied Linguistics* 30 (2): 216–235.

Brown, R. 1973. *A First Language: The Early Stages*. London: Allen and Unwin.

Brumfit, C. J. 1984. *Communicative Methodology in Language Teaching: The Roles of Fluency and Accuracy*. Cambridge: Cambridge University Press.

—— 2001. *Individual Freedom in Language Teaching*. Oxford: Oxford University Press.

—— and **Johnson, K.** (eds.). 1979. *The Communicative Approach to Language Teaching*. Oxford: Oxford University Press.

Butzkamm, W. 2001. 'Learning the language of loved ones: on the generative principle and the technique of mirroring.' *English Language Teaching Journal* 55(2): 149–154.

—— 2003. 'We only learn language once. The role of the mother tongue in FL classrooms: death of a dogma.' *Language Learning Journal* 2003 (28): 29–39.

—— and **J. A. W. Caldwell.** 2009. *The Bilingual Reform: A Paradigm Shift in Foreign Language Teaching*. Tübingen: Narr Studienbücher.

Bygate, M., P. Skehan, and **M. Swain** (eds.). 2001. *Researching Pedagogic Tasks: Language Learning, Teaching and Testing*. London: Longman.

—— and **V. Samuda.** 2005. 'Integrative planning through the use of task repetition' in R. Ellis (ed.): *Planning and Task Performance in a Second Language* 37–74. Amsterdam: John Benjamins.

Caldas-Coulthard, C. R. and **R. Iedema** (eds.). 2008. *Identity Trouble: Critical Discourse and Contested Identities*. London: Palgrave Macmillan.

Cameron, A. and **C. Jones** 1901. *The Cat Sat on the Mat*. New York: Angus and Robertson.

Cameron, D. 2000. *Good to Talk? Living and Working in a Communication Culture*. London: Sage.

Camilleri, A. 1996. 'Language values and identities: code-switching in secondary classrooms in Malta.' *Linguistics and Education* 8 (1): 85–103.

Campbell, S. 1998. *Translation into the Second Language*. New York: Addison Wesley Longman.

Canagarajah, A. S. 1999. *Resisting Linguistic Imperialism in English Teaching*. Oxford: Oxford University Press.

Candlin, C. 1984. 'Syllabus design as a critical process' in C. J. Brumfit (ed.): *General English Syllabus Design. ELT Documents 118*: 29–46. Oxford: Pergamon Press and the British Council.

—— 1987. 'Towards Task-based Learning' in C. Candlin and D. Murphy (eds.): *Language Learning Tasks*. Eaglewood Cliffs NJ: Prentice Hall.

Carter, B. and **A. Sealey.** 2007. 'Languages, nations and identities' available at http://erdt. plymouth.ac.uk/mionline/public_html/viewarticle.php?id=58&layout=html

Carter, R. and **D. Nunan** (eds.). 2001. *The Cambridge Guide to Teaching English to Speakers of Other Languages*. Cambridge: Cambridge University Press.

Catford, J. C. 1965. *A Linguistic Theory of Translation*. London: Oxford University Press.

Celik, M. 2003. 'Teaching vocabulary through code-mixing.' *English Language Teaching Journal* 57 (4): 361–9.

Chaterjee, P. 2006. 'A translator's tale.' Corpwatch. http://www.corpwatch.org/article. php?id=13992

Chernov, G. 1992. 'Message redundancy and message anticipation in simultaneous interpretation' in S. Lambert and B. Moser-Mercer (eds.): *Bridging the Gap: Empirical Research in Simultaneous Interpretation* 139–153. Philadelphia: John Benjamins.

China Education and Research Network. 2001. *Basic education curriculum reform (trial)* http://www.edu.cn/20010926/3002911.shtml.

Clark, E. L. and **A. Paran.** 2007. 'The employability of non-native-speaker teachers of EFL: A UK survey.' *System* 35 (4): 407–430.

Clark, J. 1987. *Curriculum Renewal in School Foreign Language Learning*. Oxford: Oxford University Press.

Cohen, A. D. and **S. Hawras.** 1996. 'Mental translation into the first language during foreign-language reading.' *The Language Teacher* 20 (2): 6–12.

Cook, G. 1989. *Discourse*. Oxford: Oxford University Press.

—— 1991. 'Indeterminacy, translation and the expert speaker.' *Triangle 10* (Proceedings of the 10th British Council/ Goethe Institute/ Ens-Crédif Triangle Colloquium): 127–141: Paris: Didier.

—— 1994. 'Repetition and knowing by heart: an aspect of intimate discourse.' *English Language Teaching Journal* 48 (2): 133–142.

—— 1997. 'Translation and language teaching' in M. Baker (ed.): *The Routledge Dictionary of Translation Studies* 117–120. London: Routledge (revised edn. 'Foreign language teaching' in 2009 (2nd edn.) M. Baker and G. Saldanha (eds.): 112–115).

—— 2000. *Language Play, Language Learning*. Oxford: Oxford University Press.

—— 2001a. ' "The philosopher pulled the lower jaw of the hen": ludicrous invented sentences in language teaching.' *Applied Linguistics*. 22 (3): 366–387.

—— 2001b. *The Discourse of Advertising* (2nd edn.). London: Routledge.

—— 2003. *Applied Linguistics*. Oxford: Oxford University Press.

—— 2005. 'Calm seas or troubled waters? Transitions, definitions and disagreements in applied linguistics.' *International Journal of Applied Linguistics* 15/3: 282–302.

—— 2007a. ' "This we have done". The different vagueness of poetry and PR' in J. Cutting (ed.): *Vague Language Explored* 21–40. London: Palgrave Macmillan.

—— 2007b. 'A thing of the future: translation in language learning.' *International Journal of Applied Linguistics* 17/3: 396–401.

—— 2008a. 'Advertising and public relations' in V. Koller and R. Wodak (eds.): *Handbook of Applied Linguistics Volume 3: Language and Communication in the Public Sphere* 113–138. Berlin and New York: Mouton de Gruyter.

—— 2008b. 'Plenary: an unmarked improvement: using translation in ELT' in B. Beaven (ed.): *IATEFL 2007 Aberdeen Conference Selections*: 76–86. University of Kent: IATEFL.

—— 2009. 'The Best Teacher' in R. Bhanot and E. Illes (eds.): *Best of Language Issues* 245–253. London: London South Bank University.

Cook, V. 2001a. 'Using the first language in the classroom.' *Canadian Modern Language Review* 57 (3): 399–423.

—— 2001b. *Second Language Teaching and Learning* (3rd edn.). London: Arnold.

—— 2002. 'The functions of invented sentences: a reply to Guy Cook,' *Applied Linguistics* 23 (2): 263–272.

—— and **M. Newson**. 1996. *Chomsky's Universal Grammar: An Introduction*. Oxford: Blackwell.

Cooke, M. and J. Simpson. 2008. *ESOL: A Critical Guide*. Oxford: Oxford University Press.

Copeland, R. 1995. *Rhetoric, Hermeneutics and Translation in the Middle Ages: Academic Traditions and Vernacular Texts*. Cambridge: Cambridge University Press.

Corder, S. P. 1967. 'The significance of learners' errors.' *International Review of Applied Linguistics* 4: 161–170.

—— 1973. *Introducing Applied Linguistics*. Harmondsworth: Penguin.

Coulmas, F. (ed.). 1981. *A Festschrift for Native Speaker*. The Hague, New York: Mouton.

Creese, A. 2008. 'Linguistic ethnography' in K. A. King and N. H. Hornberger (eds.): *Encyclopedia of Language and Education* (2nd edn.). *Volume 10: Research Methods in Language and Education*: 229–241. New York: Springer Science+Business Media LLC.

Cromdal, J. 2005. 'Bilingual order in collaborative word processing: on creating an English text in Sweden.' *Journal of Pragmatics* 37 (3): 329–353.

Crystal, D. 1986. *Listen to Your Child: A Parent's Guide to Children's Language*. Harmondsworth: Penguin.

—— 1997. *The Cambridge Encyclopaedia of Language* (2nd edn.). Cambridge: Cambridge University Press.

—— 2000a. 'On trying to be Crystal-clear: a response to Phillipson.' *Applied Linguistics* 21 (3): 415–423.

—— 2000b. *Language Death*. Cambridge: Cambridge University Press.

—— 2003. *English as a Global Language*. Cambridge: Cambridge University Press.

Cummins, J. 2007. 'Rethinking monolingual instructional strategies in multilingual classrooms.' *Canadian Journal of Applied Linguistics* 10 (2) 221–240.

Curran, C. A. 1976. *Counseling Learning in Second Languages*. Apple River, IL: Apple River Press.

Dalton-Puffer, C. 2007. *Discourse in Content and Language Integrated Learning (CLIL) Classrooms*. Amsterdam: John Benjamins.

Daro, V. 1990. 'Speaking speed during simultaneous interpretation: a discussion of its neuropsychological aspects and possible contributions to teaching' in L. Gran and C. Taylor (eds.): *Aspects of Applied and Experimental Research on Conference Interpretation* 83–92. Udine, Italia: Campanotta Editore.

Davies, A. 1995. 'Proficiency or the native speaker: what are we trying to achieve in ELT?' in G. Cook and B. Seidlhofer (eds.): *Principle and Practice in Applied Linguistics* 145–159. Oxford: Oxford University Press.

—— 2003. *The Native Speaker: Myth and Reality*. Clevedon: Multilingual Matters.

De Fina, A. 2003. *Identity in Narrative: A Study of Immigrant Discourse*. Amsterdam: John Benjamins.

——, D. Schiffrin, and M. Bamberg (eds.). 2006. *Discourse and Identity*. Cambridge: Cambridge University Press.

Deller, S. and M. Rinvolucri. 2002. *Using the Mother Tongue*. London: English Teaching Professional, Delta Publishing.

Dil, A. S. 1992. 'Urdu' in W. Bright (ed.): *International Encyclopaedia of Linguistics. Volume* 4: 210–212. New York, Oxford: Oxford University Press.

di Pietro, R. 1971. *Language Structures in Contrast*. Rowley, MA: Newbury House.

Dixon, R. M. W. 1980. *The Languages of Australia*. Cambridge: Cambridge University Press.

Dörnyei, Z., K. Csizér, and N. Németh. 2006. *Motivation, Language Attitudes and Globalisation: A Hungarian Perspective*. Clevedon: Multilingual Matters.

Dörnyei, Z. and T. Murphey. 2003. *Group Dynamics in the Language Classroom*. Cambridge: Cambridge University Press.

—— and E. Ushioda (eds.). 2009. *Motivation, Language Identity and the L2 Self*. Clevedon: Multilingual Matters.

Dostert, L. 1955. 'The Georgetown-IBM experiment' in W. N. Locke and A. D. Booth (eds.): *Machine Translation of Languages* 124–135. New York London: MIT Press and John Wiley.

Duff, A. 1989. *Translation*. Oxford: Oxford University Press.

Dulay, H. and M. Burt. 1973. 'Should we teach children syntax?' *Language Learning* 23 (2): 245–258.

—— and M. Burt 1974. 'Natural sequences in child language acquisition.' *Language Learning* 24 (1): 37–53.

—— and M. Burt 1975. 'Creative construction in second language learning and teaching' in M. Burt and H. Dulay (eds.): *New Directions in Second Language Learning, Teaching, and Bilingual Education* 21–32. Washington, DC: TESOL.

Edge, J. (ed.). 2006. *(Re-)locating TESOL in an Age of Empire*. London: Palgrave Macmillan.

Edstrom, A. 2006. 'L1 use in the L2 classroom: one teacher's self-evaluation.' *The Canadian Modern Language Review* 63 (2): 275–292.

Ellis, N. and D. Larsen-Freeman. 2006. 'Language emergence: implications for applied linguistics.' Introduction to the special issue. *Applied Linguistics* 27 (4): 558–590.

—— and —— (guest eds.). 2006. Special issue: 'Language Emergence.' *Applied Linguistics* 27(4).

Ellis, R. 1985. *Understanding Second Language Acquisition*. Oxford: Oxford University Press.

—— 1993. (1st edn.). *The Study of Second Language Acquisition*. Oxford: Oxford University Press.

—— 2003. *Task-based Language Learning and Teaching*. Oxford: Oxford University Press.

—— 2008. (2nd edn.). *The Study of Second Language Acquisition*. Oxford: Oxford University Press.

Fabrício, B. and D. Santos 2006. '(Re-)locating TEFL: the (re)framing process as a collaborative locus for change' in J. Edge (ed.): *(Re-)Locating TESOL in an Age of Empire* 65–83. London: Palgrave Macmillan.

Fairclough, N. 1989. (1st edn.). *Language and Power*. London: Longman.

—— 2006. *Language and Globalization*. London: Routledge.

Feinsilver, L. M. 1962. 'Yiddish Idioms in American English.' *American Speech*. 37 (3): 200–206.

Fennell, J. L. I. 1961. *The Penguin Russian Course*. Harmondsworth, Penguin.

Ferguson, G. 2003. 'Classroom code-switching in post-colonial contexts: functions, attitudes and policies.' *AILA Review* 16: 38–51.

Fillmore, C. J. 1992. 'Pronouns' in W. Bright (ed.): *International Encyclopaedia of Linguistics Volume* 3: 281–284. New York, Oxford: Oxford University Press.

Firth, J. R. 1957. *Papers in Linguistics 1934–1951*. London: Oxford University Press.

—— 1968. *Selected Papers of J. R. Firth* (F. R. Palmer ed.). London and Harlow: Longman.

Fisiak, J. (ed.) 1981. *Contrastive Linguistics and the Language Teacher*. Oxford: Pergamon.

Fries, C. C. 1945. *Teaching and Learning English as a Foreign Language*. Ann Arbor: University of Michigan Press.

Giauque, G. S. and C. M. Ely. 1990. 'Code-switching in beginning foreign language teaching' in R. Jacobson and C. Faltis (eds.): *Language Distribution Issues in Bilingual Schooling* 174–184. Clevedon: Multilingual Matters.

González Davies, M. 2004. *Multiple Voices in the Translation Classroom: Activities, Tasks and Projects*. Amsterdam: John Benjamins.

Graddol, D. 2007. 'English next: why global English may mean the end of "English as a Foreign Language"'. British Council, available at http://www.britishcouncil.org/learning-research-english-next.pdf

Granger, S. 2002. 'A bird's-eye view of learner corpus research' in S. Granger, J. Hung, and S. Petch-Tyson (eds.): *Computer Learner Corpora, Second Language Acquisition and Foreign Language Teaching* 3–33. Philadelphia: John Benjamins.

Gray, J. 2002. 'The global coursebook in English language teaching' in D. Block and D. Cameron (eds.): *Globalization and Language Teaching*. New York: Routledge.

Gregg, K. 1984. 'Krashen's monitor and Occam's razor.' *Applied Linguistics* 5 (2): 79–100.

Green, J. F. 1970. 'The use of the mother tongue and the teaching of translation.' *English Language Teaching* 24 (3).

Greenberg, R. D. 2004. *Language and Identity in the Balkans: Serbo-Croatian and Its Disintegration*. New York: Oxford University Press.

Grenfell, M. (ed.). 2002. *Modern Languages Across the Curriculum*. London: Routledge.

Guizot, F. P. G. 1821. *Oeuvres complètes de Shakespeare*. Volume 8. Paris: Didier.

Halliday, M. A. K. 1976. *System and Function in Language* (ed. G. Kress). Oxford: Oxford University Press.

—— 2007. *The Collected Works of M. A. K. Halliday* (10 volumes, ed. J. Webster). London: Continuum.

Harmer, J. 2007. *The Practice of English Language Teaching* (4th edn.). London: Longman Pearson.

Harris, R. 1998. *Introduction to Integrational Linguistics*. Oxford: Pergamon.

Hatim, B. and I. Mason. 1990. *Discourse and the Translator*. London: Longman.

He, Q. 2000. 'English language education in China' in S. J. Baker (ed.): *Language Policy: Lessons from Global Models* 225–31. Monterey, CA: Monterey Institute of International Studies.

Hedge, T. 2000. *Teaching and Learning in the Language Classroom*. Oxford: Oxford University Press.

Hewitt, B. G. 1992. 'Caucasian languages' in W. Bright (ed.): *International Encyclopaedia of Linguistics Volume* 1: 220–227. New York, Oxford: Oxford University Press.

Hickey, R. 2007. *Irish English: History and Present-day Forms*. Cambridge: Cambridge University Press.

Hobbs, V., A. Matsuo, and M. Payne. 'Code-switching in Japanese language classrooms: An exploratory investigation of native vs. non-native speaker teacher practice.' *Linguistics and Education* (forthcoming).

Hoey, M. 2005. *Lexical Priming: A New Theory of Words and Language*. London: Routledge.

Horst, M., T. Cobb, and H. Nicolae. 2005. 'Expanding academic vocabulary with an interactive on-line database.' *Language Learning and Technology* 9 (2): 90–110.

House, J. 1977. *A Model for Translation Quality Assessment*. Tübingen: Gunter Narr.

—— 1997. *Translation Quality Assessment: A Model Revisited*. Tübingen: Gunter Narr.

Howatt, A. P. R. 1984. (1st edn.) *A History of English Language Teaching*. Oxford: Oxford University Press.

—— with **H. G. Widdowson**. 2004. (2nd edn.) *A History of English Language Teaching*. Oxford: Oxford University Press.

Howells, G. 2009 'Learning, translating and teaching language: cultural resonance, individual research and the contribution of information technology' in A. Witte, T. Harden, and A. Ramos de Oliveira Harden (eds.): *Translation in Second Language Teaching and Learning* 163–180. Frankfurt: Peter Lang.

Hu, G. 2004. 'Translator-centeredness.' *Perspectives: Studies in Translatology* 12 (2): 106–117.

Hummel, K. M. 1995. 'Translation and second language learning.' *Canadian Modern Language Review* 51 (3): 444–455.

Hymes, D. 1972. 'On communicative competence' in. J. B. Pride and J. Holmes (eds.): *Sociolinguistics*. Harmondsworth, Penguin.

ITTO (International Teacher Training Organization). 2009. 'Using L1 in the TEFL classroom' available at http://www.teflcertificatecourses.com/tefl-articles/L1-teflclassroom.php

Ioup, G., E. Boustagui, M. El Tigi, and M. Moselle. 1994. 'Reexamining the critical period hypothesis: a case study in a naturalistic environment.' *Studies in Second Language Acquisition* 16 (1): 73–98.

Jakobson, R. 1959. 'Linguistic Aspects of Translation' in R. A. Brower (ed.): *On Translation*. Cambridge, MA: Harvard University Press.

—— 1960. 'Closing statement: linguistics and poetics' in T. A. Sebeok (ed.): *Style in Language* 350–377. Cambridge, MA: MIT Press.

James, C. 1980. *Contrastive Analysis*. London: Longman.

Jenkins, J. 2000. *The Phonology of English as an International Language*. Oxford: Oxford University Press.

—— 2007. *English as a Lingua Franca: Attitude and Identity*. Oxford: Oxford University Press.

Jibraa, M. J. 1986 (*The Sonnets*). Iraq: Maktabat Ash Sharq Al Awsat.

Johnson, D. C. 2009. 'The relationship between applied linguistic research and language policy for bilingual education.' *Applied Linguistics* 30 (3) (forthcoming).

Johnson, K. 1996. *Language Teaching and Skill Learning*. Oxford: Blackwell.

—— 1998. 'Curriculum' and 'Syllabus' in K. Johnson and H. Johnson (eds.): *The Encyclopaedic Dictionary of Applied Linguistics*: 93 and 312. Oxford: Blackwell.

—— 2001. *An Introduction to Foreign Language Teaching and Learning*. London: Longman.

—— and **K. Morrow.** 1979. *Communicate*. Cambridge: Cambridge University Press.

Jordan, C. 1970. *Cotton Patch Version of Matthew and John*. El Monte, CA: New Win Publishing.

Joseph, J. E. 2004. *Language and Identity: National, Ethnic, Religious*. Basingstoke: Palgrave Macmillan.

Kachru, B. 1985. 'Standards, codification and sociolinguistic realism: the English language in the Outer Circle' in R. Quirk and H. G. Widdowson (eds.): *English in the World: Teaching and Learning the Language and Literatures*: 11–30. Cambridge: Cambridge University Press.

—— 1995. 'Transcultural creativity in world Englishes and literary canons' in G. Cook and B. Seidlhofer (eds.): *Principle and Practice in Applied Linguistics* 271–289. Oxford: Oxford University Press.

Källkvist, M. 2004. 'The effect of translation exercises versus gap exercises on the learning of difficult L2 structures. Preliminary results of an empirical study' in K. Malmkjær (ed.): *Translation in Undergraduate Degree Programmes* 173–184. Philadelphia, PA: John Benjamins.

—— 2008. 'L1–L2 translation versus no translation: a longitudinal study of focus-on-formS within a meaning-focused curriculum' in L. Ortega and H. Byrnes (eds.): *The Longitudinal Study of Advanced L2 Capacities*. London: Routledge.

Kaneko, T. 1992. *The role of the first language in foreign language classrooms*. Unpublished PhD thesis: Temple University, Japan.

Kanno, Y. 2003. *Negotiating Bilingual and Bicultural Identities: Japanese Returnees Betwixt Two Worlds*. London: Lawrence Erlbaum.

Keenan, J. M., B. MacWhinney, and D. Mayhew. 1977. 'Pragmatics in memory: a study of natural conversation.' *Journal of Verbal Learning and Verbal Behaviour* 16: 549–560.

Kelly Hall, J., G. Vitanova, and L. A. Marchenkova (eds.): 2004. *Dialogue with Bakhtin on Second and Foreign Language Learning: New Perspectives*. Mahwah, NJ: Lawrence Erlbaum.

Kelly, L. G. 1969. *25 Centuries of Language Teaching: 500 B.C.–1969*. Rowley, MA: Newbury House.

Kelly-Holmes, H. 2004. *Advertising as Multilingual Communication*. London: Palgrave Macmillan.

Kenny, D. 2009. 'Equivalence' in M. Baker and G. Saldanha (eds.): *Routledge Encyclopedia of Translation Studies* (2nd edn.) 96–99. London: Routledge.

Kim, S. H. and C. Elder. 2005. 'Language choices and pedagogic functions in the foreign language classroom: a cross-linguistic functional analysis of teacher talk.' *Language Teaching Research* 9 (4): 355–380.

Koller, W. 1989. 'Equivalence in translation theory' (trans. A Chesterman): original German 1979) in A. Chesterman (ed.): *Readings in Translation Theory*. Helsinki: Finn Lectura.

Komissarov, V. 1973. *(Slovo o perevode)*. Moscow.

Kramsch, C. 1993. *Context and Culture in Language Teaching*. Oxford, Oxford University Press.

—— (ed.). 2002. *Language Acquisition and Language Socialization. Ecological perspectives*. London: Continuum.

—— 2005. 'Post 9/11: Foreign languages between knowledge and power.' *Applied Linguistics* 26 (4): 545–568.

—— 2006. 'From communicative competence to symbolic competence'. *The Modern Language Journal* 90 (2): 249–252.

—— 2008. Interview for the Open University Masters in Education (Applied Linguistics) January 2008.

—— and A. Whiteside. 2008. 'Language ecology in multilingual settings. Towards a theory of symbolic competence.' *Applied Linguistics* 29 (4): 645–672.

Krashen, S. D. 1982. *Principles and Practice in Second Language Acquisition*. Oxford: Pergamon.

—— 1985. *The Input Hypothesis: Issues and Implications*. London: Longman.

—— and T. D. Terrell. 1983. *The Natural Approach: Language Acquisition in the Classroom*. Oxford: Pergamon.

Kress, G. and T. van Leeuwen. 2001. *Multimodal Discourse*. London: Arnold.

Kumaravadivelu, B. 2003. *Beyond Methods: Macrostrategies for Language Teaching*. New Haven and London: Yale University Press.

Kupferberg, I. and E. Olshtain 1996. 'Explicit contrastive instruction facilitates the acquisition of difficult L2 forms.' *Language Awareness* 5 (3–4): 149–165.

Lado, R. 1957. *Linguistics across Cultures: Applied Linguistics for Teachers*. Ann Arbor: University of Michigan Press.

Lambert S. and B. Moser-Mercer (eds.). 1994. *Bridging the gap: Empirical Research in Simultaneous Interpretation*. Philadelphia: John Benjamins.

Lantolf, J. (ed.) 2000. *Sociocultural Theory and Second Language Learning*. Oxford: Oxford University Press.

Larsen-Freeman, D. 2000. *Techniques and Principles In Language Teaching*. Oxford: Oxford University Press.

—— and L. Cameron. 2008. *Complex Systems and Applied Linguistics*. Oxford: Oxford University Press.

Laufer, B. and **N. Girsai.** 2008. 'Form-focused instruction in second language vocabulary learning: a case for contrastive analysis and translation.' *Applied Linguistics* 29 (4): 694–716.

Le Guin, U. K. 1998. *Catwings.* New York: Scholastic.

Lee, J. 2009. 'Interpreting inexplicit language during courtroom examination.' *Applied Linguistics* 30 (1): 93–115.

Lefevere, A. 1975. *Translating Poetry.* Assen: van Gorcum.

Lenneberg, E. H. 1967. *Biological Foundations of Language.* New York: Wiley.

Levine, G. S. 2003. 'Student and instructor beliefs and attitudes about target language use, first language use, and anxiety: report of a questionnaire study.' *The Modern Language Journal* 87 (3): 343–364.

Lewis, M. 1993. *The Lexical Approach.* Hove: Language Teaching Publications.

—— 1996. 'Implementing the lexical approach.' *IATEFL Annual Conference Report.* Whitstable: IATEFL.

Lewis, M. P. (ed.). 2009. *Ethnologue: Languages of the World* (16th edn.) Dallas, TX: SIL International.

Lightbown, P. and **N. Spada.** 2006. *How Languages are Learned* (3rd edn.). Oxford: Oxford University Press.

Lin, A. (ed.) 1996. 'Bilingualism or linguistic segregation? Symbolic domination, resistance and code switching in Hong Kong schools.' *Linguistics and Education* 8 (1): 49–84.

—— 2008. *Problematizing Identity: Everyday Struggles in Language, Culture, and Education.* Mahwah, NJ: Lawrence Erlbaum.

Littlejohn, A. 1992. *Why are English language teaching materials the way they are?* Unpublished PhD thesis: Lancaster University.

—— and **D. Hicks.** 1996. *English for Schools.* Cambridge: Cambridge University Press.

Littlewood, W. 1981. *Communicative Language Teaching.* Cambridge: Cambridge University Press.

Liu, Y. 2007. 'Towards "representational justice" in translation practice' in J. Munday (ed.): *Translation as Intervention* 54–71. London: Routledge.

Long, M. 1983. 'Native speaker/non-native speaker conversation and the negotiation of comprehensible input.' *Applied Linguistics* 4 (2): 126–141.

—— 1985. 'A role for instruction in second language acquisition' in K. Hyltenstam and M. Pienemann (eds.): *Modelling and Assessing Second Language Learning*: 77–101. Clevedon: Multilingual Matters.

—— 1991. 'Focus on form: A design feature in language teaching methodology' in K de Bot, R. Ginsberg, and C. Kramsch (eds.): *Foreign Language Research in Cross-cultural Perspective* 39–53. Amsterdam: John Benjamins.

—— and **P. Robinson.** 1998. 'Focus on form: theory, research and practice' in C. Doughty, and J. Williams (eds.): *Focus on Form in Second Language Acquisition*: 15–41. Cambridge: Cambridge University Press.

Loschky, L. and **R. Bley-Vroman.** 1993. 'Grammar and task-based methodology' in G. Crookes and S. Gass (eds.): *Tasks and Language Learning: Integration Theory and Practice* 123–67. Clevedon: Multilingual Matters.

Lowell, R. 1962. *Imitations.* London: Faber and Faber.

Lozanov, G. 1978. *Suggestology and the Outlines of Suggestopedy.* New York: Gordon and Breach.

Lynch, T. 2000. 'Exploring the benefits of task repetition and recycling for classroom language learning.' *Language Teaching Research* 4 (3): 221–250.

Macaro, E. 1997. *Target Language, Collaborative Learning and Autonomy.* Clevedon: Multilingual Matters.

Macherey, P. 1978. *A Theory of Literary Production* (trans. G. Wall). London: Routledge and Kegan Paul.

MacWhinney, B. 2006. 'Emergentism – use often and with care.' *Applied Linguistics* 27 (4): 729–741.

Maier, C. 2007. 'The translator as an interventient being' in J. Munday (ed.): *Translation as Intervention* 1–18. London: Routledge.

Malmkjær, K. (ed.). 1995/1996. *Translation and Language Teaching. AILA Review No 12.*

—— (ed.). 2004. *Translation in Undergraduate Degree Programmes.* Amsterdam, Philadelphia, PA: John Benjamins.

Marlein, M. 2009. 'Improving syntactical skills through translation? Making L2 word order visible in L1 through word-by-word translation' in A. Witte, T. Harden, and A. Ramos de Oliveira Harden (eds.): *Translation in Second Language Teaching and Learning* 947–163. Frankfurt: Peter Lang.

Marsh, D. 2002. *CLIL/EMILE The European Dimension: Actions, Trends and Foresight Potential.* EU Public Services Contract 2001– 3406 /001– 001 available online at http://ec.europa.eu/education/languages/language-teaching/doc236_en.htm

Martin, J. R. 1985. *Factual Writing: Exploring and Challenging Social Reality.* Oxford: Oxford University Press.

Matthews-Breský, R. J. H. 1972. 'Translation as a testing device.' *English Language Teaching Journal* 27 (1): 58–65.

McElhinny, B. (ed.). 2008. *Words, Worlds, and Material Girls: Language, Gender, Globalization.* New York: Mouton de Gruyter.

McKay, S. 2002. *Teaching English as an International Language.* Oxford: Oxford University Press.

McLaughlin, B. 1987. *Theories of Second-Language Learning.* London: Arnold.

Medgyes, P. 1994. *The Non-Native Teacher.* London: Macmillan.

Mitchell, R. 1988. *Communicative Language Teaching in Practice.* London: CILT.

—— and F. Myles. 2004. (2nd edn.) *Second Language Learning Theories.* London: Arnold.

Morgan, B. Q. 1959. 'A critical bibliography of works on translation' in R. A. Brower (ed.): *On Translation* 270–280. Boston, MA: Harvard University Press.

Moser-Mercer, B. 2001. 'Simultaneous interpreting: cognitive potential and limitations.' *Interpreting* 5 (2): 83–94.

Munday, J. 2001. *Introducing Translation Studies: Theories and Applications.* London: Routledge.

Mustafin, Y. 1984. *The Bridge* (trans. E. Poptsova-Cook and G. Cook). Moscow: Raduga.

Myles, F. J., R. F. Mitchell, and J. V. Hooper. 1999. 'Interrogative chunks in French L2: a basis for creative construction?' *Studies in Second Language Acquisition* 21 (1): 49–80.

Nabokov, V. 1964. *Pushkin: Eugene Onegin.* London: Routledge and Kegan Paul.

Newmark, P. 1981. *Approaches to Translation.* London: Pergamon.

Newmeyer, F. and S. Weinberger. 1988. 'The ontogenesis of the field of second language learning research' in S. Flynn and W. O'Neil (eds.): *Linguistic Theory in Second Language Acquisition* 34–45. Dordrecht: Kluwer.

Nida, E. and C. R. Taber. 1969. *The Theory and Practice of Translation.* Leiden: Brill.

Nikula, T. 2007. 'Speaking English in Finnish content-based classrooms.' *World Englishes* 26 (2): 206–223.

Norris, S. 2004. *Analyzing Multimodal Interaction. A Methodological Framework.* London: Routledge.

Norton, B. 2000. *Identity and Language Learning.* New York: Pearson Education Limited.

Nunan, D. 1987. 'Communicative language teaching: making it work.' *English Language Teaching Journal* 41 (2): 136–145.

—— 1988. *Syllabus Design.* Oxford: Oxford University Press.

O'Connell, J. 2001. 'Cherishing a Minority Language: Irish Language and National Identity.' Paper given at the European Language Minorities Conference: University of Bath.

Odlin, T. 1989. *Language Transfer.* Cambridge: Cambridge University Press.

Omoniyi, T. and G. White (eds.). 2006. *The Sociolinguistics of Identity.* London: Continuum.

Pachler, N., A. Barnes, and K. Field (eds.). 2008. (3rd edn.) *Learning to Teach: Using Modern Foreign Languages in the Secondary School.* London: Routledge.

Park, J. S-Y. and L. Wee. 2009. 'The three circles redux: a market-theoretic perspective on world Englishes.' *Applied Linguistics* 30 (3): 389–406.

Pavlenko, A. 2005. 'Bilingualism and thought' in A. de Groot and J. Kroll (eds.): *Handbook of Bilingualism: Psycholinguistic Approaches* 433–454. New York: Oxford University Press.

—— and J. Lantolf. 2000. 'Second language learning as participation and the (re)construction of selves' in J. Lantolf: (9th edn.) *Sociocultural Theory and Second Language Learning* 155–179. Oxford: Oxford University Press.

—— and A. Blackledge (eds.). 2004. *Negotiation of Identities in Multilingual Contexts*. Clevedon: Multilingual Matters.

Pennycook, A. 1994. 'Incommensurable Discourses?' *Applied Linguistics* 15 (2): 115–138.

—— 2007. *Global Englishes and Transcultural Flows*. London: Routledge.

Peters, A. 1983. *The Units of Language Acquisition*. Cambridge: Cambridge University Press.

Phillipson, R. 1992. *Linguistic Imperialism*. Oxford: Oxford University Press.

—— 1999. (Review article) 'Voice in global English: unheard chords in Crystal loud and clear.' *Applied Linguistics* 20 (2): 265–275.

Pinker, S. 1994. *The Language Instinct: The New Science of Language and Mind*. London: Allen Lane.

Polio, C. G. and P. A. Duff. 1994. 'Teachers' language use in university foreign language classrooms: a qualitative analysis of English and target language alternation.' *The Modern Language Journal* 78: 313–326.

Poole, B. 1999. *A critical analysis of early start programmes in UK primary language learning*. Unpublished PhD thesis: London University Institute of Education.

Prabhu, N. S. 1984. 'Procedural Syllabuses' in T. E. Read (ed.): *Trends in Language Syllabus Design* 272–280. Singapore: Singapore University Press/RELC.

Prodromou, L. 2002. 'The liberating role of the mother tongue' in S. Deller and M. Rinvolucri (eds.): *Using the Mother Tongue: Making the Most of the Learner's Language* 5. London: English Teaching Professional and Delta Publishing.

Pym, A. 1992. *Translation and Text Transfer*. Frankfurt: Peter Lang.

—— 2009. 'The Spanish tradition' in M. Baker and G. Saldanha (eds.): *The Routledge Encyclopedia of Translation Studies* 533–542. London: Routledge.

Rampton, B. 1990. 'Displacing the "native speaker": expertise, affiliation and inheritance.' *English Language Teaching Journal* 44 (2): 97–101.

—— 1996. 'Language crossing, new ethnicities and school.' *English in Education* 30 (2): 14–26.

—— 1999a. 'Deutsch in inner London and the animation of an instructed foreign language.' *Journal of Sociolinguistics* 3 (4): 480–504.

—— 1999b. 'Dichotomies, difference and ritual in second language learning and teaching.' *Applied Linguistics* 20 (3): 316–340.

—— 2000. 'Continuity and change in views of society in applied linguistics' in Trappes-Lomax, H. (ed.): *Change and Continuity in Applied Linguistics* 97–114. Clevedon: Multilingual Matters.

—— 2005. (2nd edn.) *Crossing: Language and Ethnicity Among Adolescents* (1st edn. 1995, London: Longman). Manchester: St Jerome Press.

Richards, J. C. 2002. (2nd edn.) *The Longman Dictionary of Language Teaching and Applied Linguistics*. London: Longman.

—— and T. Rodgers. 2001. *Approaches and Methods in Language Teaching*. Cambridge: Cambridge University Press.

——, J. Platt and J. Weber. 2002. (3rd edn.) *The Longman Dictionary of Applied Linguistics*. London: Longman.

Rieu, E. V. 1953. 'Translation' in: *Cassell's Encyclopaedia of Literature*: 555. London: Cassell Publishers.

Riley, P. 2007. *Language, Culture and Identity: An Ethnolinguistic Perspective*. London: Continuum.

Ritzer, G. 1998. *The McDonaldization Thesis*. Thousand Oaks, CA: Sage.

Robertson, R. 1995. 'Glocalization: time–space and homogeneity–heterogeneity' in M. Featherstone, S. Lash, and R. Robertson (eds.): *Global Modernities* 25–4. London: Sage.

Rolin-Ianziti, J. and S. Brownlie. 2002. 'Teacher use of learners' native language in the foreign language classroom.' *Canadian Modern Language Review* 58 (3):402–426.

Roosevelt, T. 1926. *The Works of Theodore Roosevelt* (Memorial edn.) Volume 14: 554. New York: Charles Scribner's Sons.

Rubdy, R. and M. Saraceni, (eds.). 2006. *English in the World: Global Rules, Global Roles.* London: Continuum.

—— and Tan, P. (eds.). 2008. *Language as Commodity: Trading Languages, Global Structures, Local Marketplaces.* London: Continuum.

Said, E. 1994. *Culture and Imperialism*. London: Vintage.

Samuda, V. and M. Bygate. 2008. *Tasks in Second Language Learning.* Basingstoke: Palgrave Macmillan.

Santos, D. 2004. *A study of the textbook in literacy events: language, literacies and TEFL in an educational community.* Unpublished PhD thesis: University of Reading.

Sarkar, M. and L. Winer. 2006. 'Multilingual codeswitching in Quebec rap: poetry, pragmatics and performativity.' *International Journal of Multilingualism* 3 (3): 173–192.

Sarsar N. 2007. 'Low-level educational achievements in the UAE model schools' available online at http://eric.ed.gov/ERICWebPortal/custom/portlets/recordDetails/detailmini.jsp?_nfpb=true&_&ERICExtSearch_SearchValue_0=ED499085&ERICExtSearch_ SearchType_0=no&accno=ED499085

Saussure, F. de [1915] 1974. *Course in General Linguistics* (trans. W. Baskin). London: Fontana/Collins.

Schmidt, R. 1990: 'The role of consciousness in second language learning'. *Applied Linguistics* 11 (2): 129–158.

Schneiderman, E. and C. Desmarais. 1988. 'The talented language learner. Some preliminary findings.' *Second Language Research* 4 (1): 91–109.

Sealey, A. and B. Carter. 2004. *Applied Linguistics as a Social Science.* London: Continuum.

Searle, J. R. 1969. *Speech Acts: An Essay in the Philosophy of Language.* Cambridge: Cambridge University Press.

—— 1975a. 'A taxonomy of illocutionary acts' in K. Gunderson (ed.): *Language, Mind and Knowledge*, Volume 7 344–369. Minneapolis: University of Minnesota Press.

—— 1975b. 'Indirect speech acts' in P. Cole and J. L. Morgan (eds.): *Syntax and Semantics, Vol. 3, Speech Acts.* New York: Academic Press.

SEF (Secretaria de Educação Fundamental). 1998. *Língua estrangeira: Parâmetros Curriculares Nacionais* [Foreign Language, National Curricular Parameters]. Brasília, Brazil: Ministério da Educação.

Seidlhofer, B. 1999. 'Double standards: teacher education in the Expanding Circle'. *World Englishes* 18 (2): 233–245.

—— 2002. 'Closing a conceptual gap: the case for a description of English as a lingua franca.' *International Journal of Applied Linguistics* 11 (2):133–158.

—— 2010. *Understanding English as a Lingua Franca.* Oxford: Oxford University press.

Selinker, L. 1972. 'Interlanguage.' *International Review of Applied Linguistics* 10: 209–31.

Shohamy, E. 2006. *Language Policy: Hidden Agendas and New Approaches.* London: Routledge.

Sinclair, J. McH. 1991. *Corpus, Concordance, Collocation.* Oxford: Oxford University Press.

—— 2004. *Trust the Text: Language, Corpus and Discourse.* London: Routledge.

Skehan, P. 1998. *A Cognitive Approach to Language Learning.* Oxford: Oxford University Press.

Skilbeck, M. 1982. 'Three educational ideologies' in T. Horton and P. Raggat (eds.): *Challenge and Change in the Curriculum* 7–18. Sevenoaks: Hodder and Stoughton.

Smith, K. 2006. 'Rhetorical figures and the translation of advertising headlines.' *Language and Literature* 15: 159–182.

Snellings, P., A. van Gelderen, and K. de Glopper. 2002. 'Lexical retrieval: an aspect of fluent second language production that can be enhanced.' *Language Learning* 52 (4): 723–754.

Soars, J. and L. Soars. 1986 onwards. *Headway Intermediate*. Oxford: Oxford University Press.

Spada, N. and P. M. Lightbown. 1999. 'Instruction, first language influence, and developmental readiness in second language acquisition.' *Modern Languages Journal* 83 (1): 1–22.

Speight, K. 1962. *Teach Yourself Italian*. London: Teach Yourself Books.

Spolsky, B. 1989. *Conditions for Second Language Learning*. Oxford: Oxford University Press.

Sridhar, K. and S. Sridhar. 1986. 'Bridging the paradigm gap: second language acquisition theory and indigenized varieties of English.' *World Englishes* 5 (1): 3–14.

Steiner, G. 1998. (3rd edn.) *After Babel*. Oxford: Oxford University Press.

Stern, H. H. 1983. *Fundamental Concepts of Language Teaching* Oxford: Oxford University Press.

—— 1992. *Issues and Options in Language Teaching*. Oxford: Oxford University Press.

Stevick, E. 1981. *Teaching Languages: A Way and Ways*. Rowley, MA: Newbury House.

Stubbs, M. 1996. *Text and Corpus Analysis*. Oxford: Blackwell.

—— 2001. *Words and Phrases*. Oxford: Blackwell.

Swales, J. 1990. *Genre Analysis*. Cambridge: Cambridge University Press.

Swan, M. 1997. 'The influence of the mother tongue on second language vocabulary acquisition and use' in N. Schmitt and M. McCarthy (eds.): *Vocabulary: Description, Acquisition and Pedagogy* 156–181. Cambridge: Cambridge University Press.

—— 2005. 'Legislation by hypothesis: the case of task-based instruction.' *Applied Linguistics* 26 (3): 376–402.

—— 2007. 'Follow-up to Claire Kramsch's "classic" book review of Lado 1957.' *Linguistics Across Cultures: History is not what Happened: The Case of Contrastive Analysis*. *International Journal of Applied Linguistics* 17 (3): 414–419.

—— and B. Smith. 2001. (2nd edn.) *Learner English: A Teacher's Guide to Interference and Other Problems*. Cambridge: Cambridge University Press.

—— and C. Walter. 1990 onwards. *The Cambridge English Course, The New Cambridge English Course*. Cambridge: Cambridge University Press.

Sweet, H. [1899] 1964. *The Practical Study of Languages: A Guide for Teachers and Learners* (ed. R. Mackin). Oxford: Oxford University Press.

Tanaka, K. 1994. *Advertising Language: A Pragmatic Approach to Advertisements in Britain and Japan*. London: Routledge.

Tannen, D. 2007. *Talking Voices: Repetition, Dialogue, and Imagery in Conversational Discourse*. Cambridge: Cambridge University Press.

Taylor, D. S. 1988. 'The meaning and use of the term "competence" in linguistics and applied linguistics.' *Applied Linguistics* 9 (2): 148–168.

TESOL 2006. 'Position statement against discrimination of nonnative speakers of English in the field of TESOL.' TESOL USA available on-line at http://www.tesol.org/s_tesol/bin. asp?CID=32&DID=5889&DOC=FILE. pdf

Thomas, D. 1999. *Culture, ideology and educational change: the case of English language teachers in Slovakia*. Unpublished PhD thesis: London University Institute of Education.

Thomas, J. 1976. 'Translation, language teaching, and the bilingual assumption.' *TESOL Quarterly* 10 (4): 403–410.

Thomas, M. 2006. *Michel Thomas German Foundation Course: German*. Michel Thomas Series: Audiobook/audio CD (2nd edn. 29 Sep 2006): Hodder Arnold.

Thomas, S. 1998. 'Translation as intercultural conflict' in S. Hunston (ed.): *Language at Work* 98–109. Clevedon: Multilingual Matters.

Thoreau H. 1854. *Walden*. Boston and New York: Houghton, Mifflin and Company.

Titone, R. 1968. *Teaching Foreign Languages: An Historical Sketch*. Washington, DC: Georgetown University Press.

Tourey, G. 1980. *In Search of a Theory of Translation*. Tel Aviv: Porter Institute.

Towell, R. and R. Hawkins. 1994. *Approaches to Second Language Acquisition*. Clevedon: Multilingual Matters.

Truscott, J. 1996. 'The case against grammar correction in L2 writing classes.' *Language Learning* 46 (2): 327–369.

Tudor, I. 1987. 'Using translation in ESP'. *English Language Teaching Journal* 41 (4): 268–273.

van Lier, L. 1996. *Interaction in the Language Curriculum. Awareness, Autonomy and Authenticity*. London and New York: Longman.

—— 2000. 'From input to affordance: social-interactive learning in an ecological perspective' in J. P. Lantolf (ed.): *Sociocultural Theory and Language Learning* 245–260. Oxford: Oxford University Press.

—— 2004. *The Ecology and Semiotics of Language Learning. A Sociocultural Perspective*. Dordrecht: Kluwer.

Venuti, L. 1986. 'The translator's invisibility.' *Criticism* 28 (Spring): 197–212.

—— 1995. *The Translator's Invisibility: A History of Translation*. London: Routledge.

Viëtor, W. (under pseudonym Quosque Tandem). 1882. *Der Sprachunterricht Muss Umkehren! (Language Teaching Must Start Afresh)*. Heilbronn: Henninger.

von Flotow, L. 1997. *Translation and Gender: Translating in the 'Era of Feminism'*. Manchester: St. Jerome.

von Goethe, J. W. 1982. *Werke. Kommentare und Register. Hamburger Ausgabe in 14 Bänden. Band 12: Kunst und Literatur*. Hamburg: Christian Wegner Verlag.

Watts, S. 2005. *The People's Tycoon: Henry Ford and the American Century*. New York: Knopf.

White R. 1979. *Functional English*. London: Nelson.

Whorf, B. 1964. *Language, Thought, and Reality: Selected Writings of Benjamin Lee Whorf* (ed. J. B. Carroll). Cambridge, MA: MIT Press.

Whyte, J. 2003. *Bad Thoughts: A Guide to Clear Thinking*. London: Corvo.

Widdowson, H. G. 1978. *Teaching Language as Communication*. Oxford: Oxford University Press.

—— 1979. 'The deep structure of discourse and the use of translation' in *Explorations in Applied Linguistics* 101–112. Oxford: Oxford University Press.

—— 1983. *Learning Purpose and Language Use*. Oxford: Oxford University Press.

—— 1984. 'Models and fictions' in *Explorations in Applied Linguistics* 27–21 Oxford: Oxford University Press.

—— 1990a. 'Problems with solutions' in *Aspects of Language Teaching* 12–27. Oxford: Oxford University Press.

—— 1990b. 'Grammar, and nonsense, and learning' in *Aspects of Language Teaching* 79–99. Oxford: Oxford University Press.

—— 1994. 'The ownership of English'. *TESOL Quarterly* 28: 377–389.

—— 2003. *Defining Issues in English Language Teaching*. Oxford: Oxford University Press.

Wilkins, D. A. 1972. *Linguistics in Language Teaching*. London: Arnold.

—— 1976. *Notional Syllabuses*. Oxford: Oxford University Press.

Williams, M. and R. L. Burden. 1997. *Psychology for Language Teachers: A Social Constructivist Approach*. Cambridge: Cambridge University Press.

Willis, D. 1990. *The Lexical Syllabus*. London: Collins.

Willis, J. and D. Willis. 2001. 'Task based language learning' in R. Carter and D. Nunan (eds.): *The Cambridge Guide to Teaching English to Speakers of Other Languages* 173–180. Cambridge: Cambridge University Press.

Witte, A. 2009. 'From translating to translation in foreign language learning' in A. Witte, T. Harden, and A. Ramos de Oliveira Harden (eds.): *Translation in Second Language Teaching and Learning* 91–111 Frankfurt: Peter Lang.

——, T. Harden, and A. Ramos de Oliveira Harden (eds.): 2009. *Translation in Second Language Teaching and Learning*. Frankfurt: Peter Lang.

Wolfson, N. 1989. *Perspectives: Sociolinguistics and TESOL*. Cambridge, MA: Newbury House.

Wray, A. 2002. *Formulaic Language and the Lexicon*. Cambridge: Cambridge University Press.

Index